Digitalising Courts in Asia

Access to Justice in a Changing World
Series Editor: Chris Gill, Professor of Socio-Legal Studies, University of Glasgow
Series Advisory Board

Titles available in the series:
Digitalising Courts in Asia: Exploring the Mechanics of Judicial Transformations
Siddharth Peter De Souza and Julia Wellhausen (eds.)

Visit the **Access to Justice in a Changing World** website at
edinburghuniversitypress.com/series-access-to-justice-in-a-changing-world

Digitalising Courts in Asia

Exploring the Mechanics of Judicial Transformations

Edited by Siddharth Peter de Souza and Julia Wellhausen

EDINBURGH
University Press

Edinburgh University Press is one of the leading university presses in the UK. Publishing new research in the arts and humanities, EUP connects people and ideas to inspire creative thinking, open new perspectives and shape the world we live in. For more information, visit www.edinburghuniversitypress.com.

Cover image: Rachit Sharma
Cover design: Leon Strachan

Grateful acknowledgement is made to the sources listed in the List of Illustrations for permission to reproduce material previously published elsewhere. Every effort has been made to trace the copyright holders, but if any have been inadvertently overlooked, the publisher will be pleased to make the necessary arrangements at the first opportunity.

Edinburgh University Press Ltd
13 Infirmary Street, Edinburgh EH1 1LT

Typeset in 10/12pt Goudy Old Style
by Cheshire Typesetting Ltd, Cuddington, Cheshire, and
Printed and bound in the UK using 100% renewable electricity by
CPI Group (UK) Ltd

A CIP record for this book is available from the British Library

ISBN 978 1 3995 4761 1 (hardback)
ISBN 978 1 3995 4763 5 (webready PDF)
ISBN 978 1 3995 4762 8 (epub)

EU Authorised Representative:
Easy Access System Europe
Mustamäe tee 50, 10621 Tallinn, Estonia
gpsr.requests@easproject.com

MIX
Paper | Supporting responsible forestry
FSC www.fsc.org FSC® C013604

This book is printed using paper from well-managed forests, recycling and other controlled sources

Contents

Illustrations

FIGURES

TABLES

Acknowledgements

We would like to thank Stefan Samse, Carol Leong, and Dylan Yuen from Konrad-Adenauer-Stiftung Rule of Law Programme Asia for their support with organising the conference. We are grateful to Julia Wijns from Tilburg Law School for her research as well as logistical support during the conference, and Rachit Sharma from Justice Adda for his research and editorial assistance throughout the finalising of the book. We would also like to thank Tilburg University Fund for providing the support to make this book Open Access. This book is an outcome of the rich discussions, and insights from the contributors, and we are thankful for their participation.

Notes on Contributors

Varsha Aithala is an Assistant Professor and doctoral candidate at the National Law School of India University. She is Operations Lead at Justice Adda, a law and design thinking social enterprise. Her teaching and research interests cover social investment, law and technology, access to justice and legal system reform. Varsha is qualified as a solicitor in England and Wales and as an advocate in India. She has a Master's degree in corporate law from the University of Cambridge and a Bachelor's degree in law from Nalsar University of Law.

Kraiphol Aranyarat is a Judge of the Court of Justice of Thailand with over a decade of judicial experience. He holds an LLM from Columbia University, United States, and a JSD from Chulalongkorn University, Thailand. Throughout his career, Kraiphol has encountered numerous issues involving court technology and has developed a deep interest in the integration of emerging technologies within judicial practices. His research focuses on leveraging technology to enhance court efficiency while upholding the rule of law and ensuring that legal systems remain fair and just in a rapidly evolving digital world.

Rita Baramu is a writer, researcher and human rights advocate from Nepal, with over ten years of experience in the fields of human rights, land rights and digital rights. Currently pursuing Masters in Technology Governance at Australian National University, she holds academic qualifications in Gender Studies and Law. As an activist from a highly marginalised indigenous community in Nepal, she passionately advocates for gender equality and the rights of marginalised groups through her writing in national Nepali newspapers, using an intersectional lens. Rita believes that the redistribution of power and resources is essential for building a just and equitable society.

Nam-Chul Chung is a Professor of Law at Sookmyung Women's University in Seoul, South Korea. He specialises in public law (administrative law) and environmental law. He received LLB and LLM degrees from Korea University and an LLM degree from the University of Münster, Germany. In 2003, he earned his PhD in public law (Dr.iur.) from the Humboldt University of Berlin, where he was a DAAD scholarship holder. From 2011 to 2012, he was a visiting scholar at the UC Berkeley School of Law. He is one of the leading authors on public law in South Korea, having published over 150 articles.

Siddharth Peter de Souza is an Assistant Professor in AI & Society at the Centre for Interdisciplinary Methodologies, Warwick University. His work explores how data is governed globally in contested and plural settings, and he is interested in the role that social movements and civil society can play in shaping digital transformations. He is also the founder of Justice Adda, a law and design social venture in India where he works on matters related to access to justice, and legal empowerment. Siddharth has worked as a digital policy consultant with UNDP and IDLO and was previously a post-doctoral researcher at the Global Data Justice Project at Tilburg Institute for Law, Technology and Society. He is a research associate at the African Centre for Epistemology and Philosophy of Science, University of Johannesburg.

Pan Mohamad Faiz works as the Head of the Research Center of the Indonesian Constitutional Court and Lecturer on Constitutional Law at the Faculty of Law, Universitas Brawijaya, Indonesia. Faiz is also an External Research Fellow at the Centre for Public, International and Comparative Law (CPICL), the University of Queensland, Australia. He received his PhD in Constitutional Law from TC Beirne School of Law, the University of Queensland, Australia.

Mark Findlay is a distinguished Fellow at the British Institute of International and Comparative Law, and an Honorary Professorial Fellow, Law School, University of Edinburgh. The author of over thirty monographs and edited collections, Mark is currently writing on governance, freedom and ordering in the metaverse. He has held Chairs in Law Schools in the UK, Asia, Australia and the Pacific and his main research areas include data governance, globalisation and crises, law and regulation, and international criminal justice.

Ingrid Rosalie L. Gorre, currently Senior Advisor for the EU–Philippines Justice Sector Reform Programme (EU-GOJUST 2), has extensive experience in justice reform, public interest law, environmental law, and human rights. Her work spans docket decongestion, automating case management, and piloting new technologies in justice agencies. Previously, she was a Key Experts-Case Management Specialist of the Technical Assistance Team for European Union–Philippines, Justice Sector Reform Programme: Governance in Justice 1 or EU-GOJUST 1 Programme and collaborated with the Asia Foundation on justice reform. She has worked with various public interest and environmental organisations across Southeast Asia. Ms Gorre holds a BA in Political Science and a Juris Doctor from the University of the Philippines and was a Columbia Human Rights Fellow.

Tomas Kvedaras is Project Manager at Judicial Integrity Network in ASEAN, UNDP Bangkok Regional Hub. He supports anti-corruption, human rights and rule of law projects across Asia. Prior to that, he was based in Jordan, where he supported UNDP Governance and Peace Pillar implementing decentralisation, government integrity and accountability-related programmes. Before joining the United Nations, he served as a diplomat in Lithuania's Ministry of Foreign Affairs and EU's External Action Service, including in missions to the UN Security Council and Afghanistan.

Yi-Yi Lee is a Research Judge in Taiwan Constitutional Court. Since 2020, she has been engaged in the legislative debate and participated in the implementation of the Constitutional Court Procedural Act 2022 and its following amendments in 2023 and 2024. She observes the jurisprudence of the Taiwan Constitutional Court from an insider's perspective on a wide range of topics relating to fundamental rights and the separation of powers. Judge Lee obtained her LLB (2004) and LLM (2008) from National Taiwan University. She has been a criminal court judge since 2011 and and PhD from the University of Bristol, United Kingdom (2025).

Jane Loo is a senior research associate at the SMU Centre for Digital Law and adjunct faculty at Singapore Management University. Her research areas focus on AI governance and ethics, the intersection of law and technology, including how emerging technologies influence individuals' rights and vulnerability, with a focus on the digitalisation of the judicial process and the future of work. In 2023, she was awarded the Research Staff Excellence Award. Jane also designed and currently teaches two modules: Artificial Intelligence, Law and Ethics at SMU; and Artificial Intelligence Governance at the British Institute of International and Comparative Law.

Sarah McCoubrey is an Access to Justice Strategist at CALIBRATE Judicial Integrity Consultant, UNDP. She is also the founder of CALIBRATE, a consultancy where she works with small and large organisations to tackle access to justice challenges internationally, nationally and locally. She completed a Juris Doctor in Law and Masters of Education in Canada. Sarah practised law in Toronto, followed by ten years leading a civil-society organisation devoted to justice education and innovation. Her international work focuses on the rule of law, gender and equality initiatives, technology, and systemic changes in the legal sector. She has been the Strategic Advisor to the Canadian Action Committee on Access to Justice in Civil and Family Matters since 2015.

S. Muralidhar is a distinguished legal practitioner currently serving as a Senior Advocate at the Supreme Court of India. Prior to his elevation to the bench, he had an illustrious career as an advocate, practising in the Supreme

Court of India and the Delhi High Court for nearly two decades. In May 2006, he was appointed as a Judge of the High Court of Delhi, and subsequently, he served as the Chief Justice of the High Court of Orissa from 2021 to 2023. Notable achievements as Chief Justice of the High Court of Orissa included the establishment of a state-of-the-art centre for digitisation of court records.

Emilie Palamy Pradichit, the Founder and Executive Director of Manushya Foundation, is an intersectional feminist visionary and international human rights lawyer specialising in accessing justice for marginalised communities through strategic litigation before the United Nations (UN) – where her innovative work has successfully held governments and businesses accountable for their human rights abuses and violations. Working on the ground, she also endorses women and youth to speak truth to power at the forefront of their fight for justice and equality as well as defends indigenous, forest-dependent, LGBTIQ+ and marginalised communities across Asia.

Aimen Taimur is a PhD Researcher and Teaching Assistant at TILT (Tilburg University), focusing on the human rights regulation of AI-based technologies impacting cognitive liberty. Her doctoral research examines human rights protections against the challenges posed by manipulative algorithms and dark technical architecture on free thought and independent cognitive rationalisation. Previously, Aimen served as a Judicial Law Clerk at the Supreme Court of Pakistan, developing regulatory policies for technology use in judiciaries. She has also worked as a Human Rights lawyer in various IGOs, NGOs and with the National Counter Terrorism Authority of Pakistan.

Diana Torres is a Regional Governance Advisor in UNDP Bangkok Regional Hub. She leads the Governance team in Asia and the Pacific, including its three pillars: Inclusive and Future-Smart Public Goods & Services, Democratic Institutions and Processes, Inclusive Public Spheres, and Integrated Approaches to Development. She also leads the anti-corruption and local governance service offer. She has over 15 years of experience at UNDP, working at the global, regional and country levels, leading Governance solutions to accelerate sustainable development.

Letitia Visan is a dedicated human rights researcher specialising in digital rights and migrants' rights. Her work explores the intersection of technology and human rights, with a focus on the challenges faced by vulnerable people in the digital age. She co-authored the Freedom on the Net report for Thailand in 2022 and 2023.

Julia Wellhausen is a civil and criminal law judge (appointed in 2005 and 2010) as well as a (first) public prosecutor appointed (in 2008 and 2017) by the Bavarian Minister of Justice (lifetime tenure). She was on special long-term leave granted in 2021 to contribute to Konrad-Adenauer-Stiftung's Rule of Law Programme Asia (2021/2023).

Xiaohan Liang is a PhD candidate at the University of Hong Kong, specializing in procedural law, particularly in the areas of procedural justice and judicial fairness. She possesses a Master of Laws (LLM) degree from the University of Hong Kong and a Bachelor of Laws (LLB) from China University of Political Science and Law. Her research interests include the convergence of access to justice, law and technology, and empirical legal studies. Her doctoral research investigates the application and governance of AI within the legal realm to improve adjudicative processes and strengthen public confidence in the judiciary.

Chapter 1

Digitalising Courts: Leaving No One Behind

Siddharth Peter de Souza and Julia Wellhausen

A. INTRODUCTION

Courts are unique locations to witness digital transformations. Not only are they institutions upon which digitalisation is having increasing effects such as in terms of court management and adjudicatory processes, they are also institutions that are actively shaping discourses on what digitalisation means for the delivery of justice. With the advent of digitalisation in different aspects of the working of the court such as document discovery, legal research, evidence gathering and processing, workflow management, predictive sentencing, and virtual hearings, the approach taken by courts as institutions that must ensure access to justice in digital and networked spaces remains vital to a study of justice delivery.

Technology is often discussed as an enabler which allows for speedy, economic and efficient justice processes.[1] This has led to several judiciaries around the world establishing committees to find ways to address work practices on account of the escalating impacts of digital technology.

Across Asia, courts are taking different approaches to digital transformations. Some place an emphasis on building technical infrastructure. Others focus on creating enabling environments for the technology to be used, while a few are also engaging increasingly in governance considerations around the use, and regulation of technology. For instance, in 2023, the Supreme Court of India published a vision document that is designed to provide a road map for the use of technology in Indian courts through the development of a platform architecture for different digital services to be offered.[2] In Singapore, digitalising the judiciary is seen as part of the blueprint for a digital government.[3] The Japanese Supreme Court has created a new technology division to ensure that digitalisation is taking place across civil and criminal administrative processes.[4] Malaysia too has been developing an E-court system at a civil and criminal law level and has established ways to integrate the digital systems with other stakeholders including the police, prison system, department of insolvency, etc.[5]

Several concerns have emerged, from an access to justice perspective, on the use of technology in judiciaries. These include challenges to transparency and accountability of judiciaries due to their dependencies on technology, in particular where such technologies may be controlled by private entities. These developments also create challenges for public values that are at the forefront of the administration of justice, and the imperative to ensure that justice is not made subject to economic interests of private actors.[6] Digitalisation of justice also has a bearing for fair trials where there is an opacity in terms of the use of code, and the risk of potential biases that might emerge when they are used for critical judicial purposes such as sentencing. This has already been seen in the US, with the creations of risk profiles to test for recidivism which discriminated against people on the basis of race.[7] Digital divides are also a persistent challenge for judiciaries, where there is a gap in terms of how digital infrastructures are created and distributed in society. These challenges affect litigants, lawyers, as well as members of the public who might not have the ability to take part in virtual proceedings and are further alienated from the judicial process.[8]

In 2023, UNESCO conducted a survey with participants connected with the judiciary in over 96 countries, and found that 44% of respondents including lawyers, judges and prosecutors were using Artificial Intelligence (AI).[9] This included for drafting, research, as well as brainstorming. The survey also identified risks around AI systems with 27% of the judicial actors concerned about the accuracy, and the potential for falsehood with outputs from chatbots, 18% concerned about issues around data protection and data security and 14% concerned with its lack of transparency.[10] Critically, despite the increased usage, only 9% stated that there were clear guidelines or institutional training on the use. As demonstrated in this survey, while digital transformations continue to happen, they often take place in ad hoc ways without necessary preparation, caution or risk analysis, and often times driven by the promise of the 'magic' of technology,[11] and seeing justice in managerial terms.[12] It is therefore important to address this practice, as a means to avoid arbitrariness which may result if decision-making on digital transformations is not made with care.

This book emerged from a project organised by the Tilburg Institute for Law, Technology and Society and Konrad-Adenauer-Stiftung Rule of Law Programme Asia and a workshop held in Singapore in April 2023. The workshop brought together judges, academics and practitioners to reflect on digitalisation processes taking place in courts across Asia.

In this introductory chapter, we will discuss why we are focusing on Asia as a location to understand technology developments for the delivery of justice. We will thereafter discuss a framework for the digitalisation of courts based on discussions that have emerged in this book and will examine key elements of each of the aspects of the framework through reflection from the various contributions.

B. FOCUSING ON ASIA

The focus on Asia is for several reasons. The first is to tackle the increasing homogeneity of experiences that are cited by policy makers when it comes to digital transformations. This is particularly due to the fact that widely circulated case studies of digital transformations of courts are typically from the global Minority. Despite their usefulness primarily to a particular legal geography and institutional mooring, their developments are posited as 'best practices' for the rest of the world. This asymmetry of knowledge is not new but has contributed over the years, to legal transplantations, with repeated and ongoing failures of the replication of legal institutions, laws and cultures on account of a lack or difference of situated knowledges.

The second reason to focus on Asia is the need to decentre and provincialise developments in the global Minority which are often ill-suited to address the particularities of institutions in the global Majority.[13] Comparisons are often made between contexts in the global Minority with those in the global Majority, despite these comparisons needing to be force fitted to make justifications for why they are useful at all.[14] In focusing on Asia, the book takes as its starting point that Asia is not a monolith, especially given the different development and growth trajectories that judiciaries have taken, the political context of the different countries, as well as the technical capabilities that exist in these different regions.[15] However, within Asia, there are possibilities for regional learning, exchange, as well as South–South collaboration.

Thirdly, and critically, Asia is a site of new ways of seeing and doing digitalisation. This is demonstrated in innovations being undertaken by courts whether in terms of case management systems, document review, or the use of AI, where courts in some instances are also at the forefront of driving technological innovation. On the other hand, it is also as a site for the engagement with frictions, and fault lines in society, where structural inequalities demand that courts do not view digitalisation as a technical enterprise alone but as one that engages in its politics, and in the challenges of digital divides, digital discrimination, digital inequality. Thereby, foregrounding the need to situate the digital transformation processes within the development trajectory of a state.

Through discussing a variety of geographic, cultural and regulatory landscapes, the chapters in this book document the diversity and complexity of the ways in which judiciaries are seeing the promise, as well as the perils of digital transformations. In doing so, authors discuss that the emancipatory potential of technology is tied to the need to engage with the political economy of the court.[16] The chapters draw from the contextual knowledge of their contributors, who are deeply embedded in the legal cultures of their jurisdictions. Uniquely, the book brings together contributions from those with experience in the administration of technology itself to those who are actively finding ways to develop technology as a tool for adjudication. The book also includes reflections from those who are challenging the effects of technology in terms of court processes and arguing for the need for stringent policy to ensure digital justice. The pieces take the form of institutional, policy, empirical studies that each analyse the non-linearity of digital transformations. In doing so, they offer practical pathways as well as critical reflections which bridge theory and practice.

C. FRAMEWORK FOR UNDERSTANDING DIGITAL TRANSFORMATIONS IN COURTS

There are multiple points at which digital transformation is taking place in courts and changing judicial functions. Sourdin describes three trends: first, it can take the form of providing assistance through information, support, and advice apps and websites.[17] Secondly, it can also replace aspects of the judicial process typically carried out by humans such as through case management systems, chat bots, online filing platforms; and, thirdly, it can also fundamentally change how processes are being carried out such as through the use of predictive systems.[18]

These developments are significant because not only are they changing the ways in which judicial functions are taking place, but they are also changing the relations between people and courts. Refaie and Santuber outline different values of e-justice which are affected by digital transformations. These include for the independence of the judiciary due to the emergence of new technological actors with their own interests and values.[19] It also has impacts in terms of impartiality, and in terms of how information is collected, analysed and used in decision-making processes. It has implications on transparency in terms of how court activities are subject to public scrutiny, and also on privacy based on what kinds of data protection mechanisms exist to handle data.[20]

In this book, by placing justice considerations at the centre of digital transformations, we are interested in examining how the digitalisation of courts affects how people continue to have access to judicial institutions, the ways in which their participation is reshaped as a consequence of technology, and how interests of people and communities are served through technology mediated solutions.[21] From a people-centred justice lens, this involves, "taking the needs and voices of people into account when designing, delivering, implementing and evaluating public policies and services".[22] In ensuring that courts as public institutions build a people centricity to their approach to digitalisation it becomes imperative to develop a culture that empowers people, ensures that there are rights protections, and that there is rule of law that builds accountability and inclusivity.

With this in mind, the book offers a novel framework to analyse digital transformations, which considers how the court relates to different stakeholders in terms of digital transformations.

Typically, the digital transformation of courts is assessed in terms of outcomes, for instance whether a process has become more efficient or economical. Less attention is placed on the process and choices that go into undertaking a digital transformation. In addressing both process and outcomes of digital transformations, the framework looks at three sites upon which such analysis can be studied.

The first aspect is in terms of aspects of the administration of justice. The second aspect is in terms of how courts adjudicate on the implications of technology for society. Finally, the third aspect discusses the ways in which people are approaching and engaging with courts to facilitate and guarantee digital rights.

The section on *Administering technology* explores the purposes and motivations of different courts to introduce technology in the administration of justice. It examines how these developments influence transparency and accountability in the court administrative practices.

Some of the questions that are discussed include the following:

- What are the purposes and motivations of the court to introduce technology in the administration of justice?
- How are courts ensuring transparency and accountability in their administrative practices?
- What are the methods in which technology is being developed, sourced or tendered?

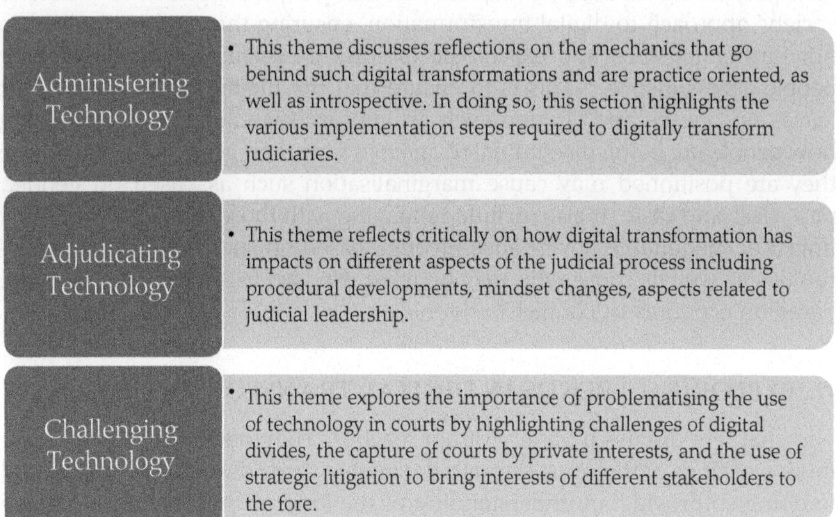

Figure 1.1 Framework for understanding the mechanics of digital transformations in courts

The section on *Adjudicating technology* discusses what sort of role the court plays in adjudicating disputes around the use of technology, particularly in terms of how technology impacts fundamental rights. Some of the motivating questions for this aspect are:

- What are some of the ways in which courts are using technology for adjudicative practices? Which functions can be enabled by technology?
- How are courts building competency for their staff on the implications of technology?
- What are the cases/areas of law wherein major technology issues are being adjudicated upon?

The section *Challenging technology* discusses the need to problematise the use of technology to account for the societal implications of its use. Some of the key questions they discuss are:

- What are the risks of digitalisation, and how to assess different kinds of risk?
- How are courts applying constitutional and fundamental rights reasoning to address the social implications of technology?
- How are groups building an understanding of digital rights in courts?

Through examining digital transformation across these three aspects, this book argues that it is critical to move beyond seeing digitalisation which prioritises economic and efficiency gains and argues for placing emphasis on equity in digital transformations.[23] In doing so, it reflects on a 'whole of society' approach to digital transformation, ensuring that such processes do not further injustice and exacerbate existing inequalities that inhibit how people access justice.[24] This is to ensure that the digitalisation of the court leaves no one behind. Taking such an approach would require examining how people are being discriminated against, how their geography and where they are positioned may cause marginalisation such as based on gender, race, class and caste. It also includes engaging with those who are affected by unjust or inequitable governance process, based on socio-economic opportunities as well as those who may be most exposed to shocks such as those based on economy or conflict.[25]

D. EXPLORING TRENDS IN DIGITAL TRANSFORMATION

The chapters discuss a variety of approaches. They offer insights from the inner workings of the court through the eyes of those designing systems, and in doing so provide an understanding of the kind of choices that are being made to manage digital transformations. They provide critique of digitalisation processes from a public interest perspective, human rights law standpoint, as well as access to justice considerations, and also offer pathways to ensure that digital transformation can be made more deliberative and careful, accounting for the people who will be affected by it.

The first cluster of chapters discuss the ways in which technology has been administered in courts. In the chapter 'Administering Technology: The Implementation of Court Technology in the Indonesian Constitutional Court', Pan Mohamad Faiz discusses the Judicial Administrative System (JAS) and the General Administrative System (GAS) that have been developed. The JAS includes e-filing, video conference hearings, case tracking system, live streaming of hearings, digital transcripts, and a digital mobile application called 'Click MK'. The GAS system includes a dynamic archival information system, real-time financial reports, talent pool system, and interactive social media of the court. The chapter highlights the importance of court technology, particularly in an archipelagic country like Indonesia, and discusses that, in addition to technology adoption, a future challenge is to work towards changing the mindsets of court employees to embrace technology.

Locating the technology transformation in contexts where there are digital divides, deep inequalities in society and structural access to justice problems is the challenge that S. Muralidhar discusses in 'Transformation through Technology: ICT Initiatives in the Odisha Judiciary'. The chapter draws from the author's work as the Chief Justice of the High Court in Odisha and discusses efforts to digitise court records, create virtual court rooms, develop e-services, as well as e-libraries, and conserve the legal heritage of the court. The chapter highlights the potential of digital transformation, but also raises concerns around questions of privacy, security, as well as mindsets of different members of the court system.

Nam-Chul Chung in his chapter 'Access to Justice and Digitalisation of Courts in South Korea' explores how the Korean Judiciary has been implementing different mechanisms for digital transformations. This chapter highlights the democratic implications of such transformations, including for judicial independence. It argues that it is critical that democratic control of the judiciary should be enhanced to ensure that the concerns of citizens are considered through creating mechanisms for public participation and access to judicial information. Further, the chapter calls for creating frameworks for risk management that ensure that the judiciary accounts for the adverse and discriminatory implications that may arise from the use of technologies, including AI in courts.

For a successful digital transformation, many aspects need to be uncovered including strong leadership, finances, technical capacity, as well as a clear and coherent strategy. This is a key contribution from Ingrid Gorre's work from the Philippines. This chapter places an emphasis on enhancing human capacity along with digital transformations. Through reflecting on the Go Just project, Gorre – in 'Digital Transformation of the Philippine Judiciary for the Filipino People' – discusses the importance of balancing people-centred needs, constitutional rights, as well as outcomes such as efficiency and consistency.

Similarly in their chapter, 'Empowering Judiciaries to Protect People's Rights in the Design of Court Technologies in ASEAN', Diana Torres, Tomas Kvedaras and Sarah McCoubrey focus on the adoption of new technologies in courts and their potential impact on justice gaps and vulnerable groups. They emphasise the importance of judges' leadership through their work at the United Nations Development Programme in ensuring a rights-based approach in the design of court technology, particularly in identifying biases and promoting rule of law and trial fairness criteria. This chapter also highlights the need for gender equality in these technology reforms and the potential risks of perpetuating inequality and eroding public confidence in the judiciary without active judicial input.

The second cluster of chapters discuss some of tensions that arise in the deployment of technology in as much as they affect the adjudicatory practices of the court. This cluster provides insights on aspects of transparency, accountability as well as fair rights considerations that might be affected through digital transformations, and offers pathways to address the challenges.

Kraiphol Aranyarat provides a framework to discuss AI adjudication in Thailand. He argues how to balance AI and human labour by examining the strengths and weaknesses of AI, and at the same time exploring the nature of judicial discretion. In 'The Division of Adjudicative Tasks in the Age of AI Adjudication in Thailand', he proposes a task division between human judges and AI to ensure a clear division of labour. Human judges are good for providing context, nuance, handling hard cases, making social contributions, and explaining decisions. AI is best suited for non-discretionary and low-stakes tasks, providing consistency, accuracy, transparency, impartiality, and predictability. The chapter proposes a three-tiered approach to task division based on the seriousness of the case and the degree of judicial discretion required.

The complexities of administering technology without affecting judicial independence are a key concern that Yi-Yi Lee discusses in the following chapter, 'The Past, Present and Future of Technology on Sentencing in Taiwan: Some Constitutional Reflections'. With the sentencing process requiring discretion by judges, she discusses three different technological systems to build transparency of sentencing. Through an analysis of each of the systems, the chapter examines the constitutional issues that emerge including in terms of the rights to a fair trial and the challenges for maintaining accountability and explainability while developing technical procedures.

In China, pioneering efforts have been made to use technology for the administration of justice. Xiaohan Yin, in 'AI and Criminal Sentencing in China: Applications, Misgivings and Prospects', discusses how AI is being used as a decisional aid, rather than a decision maker. This is because – while AI is used to build judicial efficiency and increase consistency across the judicial system – doubts remain, and concerns arise, over the manner in which the use of such technologies will facilitate harms. Yin discusses the challenges particularly in regard to aspects related to fairness, accountability, as well as the public nature of the justice process, which might be dependent on private actors.

The third cluster of chapters provide cautionary approaches around digital transformations. They raise issues of alienation, private sector capture, digital divides, as well as tech solutionism, highlighting the importance of not seeing digitalisation as a panacea to long-standing concerns of judicial systems.

In their chapter, 'The Routinisation and Depersonalisation of Justice', Jane Loo and Mark Findley discuss how digital processes result in aspects such as procedural fairness being substituted by procedural efficiency, and that digital structures create distances resulting in a lack of acknowledgement of the due process rights and existing challenges that users may have. They argue that while digitalisation does not automatically mean alienation, it must prioritise concerns of access to justice.

The concern for foregrounding access to justice considerations in legal tech developments is discussed by Varsha Aithala and Siddharth Peter de Souza in their chapter 'The Lengthening Shadow of the Legal Tech Market on the Supreme Court of India'. This chapter discusses the role of the court in promoting, participating in and regulating the nature of the legal tech market. With India emerging as one of the largest legal tech markets in the world, the chapter explores the ways in which the Supreme Court has facilitated the creation of this market. It offers a typology of the intersections between the court and the market and argues what the role of the court should be. The chapter raises concerns about how, without careful cognisance, the court can emerge as a willing party to the privatisation of judicial functions, which can further have implications for its own independence.

The next two chapters discuss the problems of a technology-first approach to digital transformations. Rita Baramu's chapter, 'A Case of Digital Rights Discourse and Advocacy within Nepali Judiciary', discusses how legal tech is currently still a new phenomenon and that, with its rise, there is also a rise of techno-solutionism, which results in little attention being paid to digital rights. She addresses how digital rights need to account for marginalised communities, and representing these experiences will enable digital transformations to be inclusive. Aimen Taimur, in 'Lessons from Pakistan's Judicial Techno-Solutionism', analyses the drawbacks of techno-solutionism in the judiciary. With Pakistan as a case study, she analyses the expeditious justice initiative and the use of AI in predictive judgment drafting and automated decision-making. This chapter emphasises the importance of addressing tech literacy, the importance of intersectionality in the South Asian context in addressing the implications of technology development in courts, highlighting sustainability concerns such as from software/hardware updates, and ensuring that resources are available to address cybersecurity, and privacy threats in Pakistan.

Lastly, Letitia Visan and Emilie Palamy Pradichit, in 'Digital Rights in Southeast Asia: Civil Society's Legal Tactics and Courts' Roles', highlight the need to uphold and protect digital rights amidst the political, economic and human rights concerns posed by technology. While technology has positive impacts such as increased efficiency and enhanced access to justice, it also has negative impacts such as targeted surveillance and similar threats. Judiciaries have a role to play in ensuring digital rights are protected. The authors discuss how, in Southeast Asia, civil society actors are approaching courts to guarantee digital rights, while facing challenges such as restrictive political environments, weak judicial systems, and digital repression. The chapter recommends promoting and advancing internet freedom, recognising and strengthening the role of courts, and urging tech companies to respect and protect human rights.

E. CONCLUSION

As this introduction has outlined, this book offers insights into the various ways in which courts are negotiating with digital transformations. Reflecting on the in-depth case studies, it becomes apparent that the path to digitalisation is not linear but fraught with unique opportunities as well as challenges that emerge from specific socio-technical environments within which these transformations are taking place. These include the development of technical infrastructures, the assessment of the choices of how technologies are designed, developed and deployed, the analysis of the policy as well as regulatory frameworks that are created to complement digital developments, and the cultivation of approaches and cultures of those who are executing these changes.

The different perspectives of digital transformations of courts across Asia demonstrate the ways in which these institutions are changing – in terms of how they perceive their own roles in society, their understandings of legal needs of justice users, and their understandings of technology. In many chapters, court administrators are wrestling with difficult decisions where on the one hand there is a need to build more efficient and effective systems for justice delivery, while on the other hand there is concern that using technology to achieve this may in fact exacerbate existing problems within the system.

By identifying three elements to interrogate these processes of digitalisation, that is, through administering technology, adjudicating technology as well as challenging technology, this book aims to provide space for dialogue for evaluating the implications of taking different pathways to digital transformations. Exploring these elements can lead to more careful and deliberative ways in which courts can digitalise.

The chapters in this book offer pathways to digital transformations that are situated, complex and at the same time driven by the goal of ensuring that no one is left behind. Together they bring to light why we need more narratives on digital transformations on courts from plural locations, and why studying developments across Asia can provide important repositories and imaginaries of engaging in socio-political and technical choices of digital development.

NOTES

1. Richard Susskind, *Online Courts and the Future of Justice* (Oxford University Press, 2021). Ethan Katsh and others, *Digital Justice: Technology and the Internet of Disputes* (Oxford University Press, 2017).
2. 'Vision Document for Phase III of eCourts Project | Official Website of E-Committee, Supreme Court of India | India' <https://ecommitteesci.gov.in/vision-document-for-phase-iii-of-ecourts-project/> (accessed 6 May 2024).
3. artificiallawyer, 'Singapore Formally Launches Its FLIP Legal Innovation Programme' (*Artificial Lawyer*, 11 January 2018) <https://www.artificiallawyer.com/2018/01/11/singapore-formally-launches-its-flip-legal-innovation-programme/> (accessed 16 August 2020).
4. 'Japanese Courts Promoting Digital Reform' (*The Japan Times*, 12 January 2022) <https://www.japantimes.co.jp/news/2022/01/12/national/courts-digital-reform/> (accessed 6 July 2022).
5. 'MyGOV – Whole of Government | Legislation | e-Judiciary System For Courts Nationwide' <https://www.malaysia.gov.my/portal/content/31135> (accessed 6 July 2022).
6. Giulia Gentile and Giovanni De Gregorio, 'The Digitisation of Justice Risks Blurring the Lines between Public and Private Actors' (*EUROPP*, 23 June 2023) <https://blogs.lse.ac.uk/europpblog/2023/06/23/the-digitisation-of-justice-risks-blurring-the-lines-between-public-and-private-actors/> (accessed 9 July 2023). Siddharth Peter de Souza, Varsha Aithala and Srishti John, 'The Supreme Court of India's Vision for e-Courts: The Need to Retain Justice as a Public Service' (2021) <https://www.thehinducentre.com/publications/policy-watch/article34779031.ece> (accessed 31 August 2021).
7. Julia Angwin and others, 'Machine Bias' (*ProPublica*, 23 May 2016) <https://www.propublica.org/article/machine-bias-risk-assessments-in-criminal-sentencing> (accessed 16 February 2018).
8. Victor D Quintanilla and others, 'Digital Inequalities and Access to Justice: Dialing into Zoom Court Unrepresented' in David Freeman Engstrom (ed.), *Legal Tech and the Future of Civil Justice* (Cambridge University Press, 2023); Varsha Aithala and Siddharth Peter de Souza, 'Administering Virtual Justice in Times of Suffering During COVID-19' in Anindita Pattanayak and others (eds), *Constitutional Ideals – Development and Realisation Through Court-led Justice* (2023) <https://www.oakbridge.inconstitutional-ideals-%E2%80%93-development-and-realisation-through-court-led-justice> (accessed 9 October 2024).
9. 'UNESCO Survey Uncovers Critical Gaps in AI Training Among Judicial Operators | UNESCO' <https://www.unesco.org/en/articles/unesco-survey-uncovers-critical-gaps-ai-training-among-judicial-operators-0> (accessed 20 September 2024).

10. Ibid.
11. Alexander Campolo and Kate Crawford, 'Enchanted Determinism: Power without Responsibility in Artificial Intelligence' (2020) 6 *Engaging Science, Technology, and Society* 1.
12. Siddharth Peter de Souza, 'Epistemic Diversity and Voices from the Global South: Countering the Managerial Implications of Measuring Justice', *Designing Indicators for a Plural Legal World* (Cambridge University Press, 2022).
13. Siddharth Peter de Souza, Hellen Mukiri Smith and Linnet Taylor, 'Decolonial Data Law and Governance' (2024) *Technology and Regulation* 1. Patricia Boshe and Carolina Goberna Caride, 'Is the Brussels Effect Creating a New Legal Order in Africa and Latin America and the Caribbean?' (2024) *Technology and Regulation* 12.
14. Lena Salaymeh and Ralf Michaels, 'Decolonial Comparative Law: A Conceptual Beginning' (Social Science Research Network, 26 January 2022) <https://papers.ssrn.com/abstract=4014459> (accessed 11 October 2024).
15. Sunil Khilnani, Vikram Raghavan and Arun K. Thiruvengadam, *Comparative Constitutionalism in South Asia*, vol. 22 (Oxford University Press, New Delhi, 2013); Rosalind Dixon and Tim Ginsburg, *Comparative Constitutional Law in Asia* (Edward Elgar Publishing, 2014); Ngoc Son Bui and Mara Malagodi, *Asian Comparative Constitutional Law, Volume 1: Constitution-Making* (Bloomsbury Publishing, 2023).
16. Molly K. Land and Jay D. Aronson, 'Human Rights and Technology: New Challenges for Justice and Accountability' (2020) 16 *Annual Review of Law and Social Science* 223. Payal Arora and Rumman Chowdhury, 'Cross-Cultural Feminist Technologies' (2021) 2 *Global Perspectives* <https://online.ucpress.edu/gp/article/2/1/25207/117801/Cross-Cultural-Feminist-Technologies> (accessed 21 March 2022).
17. Tania Sourdin, 'Judges and Technology', *Judges, Technology and Artificial Intelligence* (Edward Elgar Publishing, 2021) <https://www.elgaronline.com/monochap/9781788978255.00005.xml> (accessed 13 October 2024).
18. Ibid.
19. Reem Abou Refaie and Joaquin Santuber, 'Risks and Challenges to E-Justice Principles: Governing Remote Work, Online Hearings and the Use of Social Media in Chilean Courts' (2023) 15 *JeDEM – eJournal of eDemocracy and Open Government* 118.
20. Ibid.
21. 'Detroit Digital Justice Coalition Principles' (*Detroit Digital Justice Coalition*) <https://www.detroitdjc.org/principles> (accessed 13 October 2024).
22. OECD, *OECD Framework and Good Practice Principles for People-Centred Justice* (OECD 2021) <https://www.oecd-ilibrary.org/governance/oecd-framework-and-good-practice-principles-for-people-centred-justice_cdc3bde7-en> (accessed 4 June 2024).
23. Kanan Dhru, Manasi Nikam and Maurits Barendrecht, 'Use of Digital Technologies in Judicial Reform and Access to Justice Cooperation' <https://www.hiil.org/research/digital-technology-and-judicial-reform/> (accessed 13 October 2024).
24. 'UNDP – Digital Strategy 2022–2025' <https://digitalstrategy.undp.org/> (accessed 7 May 2024).
25. 'What Does It Mean to Leave No One Behind?' (*UNDP*) <https://www.undp.org/publications/what-does-it-mean-leave-no-one-behind> (accessed 6 May 2024).

REFERENCES

Aithala, V. and de Souza, S. P., 'Administering Virtual Justice in Times of Suffering During COVID-19' in Anindita Pattanayak and others (eds), *Constitutional Ideals – Development and Realisation Through Court-led Justice* (2023) <https://www.oakbridge.inconstitutional-ideals-%E2%80%93-development-and-realisation-through-court-led-justice> (accessed 9 October 2024).

Angwin, J. and others, 'Machine Bias' (*ProPublica*, 23 May 2016) <https://www.propublica.org/article/machine-bias-risk-assessments-in-criminal-sentencing> (accessed 16 February 2018).

Arora, P. and Chowdhury, R., 'Cross-Cultural Feminist Technologies' (2021) 2 *Global Perspectives* <https://online.ucpress.edu/gp/article/2/1/25207/117801/Cross-Cultural-Feminist-Technologies> (accessed 21 March 2022).

artificiallawyer, 'Singapore Formally Launches Its FLIP Legal Innovation Programme' (*Artificial Lawyer*, 11 January 2018) <https://www.artificiallawyer.com/2018/01/11/singapore-formally-launches-its-flip-legal-innovation-programme/> (accessed 16 August 2020).

Boshe, P. and Caride, C. G., 'Is the Brussels Effect Creating a New Legal Order in Africa and Latin America and the Caribbean?' (2024) *Technology and Regulation* 12.

Bui, N. S. and Malagodi, M., *Asian Comparative Constitutional Law, Volume 1: Constitution-Making* (Bloomsbury Publishing, 2023).

Campolo, A. and Crawford, K., 'Enchanted Determinism: Power without Responsibility in Artificial Intelligence' (2020) 6 *Engaging Science, Technology, and Society* 1.

de Souza, S. P. (ed.), 'A Capability Approach to Access to Justice in Plural Legal Systems', *Designing Indicators for a Plural Legal World* (Cambridge University Press, 2022) <https://www.cambridge.org/core/books/designing-indicators-for-a-plural-legal-world/capability-approach-to-access-to-justice-in-plural-legal-systems/3BC8F0B482818E5AE7B7905F1729A706> (accessed 13 March 2023).

de Souza, S. P. (ed.), 'Epistemic Diversity and Voices from the Global South: Countering the Managerial Implications of Measuring Justice', *Designing Indicators for a Plural Legal World* (Cambridge University Press, 2022).

de Souza, S. P., Aithala, V. and John, S., 'The Supreme Court of India's Vision for e-Courts: The Need to Retain Justice as a Public Service' (2021) <https://www.thehinducentre.com/publications/policy-watch/article34779031.ece> (accessed 31 August 2021).

de Souza, S. P., Smith, H. M. and Taylor, L., 'Decolonial Data Law and Governance' (2024) 2024 *Technology and Regulation* 1.

'Detroit Digital Justice Coalition Principles' (*Detroit Digital Justice Coalition*) <https://www.detroitdjc.org/principles> (accessed 13 October 2024).

Dhru, K., Nikam, M. and Barendrecht, M., 'Use of Digital Technologies in Judicial Reform and Access to Justice Cooperation' <https://www.hiil.org/research/digital-technology-and-judicial-reform/> (accessed 13 October 2024).

Dixon, R. and Ginsburg, T., *Comparative Constitutional Law in Asia* (Edward Elgar Publishing, 2014).

Gentile, G. and De Gregorio, G., 'The Digitisation of Justice Risks Blurring the Lines between Public and Private Actors' (*EUROPP*, 23 June 2023) <https://blogs.lse.ac.uk/europpblog/2023/06/23/the-digitisation-of-justice-risks-blurring-the-lines-between-public-and-private-actors/> (accessed 9 July 2023).

'Japanese Courts Promoting Digital Reform' (*The Japan Times*, 12 January 2022) <https://www.japantimes.co.jp/news/2022/01/12/national/courts-digital-reform/> (accessed 6 July 2022).

Katsh, E. and others, *Digital Justice: Technology and the Internet of Disputes* (Oxford University Press, 2017).

Khilnani, S., Raghavan, V. and Thiruvengadam, A. K., *Comparative Constitutionalism in South Asia*, vol. 22 (New Delhi: Oxford University Press, 2013) <https://www.academia.edu/download/102520419/bd8c89bab22e83f0ff3a0ca335ddac41b020.pdf> (accessed 11 October 2024).

Land, M. K. and Aronson, J. D., 'Human Rights and Technology: New Challenges for Justice and Accountability' (2020) 16 *Annual Review of Law and Social Science* 223.

'MyGOV – Whole of Government | Legislation | e-Judiciary System For Courts Nationwide' <https://www.malaysia.gov.my/portal/content/31135> (accessed 6 July 2022).

OECD, 'Equal Access to Justice for Inclusive Growth – Putting People at the Centre' (2019) <https://www.oecd.org/governance/equal-access-to-justice-for-inclusive-growth-597f5b7f-en.htm> (accessed 31 July 2019).

OECD, *OECD Framework and Good Practice Principles for People-Centred Justice* (OECD 2021) <https://www.oecd-ilibrary.org/governance/oecd-framework-and-good-practice-principles-for-people-centred-justice_cdc3bde7-en> (accessed 4 June 2024).

Quintanilla, V. D. and others, 'Digital Inequalities and Access to Justice: Dialing into Zoom Court Unrepresented' in David Freeman Engstrom (ed.), *Legal Tech and the Future of Civil Justice* (Cambridge University Press, 2023) <https://www.cambridge.org/core/books/legal-tech-and-the-future-of-civil-justice/digital-inequalities-and-access-to-justice/283CB78FAD49783FF3AB4CD94B5DB4AC> (accessed 9 October 2024).

Refaie, R. A. and Santuber, J., 'Risks and Challenges to E-Justice Principles: Governing Remote Work, Online Hearings and the Use of Social Media in Chilean Courts' (2023) 15 *JeDEM – eJournal of eDemocracy and Open Government* 118.

Salaymeh, L. and Michaels, R., 'Decolonial Comparative Law: A Conceptual Beginning' (Social Science Research Network, 26 January 2022) <https://papers.ssrn.com/abstract=4014459> (accessed 11 October 2024).

Sourdin, T., 'Judges and Technology', *Judges, Technology and Artificial Intelligence* (Edward Elgar Publishing, 2021) <https://www.elgaronline.com/monochap/9781788978255.00005.xml> (accessed 13 October 2024).

Susskind, R., *Online Courts and the Future of Justice* (Oxford University Press, 2021).

'UNDP – Digital Strategy 2022–2025' <https://digitalstrategy.undp.org/> (accessed 7 May 2024).

'UNESCO Survey Uncovers Critical Gaps in AI Training Among Judicial Operators | UNESCO' <https://www.unesco.org/en/articles/unesco-survey-uncovers-critical-gaps-ai-training-among-judicial-operators-0> (accessed 20 September 2024).

'Vision Document for Phase III of eCourts Project | Official Website of E-Committee, Supreme Court of India | India' <https://ecommitteesci.gov.in/vision-document-for-phase-iii-of-ecourts-project/> (accessed 6 May 2024).

'What Does It Mean to Leave No One Behind?' (*UNDP*) <https://www.undp.org/publications/what-does-it-mean-leave-no-one-behind> (accessed 6 May 2024).

Part I

Administering Technology

Chapter 2

Administering Technology: The Implementation of Court Technology in the Indonesian Constitutional Court

Pan Mohamad Faiz

A. INTRODUCTION

The Indonesian Constitutional Court was established on 13 August 2003, based on the results of the amendments of the Indonesian Constitution to strengthen the checks and balances mechanism in the system of separation of state power in Indonesia. Pursuant to Article 24C paragraph (1) of the Indonesian Constitution, the Court has granted five constitutional authorities. The Court has powers to review the constitutionality of laws, resolve disputes of authority between state institutions, decide political parties' dissolution, settle disputes over the general election results, and decide on legal issues related to the impeachment of the President and Vice President.[1] With this authority, the Indonesian Constitutional Court functions as the guardian of the Constitution and the principles of democracy and the protector of citizens' constitutional rights.[2]

The Constitutional Court in Indonesia is an independent court on equal footing with the Supreme Court.[3] Therefore, as a judicial institution, the Court has a vision and acts as a means of reference in carrying out its duties and authorities. In realising the goal of being recognised as a modern and trusted judicial institution, five strategic objectives were set.[4]

1. Increasing the institutional capacity of the Constitutional Court in carrying out its constitutional authority.
2. Improving court administration services and general administration in resolving constitutional cases.
3. Enhancing the support for facilities and infrastructure of constitutional justice based on ICT.
4. Strengthening the role of the Constitutional Court in encouraging the realisation of a democratic rule of law on a national, regional and global level.
5. Increasing public knowledge and understanding of the values of the *Pancasila* and constitutional norms in the society, nation and state.[5]

Based on the 20-year journey since its establishment, the presence of the Constitutional Court has been a significant achievement for the constitutional system and the development of democracy in Indonesia. As of April 2023, the Constitutional Court has ruled 1,628 cases of judicial review, 29 cases of dispute over the authority of state institutions, 676 cases of legislative elections, 5 cases of presidential elections, and 1,136 cases of disputes over the results of regional elections.[6] Thus far, no applications have been submitted to the Constitutional Court related to the dissolution of political parties and alleged violations of the Constitution by the President or Vice President. Thus, the details of the Constitutional Court's decisions are presented in Table 2.1.

An increase in citizens' understanding and constitutional awareness correlates with their increasing desire to submit cases to the Constitutional Court. Therefore, this presents the challenge of providing excellent judicial services for justice seekers who litigate in the Constitutional Court. To achieve this goal, applying court technology in the Constitutional Court is an inevitable necessity, reflected in the aforementioned strategic objectives.

This chapter will examine how the Indonesian Constitutional Court uses technology for its day-to-day functioning. It will discuss the importance of technology for the court, followed by the implementation of court technology in the Indonesian Constitutional Court, an analysis of its implications and an evaluation of the challenges faced.

B. THE IMPORTANCE OF COURT TECHNOLOGY

Judicial institutions in various countries that seemingly competed to implement court technology have proved to be successful examples of utilising technological advancements to facilitate the business process in their judicial institutions. In the Case Management or Electronic Case File (CM/ECF) service in the US Supreme Court, for instance, technological innovation has played a critical role in the performance of the judiciary. Greenwood and Brinkema explained that this service system is the oldest and largest in the world with an integrated case management and e-filing system. This system was fully developed by a group of highly qualified and experienced programmers, system analysts, computer scientists and other IT professionals employed by the US Court Administration Office (AOUSC). In addition, US Judicial Branch agents were responsible for all lower federal court administration and management support.[7]

Furthermore, the European Commission on Justice Efficiency (CEPEJ) has illustrated that information technology can be utilised in three ways: (1) direct support for judges and staff; (2) support for court management; and (3) support for interaction between courts and parties.[8] According to Reiling, the interaction developed between the judiciary and its users will increase

Table 2.1 Constitutional Court decisions (as of April 2023)

Jurisdiction	Granted	Rejected	Dismissed	Withdrawn	Others	Total
Judicial Review	298	614	509	118	39	1,628
Disputes between State Institutions	1	2	18	7	–	29
Disputes on Legislative Elections	53	423	148	13	34	671
Disputes on Presidential Elections	–	5	–	–	–	5
Disputes on Local Elections	83	495	509	35	14	1,136

Source: Registry Office and Secretariat General of the Constitutional Court.

opportunities to improve the administration of justice and the ongoing handling of cases.[9] Moreover, the use of court technology can reduce costs incurred by parties to gain access to legal information provided by the court. Likewise, publishing legal information and court decisions on the website will increase public understanding of the constitutional justice system and create more accessible judicial institutions.[10]

The Indonesian Constitutional Court also uses technology in the administration of justice. It has become necessary because the Constitutional Court has the vision to 'Uphold the Constitution through a Modern and Reliable Court'. The modern court means a court with an Information and Communication Technology (ICT) based working system and a progressive mindset and culture set. The purpose and motivation for utilising court technology in the Indonesian Constitutional Court are to reduce costs and time processes, create transparent, accountable and reliable work processes, and improve the quality of public services.

Responding to Disruption Era,[11] the Indonesian Constitutional Court provides online applications, digital transcripts, live streaming hearings, and conducts hearings remotely to simplify judicial processes. These court technologies developed by the Court aim to ensure transparency and accountability in the administration of justice. It is carried out directly by the Court IT staff under the Center for Information and Communication Technology (*Pusat TIK*) in collaboration with IT professionals. They built a grand design of a court technology system that can strengthen transparency and accountability in implementing judicial administration.

C. COURT TECHNOLOGY IN THE INDONESIAN CONSTITUTIONAL COURT

Even though it is still relatively young, the Constitutional Court is an institutional icon in establishing a modern court in Indonesia, as it can continue to follow new developments and progress at any time. Court technology is a handy tool for the Constitutional Court in resolving cases and providing access to information that is open to parties and the broader public regarding case examination. In addition, it enables transparency and accountability in each stage of case settlement.

The court technology system in the Indonesian Constitutional Court has two main systems. First, the Judicial Administrative System (JAS), including electronic filing (e-Filing), video conferencing, a case tracking system, live-streaming of hearings, digital transcripts, and a digital mobile application. Second, the General Administrative System (GAS) covers a dynamic archival information system, real-time financial reports, a talent pool system and social media. These systems will be examined below.

I. Electronic filing (e-Filing)

With the online application system, applicants do not need to come directly to the Constitutional Court building to submit their documents. In particular, the presence of an online application is beneficial in handling cases that require a quick examination, especially in resolving disputes over election results. As described in the case statistics above, election disputes form the most considerable percentage of cases decided by the Constitutional Court. However, the election law in Indonesia has outlined strict deadlines for applicants to submit disputes within 3 × 24 hours after the General Election Commission has determined the election results. If the application is submitted beyond the deadline, the case will be dismissed.[12]

This short period would be sufficient for the applicants if transportation options were not limited. However, as the largest archipelago in the world, candidates do not have the same accessibility to file a dispute over election results. For example, due to the great distance, election participants in areas such as Papua and West Papua in eastern Indonesia need more than one day to get to the Constitutional Court building in the nation's capital, Jakarta. Aside from distance and time, a further obstacle is transporting many documents needed as supporting evidence. Therefore, an online application system can avoid the expiration of the period if filing an election dispute to the Constitutional Court is possible. The biggest challenge is to change the habits of the parties to move on from the conventional mechanism that carries the application file and physical evidence to the paperless mechanism by sending all the application files and evidence through an online system.

Given that not all justice seekers understand the online application technology, the Constitutional Court needs to issue a mandatory requirement for applicants to submit their applications online gradually. Indeed, it is not required for applicants in the Constitutional Court to be accompanied by a lawyer, resulting in self-represented litigants being able to submit their applications to the Constitutional Court directly. This policy is carried out to provide broader access to justice and public service. However, when the COVID-19 pandemic occurred, all applications had to be submitted online. Under conditions of compulsion, they realised how beneficial court technology is in supporting their cases before the Court, particularly in judicial review cases. This practice is illustrated by the line chart in Figure 2.1, which shows a significant increase in online applications during the COVID-19 pandemic.

Indonesia is a vast archipelagic country with around 17,000 islands, while the Indonesian Constitutional Court is only located in Jakarta. Therefore, the Court seeks to provide easier access to justice for citizens who want to fight for their constitutional rights. In this context, a court hearing in the Indonesian Constitutional Court can also be conducted using video conferencing. The Court has cooperated with more than forty-two universities in

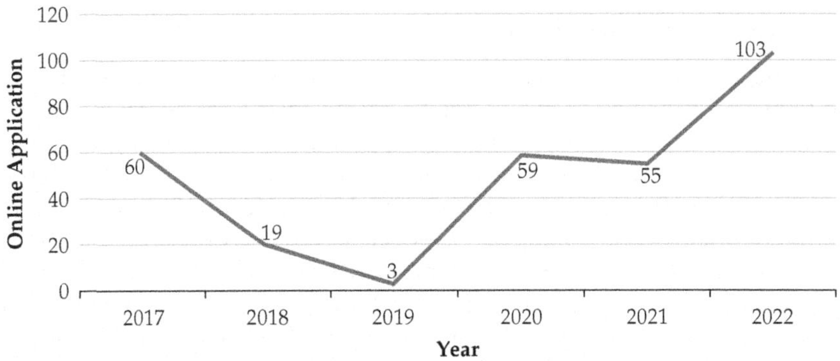

Figure 2.1 Statistics of online applications (2017–2022)
Source: ICT Center of the Constitutional Court.

all thirty-eight provinces in Indonesia to place its video conference facilities and devices.[13]

The Constitutional Court owns the facilities and devices, but daily maintenance is carried out by local officers assigned by the local university. With this video conference, all regions of Indonesia are connected to the Constitutional Court located in Jakarta, the capital of Indonesia. The parties can simply go to their nearest university to conduct the hearings. Thus, remote hearings using this video conference have created a more effective process. For example, experts or witnesses who are involved in resolving disputes over election results, particularly in national legislative election disputes, do not need to be flown to Jakarta to provide their expertise or testimony, instead attending via the university closest to them (see Figures 2.2 and 2.3).

This video conference facility is not only used by parties from Indonesian territories but also to listen to experts from different continents, such as the Americas, Europe and Australasia. When this facility is not being used for court hearing purposes, it can be utilised instead by holding public lectures with universities within Indonesia and abroad, enabling a large number of students to participate. To show its dedication to academia, the Constitutional Court goes as far as facilitating a schedule for various educational activities to ensure there are no collisions in timetabling.

With current technological advances, primarily since the COVID-19 pandemic, the Constitutional Court also uses Zoom to hold court hearings. This application was chosen because the system is easy to understand and has a more stable network where everyone can use it from their office, home, or other places as long as they are connected to the internet. Almost all court hearings during the COVID-19 pandemic from 2020 to 2022 were conducted online. The use of video conference hearings has dramatically assisted the Constitutional Court in continuing to sit in the midst of a pandemic. Until now, the court hearings via video conference have also been

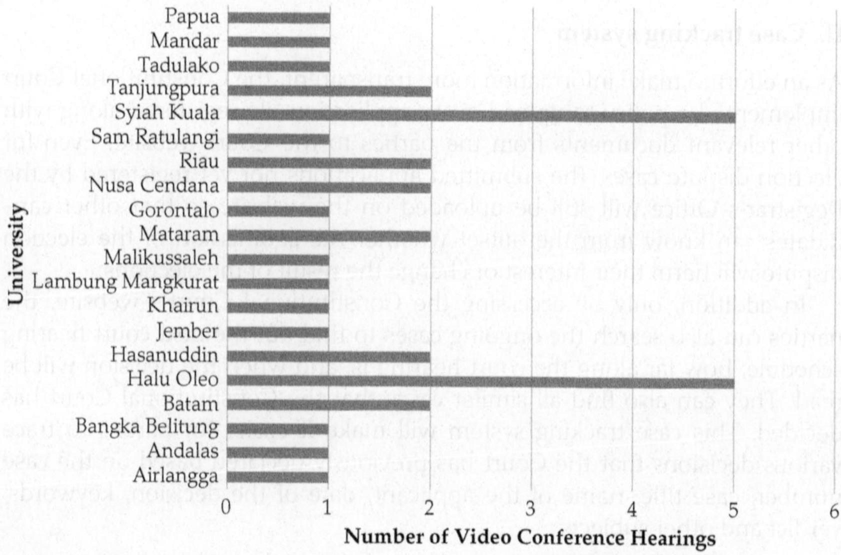

Figure 2.2 Video conference hearings on national legislative election dispute 2019

Source: ICT Center of the Constitutional Court.

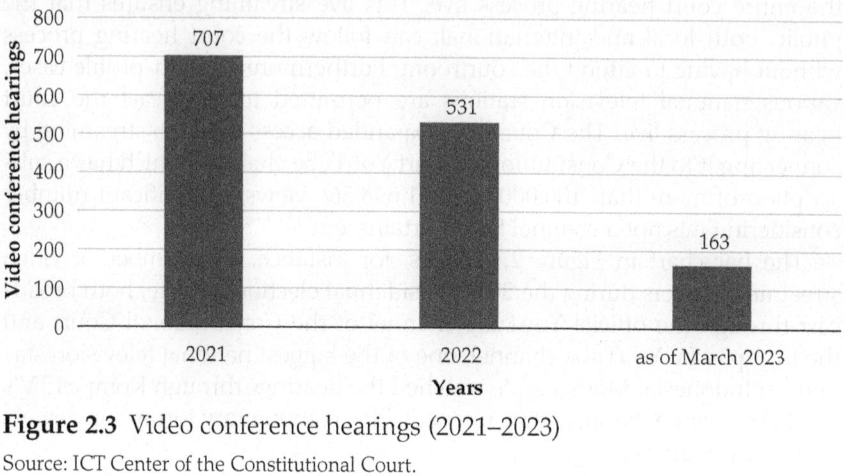

Figure 2.3 Video conference hearings (2021–2023)

Source: ICT Center of the Constitutional Court.

maintained if there is a request from parties. Currently, the Constitutional Court is also building smartboard mini-courtrooms at various universities so that the examination process will run as if it were in the middle of a courtroom.

II. Case tracking system

As an effort to make information more transparent, the Constitutional Court implemented a policy to upload every application file registered along with other relevant documents from the parties to the Court website. Even for election dispute cases, the submitted applications not yet registered by the Registrar's Office will still be uploaded on the website so that other candidates can know from the outset whether the submission of the election dispute will harm their interest or change the result of the elections.

In addition, only by accessing the Constitutional Court's website, the parties can also search the ongoing cases to find out the next court hearing schedule, how far along the court hearing is, and when the decision will be read. They can also find all similar cases that the Constitutional Court has decided. This case tracking system will make it easier for parties to trace various decisions that the Court has previously declared based on the case number, case title, name of the applicant, date of the decision, keywords, verdict and other subjects.

III. Live streaming of hearings

The use of court technology is also implemented through the video streaming facility available on the website of the Constitutional Court by broadcasting the entire court hearing process live. This live streaming ensures that the public, both local and international, can follow the court hearing process without having to attend the courtroom. Furthermore, in high-profile cases, various national television stations are permitted to broadcast the court hearing process live. The Court also expanded access to video streaming by connecting it to the Constitutional Court YouTube channel, which has a subscription of more than 100,000 with 11,698,566 views, a significant number considering it is not a channel for entertainment.[14]

The bar chart in Figure 2.4 shows, for instance, the number of video streaming viewers during the 2019 Presidential election dispute, both broadcast through the official YouTube channel of the Constitutional Court and the Kompas TV YouTube channel, one of the biggest national television stations in Indonesia. More people watched the hearings through Kompas TV's YouTube channel because they opened a live commentary forum for viewers during the court hearings.

The combination of online and offline access to information and court hearing services has also resulted in the Constitutional Court obtaining another award from the Indonesian World Record Museum for having 'the most transparent court hearing process'.[15] The court hearings of the 2019 presidential election were broadcast live by almost all national television channels and their respective YouTube channels. In addition, based on data held by the Public Relations Division of the Constitutional Court, those

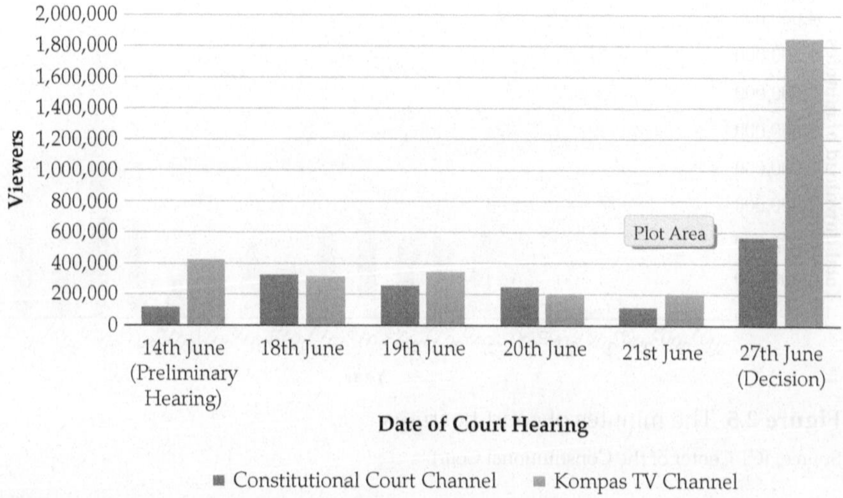

Figure 2.4 YouTube viewers on presidential election dispute settlement 2019

Source: ICT Center of the Constitutional Court.

hearings were covered by 544 journalists consisting of 74 online media outlets, 130 domestic and foreign media outlets, 39 TV stations, 9 radio stations, 16 print media outlets, and 80 other countries monitored through the Court's website. With such wide access, the Indonesian public and people from abroad were able to follow the proceedings in real time.

IV. Digital transcripts

One of the strengths of the use of court technology in the Indonesian Constitutional Court can also be seen in the availability of digital transcripts or minutes from each court hearing. Records from every court hearing are recorded in an audio and visual format, and then converted into a transcript or written document. The standard operating procedure for uploading transcripts and audio recordings to the Court website is no later than six hours after a court hearing is closed. These must be uploaded regardless of whether the court hearing is lengthy.

The most extreme example is the court hearing of the presidential election dispute in 2019, which won an award from the Indonesian World Record Museum for being the 'Longest Non-Stop Court Hearing' for twenty hours.[16] It consisted of a non-stop court hearing for nineteen hours and fifty-two minutes, beginning on Wednesday, 19 June 2019 at 9.08 am and terminating on Thursday, 20 June 2019 at 5.00 am. Within six hours after the court hearing was closed, a 917-page digital transcript was completed and could be accessed immediately from the Court website.

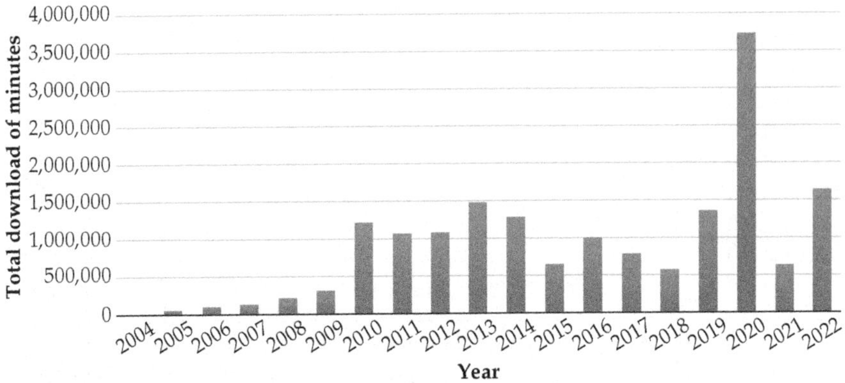

Figure 2.5 The minutes of court hearings

Source: ICT Center of the Constitutional Court.

This digital transcript could be done using an automatic audio conversion machine supervised by a team of transcribers and editors. However, on account of Indonesia's diverse cultural and ethnic backgrounds, the machine was unable to differentiate between the various dialects spoken by Indonesians, resulting in a low accuracy rate of 60%.[17] Professional staff was necessary to work alongside it to prepare the minutes of the hearing. Having said this, the Court still cooperates with technology institutions in Indonesia to develop the automatic transcript machine to improve its accuracy level. This improvement is necessary to ensure that subsequent hearings are more accountable. The availability of the minutes is pivotal to the accuracy of the data and facts. Justices of the Court and all parties can read and re-examine the matters that have been debated, examined and proven in previous court hearings.

V. Digital mobile application

With regard to the various court technology systems discussed above, the Constitutional Court has also transformed them in the form of a digital application called 'Click MK' which can be installed on Android and iOS-based gadgets (Figure 2.6). This application enables users to follow the court hearing process through live streaming, the progress of the case with the case tracking system, read the minutes of the hearings and view the decision made. Documents that previously could only be obtained by visiting a court can now be found quickly and easily at any time using their respective smartphones or gadgets.

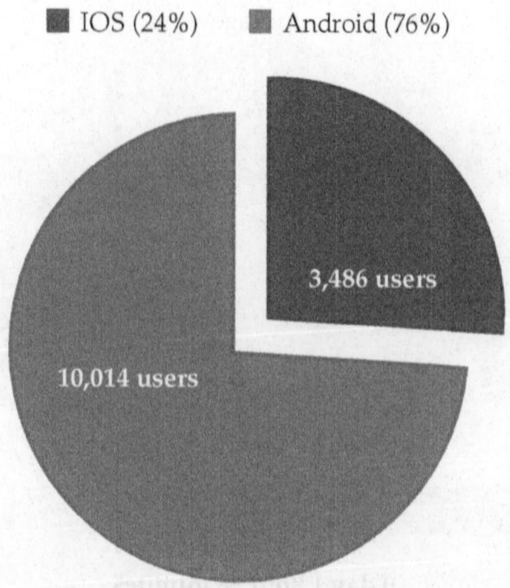

Figure 2.6 Digital mobile application installation
Source: ICT Center of the Constitutional Court.

VI. Dynamic Archival Information System (SIKD)

In the general administration system, the Constitutional Court applies a new technology called a Dynamic Archival Information System (*Sistem Informasi Kearsiapan Dinamis,* SIKD), which has shifted the administration model from a print-out system to an online system. For internal purposes, only a few essential documents are printed. Using the SIKD, all instructions and directives from the court leadership are carried out through an online system, so there are no longer piles of documents on the desks of Court employees.

This SIKD can be accessed from anywhere using a unique VPN that employees of the Constitutional Court own. During the COVID-19 pandemic, the SIKD was very useful for completing work from home so that, even though a pandemic was occurring, various preparations for online hearings could be carried out optimally. Moreover, the SIKD system developed by the Constitutional Court now serves as an example and a reference for other state institutions in Indonesia, including non-judicial institutions, to be adopted in their respective institutions.

VII. Real-time financial reports

The Constitutional Court is also a pioneer in introducing real-time financial reports announced on its official website to implement judicial transparency and accountability in the general administration system. Therefore, anyone can evaluate the use of the budget allocated for the Constitutional Court at any time.[18]

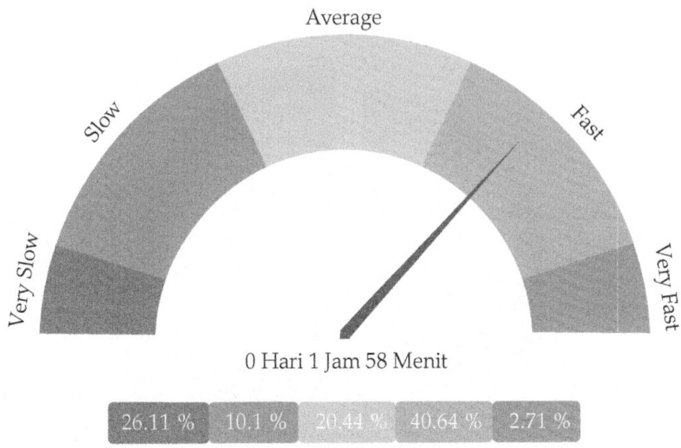

0 day 1 hour 58 minutes

Average response time for all Court employees:
0 day 4 hour 14 minutes

Figure 2.7 Response time of the author as of April 2023

Source: Talent Pool System at the Indonesian Constitutional Court.

This real-time financial report is also prepared in detail based on monthly periods, working units, programs, and activities. With these reports, the House of Representative members or the Ministry of Finance staff can also control and supervise the use of the judicial budget at the Constitutional Court.

VIII. Talent pool system

Currently, the Constitutional Court is developing and implementing a talent pool system (Talent Management) to select and promote employees to higher positions. This system uses technology to evaluate employee performance and potential. The assessment of this talent pool system consists of several criteria, namely employee potential (30%), competency (30%), track record (15%) and other criteria (25%), such as foreign language skills and collaborative awards.

This talent pool system can also show how fast each employee responds in following up on the directives they receive through a Dynamic Archival Information System (SIKD), as described above (see Figure 2.7). Based on the data displayed in this system, the Constitutional Court can determine the successor candidates who will fill strategic and structural positions in the future. The higher the performance of an employee, the greater the chance of getting a promotion to a judicial administration position.

IX. Social media of the Court

In addition to the technology system implemented above, the use of social media applications owned by the Constitutional Court also helps disseminate information on case developments and the various Court activities. In some countries, judicial institutions have also begun to have social media accounts to disseminate information about their decisions.[19] Social media applications run by the Indonesian Constitutional Court, among others, are Twitter, Facebook, Instagram and TikTok. Through these social media accounts, the Constitutional Court can provide the latest developments on a daily basis for hearings that will be or have just been held. Presently, the number of people who follow the Constitutional Court's social media accounts is 131,500 on Twitter (@officialMKRI), 20,220 on Facebook (Mahkamah Konstitusi Republik Indonesia), 178,000 on Instagram (@mahkamahkonstitusi) and 2,845 on TikTok (@officialmkri).

These accounts' followers are still relatively small compared to other influencers' accounts. However, the Constitutional Court shows its commitment to sharing information that can be accessed openly. The use of social media for a judiciary can have pros and cons. Nevertheless, as long as the information disseminated is public, the use of social media helps inform the broader community, particularly the younger generation.[20]

D. THE FUTURE CHALLENGES

Based on extensive evaluation, an ongoing target is to connect the court technology system established in the Constitutional Court with other state institutions, such as the House of Representatives, the Ministry of Law and Human Rights and the Supreme Court. Furthermore, this e-Court system should be built integratively to make the case examination process more measurable and of better quality.

The experience of various courts in many countries shows that the main challenge often faced in administering court technology is more than financial support. However, it lies in the mindset of internal or external parties to take the initiative and to make changes to routines that have been done conventionally to become more modern, progressive, and out of the box. The mindset that wants to maintain conventional methods will undoubtedly hinder the development and application of court technology. In fact, in this disruptive era, creative and innovative ideas are urgently needed to anticipate future challenges so that reformers can overcome them.[21]

In addition, as also conveyed by Dory Reiling,[22] the Indonesian Constitutional Court also faces the challenge of changing the culture and mindset of its employees, some of whom still have concerns regarding the failure of the court technology, especially senior Justices and employees. These concerns can affect innovations in the development of e-Court in the

Indonesian Constitutional Court. However, as most of its employees are under forty years old, the transition to applying and using the court technology will be smoother as they are more inclined to adapt.

Furthermore, when handling disputes over election results, the Indonesian Constitutional Court always receives many documents of evidence. For instance, in the 2019 presidential election dispute, the Court received approximately 11,000 boxes containing documents of evidence. As a result, the Court must introduce electronic evidence in the form of soft files. The International Criminal Court has successfully implemented this electronic evidence system.[23] If the Indonesian Constitutional Court also applies this system, there will be a reduction in the number of documents that accumulate in the Constitutional Court building. It will also reduce the use of paper. This transition should be done gradually: although it can be quickly implemented, the public needs time to understand the switch to an electronic evidence system.

E. CONCLUSION

Some of the ICT systems discussed above have provided an overview of the kinds of court technology developed by the Indonesian Constitutional Court related to the administration of justice. However, the court technology provided by the Constitutional Court still needs to be improved. Therefore, the Court must conduct more profound research on the best practices for implementing court technology in other countries.

For this reason, the Indonesian Constitutional Court needs to learn and join the consortium of leading courts in order to exchange experiences of using appropriate technology in the administration of justice. The technological system applied in the Indonesian Constitutional Court may be superior to other judicial institutions in Indonesia. However, the system needs to catch up compared to other developed countries.[24]

Based on the discussion and data presented above, the use of court technology in Indonesia also gained momentum during the COVID-19 pandemic, when it was impossible to have face-to-face physical hearings. At that time, court technology at the Constitutional Court was optimally used, especially for the online submission of applications and case examinations using a video conferencing system.

Given that science and technology are constantly developing, the Indonesian Constitutional Court must be active in carrying out various innovations in applying court technology in its judicial institution. Thus, the Court can create a more efficient and effective system, not only for the Judicial Administration System (JAS) and the General Administration System (GAS) but also for improving public services for justice seekers in Indonesia. Equally important, information and communication technology (ICT) must be used with principles of integrity, cleanliness and trustworthiness (ICT).

If technology is understood merely as a tool, then the person behind the tool will not be able to use the technology properly. Therefore, integrity, cleanliness and trustworthiness are inseparable from the court technology applied at the Indonesian Constitutional Court.

NOTES

1. S. Butt, *The Constitutional Court and Democracy in Indonesia* (Brill Nijhoff, 2015); S. Hendrianto, *Law and Politics of Constitutional Courts: Indonesia and the Search of Judicial Heroes* (Routledge, 2018); I. D. G. Palguna, S. Isra and P. M. Faiz, *The Constitutional Court and Human Rights Protection in Indonesia* (Rajawali Pers, 2022).
2. S. Isra and P. M. Faiz, *Indonesian Constitutional Law: Selected Articles on Challenges and Developments in Post-Constitutional Reform* (Rajawali Pers, 2021).
3. Constitution of Indonesia, art. 24(2), states: 'Judicial power shall be exercised by a Supreme Court and its inferior courts in the jurisdiction of general courts, the religious affair courts, the military tribunal, the state administrative courts, and by a Constitutional Court.'
4. Mahkamah Konstitusi Republik Indonesia, *Dokumen Rencana Strategis Mahkamah Konstitusi 2015–2019* [*Constitutional Court Strategic Plan Document 2015–2019*] (Kepaniteraan and Sekretariat Jenderal, 2015).
5. *Pancasila* (five principles) is the Indonesian state philosophy, namely: (1) the belief in the One and Only God; (2) just and civilised humanity; (3) Indonesian unity; (4) democracy led by the wisdom of the representative of the People; and (5) social justice for all the peoples of Indonesia.
6. Statistics of the Indonesian Constitutional Court decisions can be accessed at www.mkri.id.
7. M. J. Greenwood and J Brinkema, 'E-Filing Case Management Services in the US Federal Courts: The Next Generation: A Case Study' (2015) IJCA 3, 3.
8. D. Reiling, 'Technology in Courts in Europe: Opinions, Practices and Innovations' (2012) IJCA 1, 2.
9. D. Reiling, 'Understanding IT for Dispute Resolution' (2011) ICJA 1, 6.
10. R. van den Hoogen, 'Will E-Justice still be Justice? Principles of a fair electronic trial' (2008) IJCA 65, 66.
11. The term denotes the significant transformation initiated by the Fourth Industrial Revolution (Industry 4.0), which is defined by the incorporation of advanced digital technologies across various sectors, including the judiciary. This revolution is characterised by the emergence of technologies such as artificial intelligence (AI), the Internet of Things (IoT), big data, automation, and cloud computing.
12. Constitutional Court Regulation Number 2 of 2023 on Procedural Law on Disputes of Legislative Election Result, art. 7(1) (Indonesia).
13. The legal validity of this video conference is regulated based on Regulation of the Indonesian Constitutional Court Number 18/PMK/2009 on Guideline of Electronic Filing and Video Conference Examination, which has been changed by Regulation of the Indonesian Constitutional Court Number 1 of 2021 on Organizing Remote Hearings.
14. Indonesian Constitutional Court, YouTube Channel <www.youtube.com/@mahkamahkonstitusi> (accessed 15 February 2024).

15. A. Dwi, 'Mahkamah Konstitusi Catatkan Tiga Rekor MURI [Constitutional Court receives three records from MURI]' *Media Indonesia* (August 2019) <https://mediaindonesia.com/hut-ri/253568/mahkamah-konstitusi-catatkan-tiga-rekor-muri> (accessed 14 February 2024).
16. Dwi (n. 15).
17. Based on data released by the Language Development Board of the Ministry of Education and Culture, the number of local languages in Indonesia in 2018 was 652. These local languages also influence the dialect used by different people when they speak Bahasa Indonesia. See 'Badan Bahasa Petakan 652 Bahasa Daerah di Indonesia [The Language Agency maps 652 Regional Languages in Indonesia]' (*Ministry of Education and Culture*) <kemdikbud.go.id/main/blog/2018/07/badan-bahasa-petakan-652-bahasa-daerah-di-indonesia> (accessed 16 January 2023).
18. 'Grafik Informasi Anggaran [Budget Information Graph],' (Constitutional Court of Indonesia) <www.mkri.id/index.php?page=web.Keuangan&id=2&pages=1&menu=7> (accessed 2 February 2023).
19. J. Gibson, 'Social Media and the Electronic "New World" of Judges' (2016) IJCA 1, 1.
20. Gibson (n. 19), 2.
21. P. M. Faiz, 'MK dan e-Court di Era Disruptif [Constitutional Court and e-Court in Disruptive Era]', *Konstitusi No. 134* (Jakarta, April 2018), 80.
22. A. Wallace, 'Developing IT for Courts – Ten Questions for Dory Reiling' (2019) IJCA 1, 2.
23. M. Dillon and D. Beresford, 'Electronic Courts and the Challenges in Managing Evidence: A View from Inside the International Criminal Court' (2014) IJCA 1, 5.
24. For instance, when Indonesia just began to implement the e-filing system, the US Federal Courts had developed the second generation of e-filing. See Greenwood and Brinkema, 'E-Filing …' (n. 7), 3.

REFERENCES

Butt, S., *The Constitutional Court and Democracy in Indonesia* (Leiden, Netherlands: Brill Nijhoff, 2015).

Constitutional Court of Indonesia, 'Grafik Informasi Anggaran [Budget Information Graph]', *Constitutional Court of Indonesia*, www.mkri.id/index.php?page=web.Keuangan&id=2&pages=1&menu=7, (accessed 2 February 2023).

Constitutional Court of Indonesia, *Dokumen Rencana Strategis Mahkamah Konstitusi 2015–2019* [*Constitutional Court Strategic Plan Document 2015–2019*], Jakarta, Indonesia, Kepaniteraan and Sekretariat Jenderal, 2015.

Constitutional Court Regulation Number 1 of 2021 on Organizing Remote Hearings (Indonesia).

Constitutional Court Regulation Number 18/PMK/2009 on Guideline of Electronic Filing and Video Conference Examination (Indonesia).

Constitutional Court Regulation Number 2 of 2023 on Procedural Law on Disputes of Legislative Election Result, art. 7(1) (Indonesia).

Dillon, M. and Beresford, D., 'Electronic Courts and the Challenges in Managing Evidence: A View from Inside the International Criminal Court', *International Journal for Court Administration*, vol. 6, no. 1, 2014, pp. 29–36.

Dwi, A., 'Mahkamah Konstitusi Catatkan Tiga Rekor MURI [Constitutional Court receives three records from MURI]', *Media Indonesia*, August 2019, https://mediaindonesia.com/hut-ri/253568/mahkamah-konstitusi-catatkan-tiga-rekor-muri (accessed 14 February 2024).

Faiz, P. M., 'MK dan e-Court di Era Disruptif [Constitutional Court and e-Court in Disruptive Era]', *Konstitusi*, no. 134, April 2018, p. 80.

Gibson, J., 'Social Media and the Electronic "New World" of Judges', *International Journal for Court Administration*, vol. 7, no. 2, 2016, pp. 1–9.

Greenwood, M. J. and Brinkema, J., 'E-Filing Case Management Services in the US Federal Courts: The Next Generation: A Case Study', *International Journal for Court Administration*, vol. 7, no. 1, 2015, pp. 3–17.

Hendrianto, S., *Law and Politics of Constitutional Courts: Indonesia and the Search of Judicial Heroes* (New York: Routledge, 2018).

Hoogen, R. van den, 'Will E-Justice still be Justice? Principles of a fair electronic trial', *International Journal for Court Administration*, vol. 1, no. 1, 2008, pp. 65–73.

Isra, S. and Faiz, P. M., *Indonesian Constitutional Law: Selected Articles on Challenges and Developments in Post-Constitutional Reform* (Depok, Indonesia: Rajawali Pers, 2021).

Ministry of Education and Culture of Indonesia, 'Badan Bahasa Petakan 652 Bahasa Daerah di Indonesia [The Language Agency maps 652 Regional Languages in Indonesia]', *Ministry of Education and Culture* <kemdikbud.go.id/main/blog/2018/07/badan-bahasa-petakan-652-bahasa-daerah-di-indonesia> (accessed 16 January 2023).

Palguna, I. D. G., Isra, S. and Faiz, P. M., *The Constitutional Court and Human Rights Protection in Indonesia* (Depok, Indonesia: Rajawali Pers, 2022).

Reiling, D., 'Technology in Courts in Europe: Opinions, Practices and Innovations', *International Journal for Court Administration*, vol. 4, no. 2, 2012, pp. 11–20.

Reiling, D., 'Understanding IT for Dispute Resolution', *International Journal for Court Administration*, vol. 3, no. 2, 2011, pp. 34–44.

Wallace, A., 'Developing IT for Courts – Ten Questions for Dory Reiling', *International Journal for Court Administration*, vol. 10, no. 1, 2016, pp. 1–3.

Chapter 3

Transformation through Technology: ICT Initiatives in the Odisha Judiciary*

S. Muralidhar

A. INTRODUCTION

The judiciary in India is structured in a broad hierarchy of the District Courts, the High Courts and the Supreme Court. India has had to grapple with numerous challenges, including case backlogs, limited accessibility, inefficiencies and transparency issues. In 2005,[1] the first Vision Document of the Indian Judiciary was released which attempted a blueprint for overall improvement in judicial infrastructure, with a special focus on digitalisation. It advocated the extensive adoption of Information and Communication Technology (ICT) to achieve the targets set for itself in the said document.

The Odisha judiciary has, since 2021, adopted several measures towards this digital transformation. From digitising case records and administrative files to introducing virtual hearings and live streaming of court proceedings, the Odisha judiciary has embraced a comprehensive approach leveraging technology. This chapter provides an overview of the ICT initiatives undertaken by the Odisha judiciary, highlighting its position as one of India's largest and most progressive judicial systems. It delves into the digitisation of case records, the introduction of virtual courtrooms, the establishment of e-libraries and e-services, and the preservation of legal heritage.

Moreover, this chapter aims to share the experiences and best practices of the Odisha judiciary with an international audience, particularly developing and emerging countries seeking to modernise their judicial systems through ICT. By contributing to the global discourse on the opportunities and challenges of ICT in the judiciary, it seeks to advocate for a more accessible and sustainable justice system worldwide.

* This is a modified version of a talk delivered online on 28 April 2023 at the 'Access to Justice, Technology and Courts in Asia Conference' at the Ibis on Bencoolen in Singapore. The author wishes to thank Rachit Sharma of Justice Adda, India and Sri Sai Santosh R, Final Year B. Com LLB, SASTRA University for their assistance in the preparation of this piece.

B. THE EVOLUTION OF DIGITALISATION IN THE INDIAN JUDICIARY

The digitisation[2] journey of the Indian judiciary commenced in 1989, with the introduction of computers at the Supreme Court for caveat matching.[3] This marked the initiation of a transformative phase in legal technology. In the subsequent decade, various states, led by Karnataka, attempted district-level computerisation, facing challenges due to the diverse applications and platforms in use.

By 1997, the National Informatics Centre (NIC)[4] computerised 430 district courts, supported by funding from the Ministry of Electronics and Information Technology (MeitY), signifying a significant milestone in streamlining court registry operations. Additionally, complete computerisation of twenty-seven district courts commenced in Nanded District, Maharashtra, in 1998.

In the early 2000s, focused efforts were directed towards comprehensive computerisation. A centrally sponsored scheme aimed at computerising 700 city courts across Delhi, Kolkata, Mumbai and Chennai was initiated in 2003/04.[5] However, this phase primarily focused on back-office tasks rather than holistic digitisation.

In July 2004, the Chief Justice of India (CJI) proposed the formation of an e-Committee to formulate a National Policy on the computerisation of the Indian Judiciary.[6] Subsequently, the e-Committee, chaired by Dr Justice G. C. Bharuka, meticulously crafted a strategic plan presented to the CJI in May 2005.[7] This laid the foundation for a national policy and action plan, emphasising judicial autonomy in technology adoption.

Early on in the journey towards digitalisation, a significant decision was made to opt for what is known as open-source software, specifically the Linux system. This choice, driven by budget considerations and the appeal of free and open-source software, presented both advantages and challenges. While Linux offered cost savings and accessibility, its compatibility issues with proprietary software posed significant hurdles. The efforts of the e-Committee during the 1990s at standardising procedures and devising uniform formats for legal documents in the various courts faced several hurdles including, at a broad level, resistance to change from the legal fraternity, including lawyers and their clerks.

In a market dominated by generic licensed products, including pre-bundled software sold with desktop computers and laptops, the preference of the judiciary in most states for an open-source system like Linux meant that the progress of digitalisation across courts remained uneven. Having a separate unit of skilled technical manpower helped some of the courts, including the Delhi High Court, adopt innovations faster than other courts.

In parallel, the e-Courts Project, launched in October 2005, aimed at universal computerisation of courts. The project evolved through three phases, emphasising citizen-centric services, software development models, and migration to cloud infrastructure.

Despite challenges, states like Kerala, Delhi and Odisha made significant strides. However, concerns over the digital divide prompted gradual implementation strategies, including training programmes and assistance centres for e-filing.

The milestones achieved during Phase I of the e-Courts Project were the automation of case workflows, the establishment of virtual courts, and the introduction of mobile-based services, underscoring India's commitment to enhancing accessibility and efficiency. This phase began in 2007 and concluded with extended timelines up to 30 March 2015. Phase II,[8] marked by the consolidation of available technology and innovation, laid the groundwork for future advancements, including the migration to cloud computing and the integration of big data mining and artificial intelligence. The government of India sanctioned the project on 4 August 2015 and this phase concluded in 2023.

The eCourts Vision Plan Phase III,[9] from 2023 onwards and projected over a period of four years, aims to revolutionise the Indian judicial system. Guided by the principles of 'access and inclusion', it focuses on creating digital courts, simplifying procedures and establishing a robust digital infrastructure. Through decentralised implementation and leveraging emerging technologies like AI and Machine Learning, Phase III aims to bridge the digital divide, streamline processes, reduce case backlogs, and make the justice delivery system more accessible, cost-effective and citizen-centric.

As we reflect on our journey thus far, it is imperative to recognise that our efforts extend beyond mere technological adoption. They embody a collective vision for a more accessible, transparent and efficient justice system – one that upholds the principles of fairness and equity for all.

I. Digitisation of judicial and administrative files

Recognising the challenges and limitations of conventional paper-based record management, the High Court of Orissa has since 2021[10] adopted various projects and strategies to digitise and manage the records of disposed-of, new and pending cases, as well as administrative files. These initiatives have addressed the issues of space, preservation, retrieval and verification of records, and have enhanced the efficiency and accessibility of record-keeping.

One of the major initiatives undertaken by the High Court of Orissa was the digitisation of disposed-of case records. To achieve this, a dedicated committee of six High Court Judges was formed to oversee the ambitious digitisation project. Their primary responsibility was to monitor the scanning and digitisation processes in both the High Court and the District Courts periodically. Further, relevant changes to incorporate digitisation were made to the General Rules through the Circular Orders of the High Court.[11] The new Rules outlined a clear procedure for record disposal.

This initiative not only addressed the immediate challenge of space management but also ushered in an era of efficient, digitised record-keeping, guaranteeing the preservation of important legal records for future generations. To facilitate this process, the Record Room Digitization Centre (RRDC) was inaugurated in September 2021, as part of record management and preservation efforts. The RRDC presented a modern efficient solution to the long-standing challenge of managing civil and criminal records. Maintaining the servers within the RRDC ensured that the repository of scanned records was accessible not only within the RRDC itself but also in courtrooms and offices of the High Court, enhancing accessibility and efficiency. One notable aspect of the RRDC's operations was its strong commitment to data accuracy, ensuring reliable records for all users. Before records were uploaded, a thorough verification process was undertaken to uphold the integrity of the digitised documents. A systematic three-step verification process was instituted, followed by the secure shredding of digitised physical records. Figure 3.1 explains the workflow at the RRDC.[12]

As of 31 January 2024, in the Record Room Digitization Centre (RRDC), the number of case records scanned is 9,77,436, the number of case records uploaded to the server is 9,90,778, and the number of records shredded is 8,94,509.[13]

One of the most salient revelations is the remarkable reduction in the turnaround time for retrieving and providing copies of records. In instances where a record has been successfully scanned and uploaded onto the Document Management System (DMS) server, the entire process of generating a hard copy can be accomplished in a matter of minutes.[14]

Traditionally, in a conventional procedure, when a litigant or advocate requested a copy of a record, the Copying Section would initiate a requisition to the relevant section or the Record Room. The provision of a copy was contingent upon the retrieval of the physical record, a process that inherently introduced delays and uncertainties. In stark contrast, the digitisation process has ushered in a transformation in the efficiency of record retrieval and reproduction. With digitisation, the Copying Section now possesses the capability to swiftly locate and access the required file within the DMS. This transformation applies not only to current records but extends to the legacy records that have undergone digitisation.

The District Court Digitization Centres (DCDCs), aimed at extending the principles of storage, scanning, preservation and retrieval of legacy records to district and taluka courts, commenced with a pilot phase encompassing four major District Courts of Cuttack, Ganjam, Sambalpur and Balasore. The project was subsequently expanded to an additional ten districts, highlighting its ongoing progress and potential for broader implications. One key observation is the strategic approach taken in formulating and disseminating

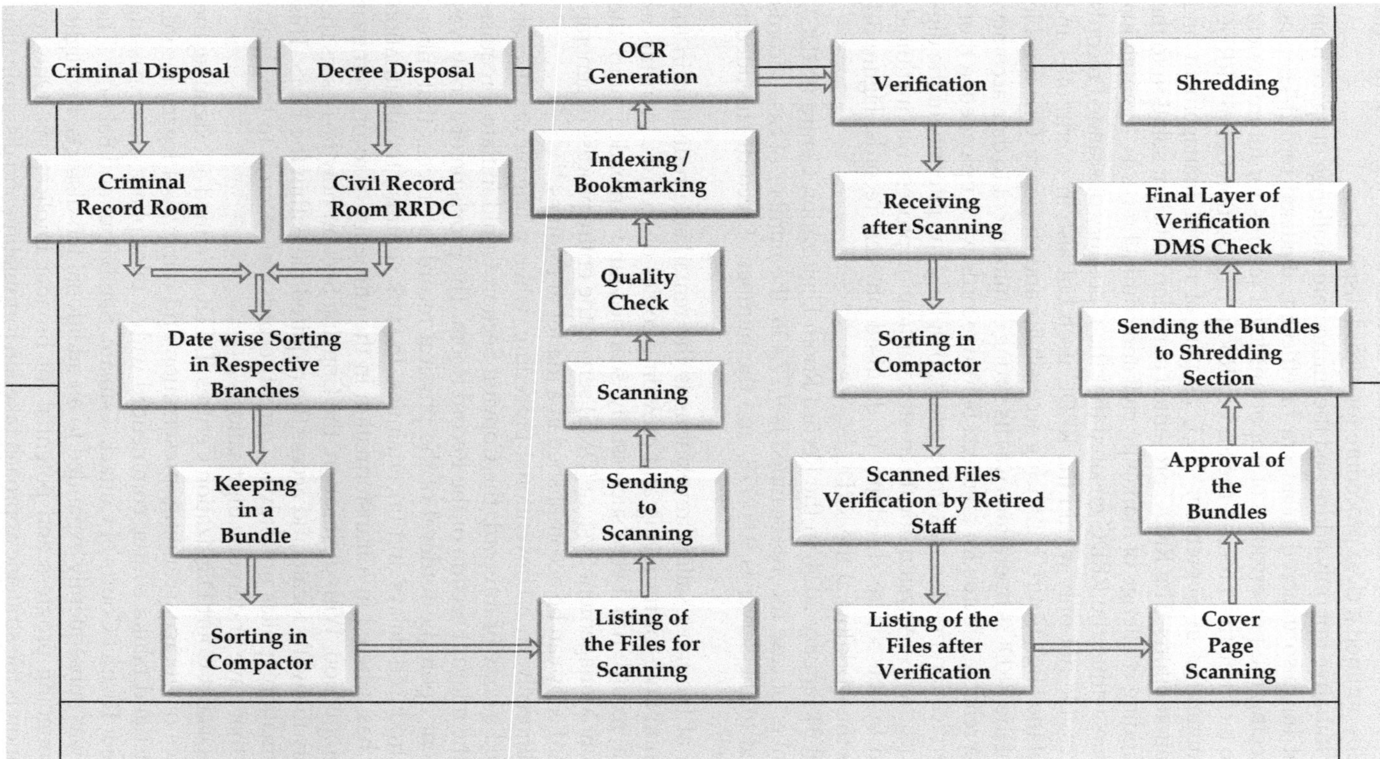

Figure 3.1 Workflow at Record Room Digitization Centre

Standard Operating Procedures (SOPs) to guide the uniform execution of storage and scanning processes across all DCDCs. Furthermore, the transformation of these fourteen DCDCs into 'Digitization Hubs' for the remaining sixteen Districts stands out as a pragmatic and scalable solution. The fourteen District Court Digitization Centres (DCDCs) are tasked with scanning pending records for the Paperless Courts. This approach not only optimises resource utilisation but also positions these centres as pivotal drivers of digital transformation within the legal landscape. The concept of utilising these hubs to scan pending records for the realisation of Paperless Courts aligns with contemporary trends towards greater efficiency and sustainability.[15] As of 31 January 2024, there are eighteen judgeships across fourteen District Court Digitization Hubs/Centres, the number of case records scanned is 19,81,158, and the number of case records uploaded to the server is 9,57,927.[16]

II. The e-Filing Section and Centres

The e-Filing Section and Centre, within the High Court of Orissa, have been instrumental in the efficient processing and integration of legal petitions, cases and related documentation. This systematic approach includes both physically filed submissions by advocates and electronically submitted documents, supporting the Paperless court system. Within this context, the Filing Section plays a pivotal role by promptly scanning and processing all newly filed petitions and cases, as well as accompanying documents like annexures and affidavits, on the same day they are received. Simultaneously, the e-Filing Section is responsible for the reception and processing of petitions, cases and documents submitted electronically by Advocates. These materials are efficiently processed within this specialised division and subsequently transmitted to the Judicial Sections of the Court for further proceedings.

The e-Filing Section and Centre have also facilitated the extension of e-filing capabilities across the state of Odisha, marking a significant milestone with the introduction of this feature in 244 court establishments, encompassing all thirty districts within the state. Additionally, a total of thirty-four Paperless Courts were inaugurated as part of this initiative. In these Paperless Courts, judges utilise a specialised device known as 'WACOM' to access scanned and bookmarked copies of case records. This custom device streamlines the process, allowing judges to navigate through extensive case records with the simple click of a mouse button.[17]

III. Paperless Courts

The other major initiative undertaken by the High Court of Orissa was the digitisation of pending case records for Paperless Courts. The High Court of Orissa has embarked on a substantial initiative aimed at the transformation of its judicial operations into a paperless environment. The inception of this transition was set in motion on 11 September 2021, with the inauguration of the Paperless Court of the Chief Justice, High Court of Orissa. As of 31 March 2023, a total of twelve benches within the High Court of Orissa successfully transitioned into a paperless mode, marking significant progress in this transformative journey. In an effort to facilitate and support the transition to e-filing, the High Court of Orissa established e-facilitation centres and e-filing stations. These centres serve as valuable resources for advocates seeking to adopt e-filing practices, particularly those who may lack the necessary knowledge or means to do so independently.

The Paperless Office initiative, launched within the High Court of Orissa on 2 April 2022, has been made possible through the implementation of the Odisha Judicial Workflow Automation System (OJWAS). It has enabled the Chief Justice's administrative office to operate in a paperless mode, eliminating the need for physical files to be presented for the Chief Justice's approval. This digital platform is accessible to the Chief Justice and the offices of the Registry, not only from their workplaces but also from their residences, all while maintaining the highest levels of security through a Virtual Private Network. It is worth noting that this automation initiative has resulted in the digitisation of nearly all administrative processes, creating a digital ecosystem that no longer relies on traditional paper-based files.[18]

Within this context, the evolution towards a paperless paradigm has extended to various committees operating within the legal framework. One such is the Information Technology and Artificial Intelligence (IT and AI) Committee, which set a significant precedent by becoming the first committee to transition into paperless mode. Subsequently, a growing number of committees have embraced this paperless transformation. Notably, these committees have adopted the Odisha Judicial Workflow Automation System (OJWAS) to manage their administrative processes, thereby enhancing efficiency and accessibility. The transition to a paperless environment has not only streamlined administrative processes but also significantly reduced the physical space required for file storage.[19]

Another initiative of the Odisha judiciary was the e-LCR System, which streamlined the record access and management, eliminating the need for physical LCRs (Lower Court Records). The High Court of Orissa equipped every District Court complex with high-speed ADF scanners to meet the demands of official scanning requirements. District Courts have been directed to scan and send electronic copies of LCRs or e-LCRs whenever requested by the High Court. This digital approach has enabled the High Court to readily access LCRs in electronic format without impinging upon the accessibility of the original case records by the respective Subordinate Courts. This marks a significant departure from the previous practice, where District and Subordinate Courts would dispatch physical LCRs after producing photocopies, which incurred substantial resources in terms of transportation, receipt, storage and retrieval of the LCRs.[20]

IV. Digitisation of court proceedings and services

The High Court of Orissa, under the guidance of the e-Committee of the Supreme Court of India, has embarked on a journey of digitisation and transformation of court proceedings and services.

The Odisha judiciary transformed the physical hearings into virtual hearings, by introducing the Hybrid Hearing System in February 2021. This system, combining physical courtroom proceedings with remote participation through video conferencing, was a response to the potential issues arising from the digital divide, where access to ICT devices was limited. The High Court proactively addressed this by installing video conferencing cabins within their premises and equipping district court VC cabins accordingly. State-of-the-art audio and video equipment in functional courtrooms facilitated a seamless interface for lawyers, enabling them to address the bench whether physically present or connected remotely. The Hybrid Hearing System was supported by a comprehensive Standard Operating Procedure (SOP), which granted parties the flexibility to choose between physical and virtual appearances and established strict entry and exit protocols, preventive measures, and general etiquette for physical hearings. The SOP aimed to ensure the smooth conduct of hybrid hearings while prioritising the health and safety of all participants.[21]

Building on the Hybrid Hearing System, two Model Virtual Courtrooms in the District Court complexes of Angul and Nayagarh were launched in November 2021, and operational in twenty-four districts by November 2022.[22] These Model Virtual Courtrooms (Figure 3.2) were equipped with advanced audio and visual equipment allowing the accused or litigant (whether in a criminal or civil case) to attend court virtually. Remote point coordinators were appointed for each of these Courts.

Since 2 August 2021, Virtual Courts have enabled the online adjudication of cases, especially traffic challan cases, which can now be settled online by the litigants and their advocates within the Cuttack-Bhubaneswar Commissionerate area.[23]

Further, Virtual Centres of the High Court were established in all thirty District Courts. These Virtual Centres (Figure 3.3) are equipped with

Figure 3.2 Virtual courtroom in Angul (left) and Nayagarh (right)

Figure 3.3 Virtual Centres

video conferencing facilities and include a vital 'Back Office' to support lawyers in e-filing their cases, facilitating the transition to digital operations. Additionally, for individuals less proficient with computers, the Back Office employs dedicated staff to assist in tasks such as scanning, preparing, and e-filing petitions and documents.

The Odisha judiciary also made a progressive step in enhancing the transparency and accessibility of court proceedings by introducing the live streaming of court proceedings in the Chief Justice's Court in August 2021. This groundbreaking initiative, accessible through the official High Court YouTube channel,[24] provides a direct window into the legal proceedings. The live streaming of court proceedings was enabled by the implementation of the 'High Court of Orissa Live Streaming of Court Proceedings Rules, 2021', which extended the Open Court concept to physical, virtual and hybrid hearings. The rules provide a detailed framework for the conduct of live streaming, including the categories of cases that are excluded, the responsibilities of authorised personnel, the restrictions on public participation, and the measures to address disruptions. The rules also emphasise the adaptability of the framework, subject to further modification as required.

To serve as an aid to these hybrid hearings, paperless and virtual courts and as well as to digitise the whole system, many services were introduced to make it truly digital and leverage the technology to our advantage. Some of the main services that were introduced are:

1. The e-Filing 3.0,[25] a web portal designed by the National Informatics Centre (NIC) to cater to the needs of advocates and litigants engaging with High Courts and Subordinate Courts throughout the country. This web portal, launched across 244 court establishments spanning all districts within the state, allows users to file cases, documents and fees online, without having to visit the court premises physically. It also provides users with features such as e-verification, e-signature, e-stamping, e-acknowledgement and e-tracking of case status. The e-Filing portal has significantly enhanced the efficiency and convenience of filing cases, as well as reducing the paper consumption and environmental impact of court operations.[26]

2. Another initiative of the Odisha judiciary was the establishment of e-Inspection Centres,[27] which improved the accessibility to legal case records. After the comprehensive scanning of pending case records, these records became available not only to the judicial sections but also to advocates and law clerks. This represented a departure from the previous practice, where advocates often experienced significant waiting periods for the physical retrieval and inspection of records. With the implementation of the e-Inspection Centre, records are now accessible within seconds, saving time and resources for the users.
3. The Odisha judiciary also introduced the e-Payment of Court Fees and e-Facilitation Centre, which offered advocates and litigants a convenient and efficient way to handle financial transactions related to court fees. The e-Payment of Court Fees was facilitated through the e-Committee's e-Pay Portal,[28] which allowed users to pay court fees online using various modes of payment, such as debit cards, credit cards, net banking, and UPI. Furthermore, a dedicated Facilitation Centre for e-Payment of Court Fees was established within the High Court of Orissa to provide assistance to advocates and litigants in navigating e-Payment procedures.[29]
4. The National Judicial Data Grid (NJDG) is a prime example, serving as a comprehensive database that provides case details, orders and judgments from courts across the nation, enhancing transparency and accessibility. Complementing this is the e-Notification System (e-NS), a paperless method of circulating court notices among court employees, improving efficiency and reducing environmental impact.[30]
5. The Order Communication Portal (OCP) further bolsters this efficiency by providing a secure platform for transmitting orders and judgments to subordinate courts, reducing potential delays and errors. The e-Custody Certificate System streamlines the process of obtaining custody certificates by providing prisoner information to applicants before the High Court's bench.[31]
6. In an effort to keep relevant parties informed about developments in their cases, the Automated E-Mail Alert System collects and dispatches orders and judgments involving government departments to the designated nodal officers.[32] Similarly, the Automated SMS Alert System sends real-time notifications to advocates and litigants about the status and scheduling of their cases.
7. The High Court of Orissa eServices Mobile App[33] extends these services to mobile platforms, offering features such as case status, cause lists, display boards, judgments and orders, and free-text searches. Finally, the court's presence on social media platforms like YouTube and Telegram expands the reach and dissemination of court-related information, allowing the court to engage with a wider audience and provide timely updates.[34]
8. The Odisha judiciary also introduced e-Sewa Kendras,[35] which bridges the digital divide by providing e-services to advocates and litigants who may

not have access to ICT tools, ensuring equitable access to legal services. These centres, including one within the High Court of Orissa and 109 in District and Taluka Court complexes, provide assistance to users in accessing various online platforms and features, such as e-filing, e-payment, e-inspection, e-notification, e-custody, e-libraries, NJDG, OCP, e-NS, and eServices Mobile App.[36]

9. The Odisha judiciary also introduced the Vulnerable Witnesses Deposition Centres (VWDCs),[37] which function as secure spaces for witnesses involved in both criminal and civil trials, ensuring they can testify without fear or coercion. These centres, established in accordance with directives from the Honourable Supreme Court of India, consist of three distinct rooms: a virtual courtroom equipped with electronic devices and cameras, a waiting room for the witness, and a separate room for the accused. The virtual courtroom is equipped with a two-way mirror, allowing the judge and the lawyers to observe the witness without being seen. The witness's testimony is recorded and transmitted live to the courtroom, ensuring that the proceedings are conducted in a fair and transparent manner. These centres have been established in all thirty districts of Odisha, ensuring that vulnerable witnesses are provided with a safe and secure environment to testify.[38]

C. ACCESS TO INFORMATION AND CASE LAW

Over the years, the Odisha judiciary has undertaken various projects and strategies to provide access to case law and legal heritage, both to the legal community and the general public. These initiatives have facilitated legal research and knowledge sharing among legal professionals, and have preserved and showcased the rich and diverse judicial history of Odisha. The initiatives are as follows:

1. SCC Online is a comprehensive online legal database that offers access to judgments, statutes, parliamentary bills, and scholarly articles from various tribunals, High Courts and the Supreme Court of India. In February 2022, the provision of SCC Online facility access was extended to every judicial officer in the state, marking the beginning of an era characterised by increased accessibility to an extensive reservoir of legal knowledge. Judicial officers now enjoy unrestricted access to SCC Online, enhancing their access to essential legal resources. This initiative has empowered judicial officers to conduct thorough and efficient legal research and to stay updated with the latest developments and trends in the field of law. Furthermore, it has enabled them to deliver well-reasoned and informed judgments, thereby strengthening the quality and credibility of the judicial system in Odisha.[39]
2. The Odisha judiciary also introduced e-Libraries for Advocates, which empower them with access to an extensive array of online law journals,

statutes, parliamentary bills, scholarly articles, and case law summaries and commentaries. These initiatives, launched in March 2022, were strategically set up at the headquarters of all thirty districts in Odisha, with additional stations in Rourkela and Koraput. They also provide access to prominent sources like AIR ONLINE and MANUPATRA FAST. They also enable judicial officers to exchange and review case law summaries and commentaries, fostering an interactive environment for professional discussions and knowledge sharing.[40]

3. Similarly, the Case Law Portal (CLP) is an online platform that was introduced in May 2022. This platform empowers judicial officers to exchange and review case law summaries and commentaries, fostering an interactive environment for professional discussions and knowledge sharing. Access to the portal is exclusively available to judicial officers, promoting a collaborative space tailored to their needs. The portal allows judicial officers to upload and download case law summaries and commentaries, and to provide feedback and suggestions to their peers. The portal also features a rating system, where judicial officers can rate the quality and usefulness of the summaries and commentaries. The portal serves as a valuable tool for enhancing the analytical and writing skills of the judicial officers, and for encouraging them to engage in constructive and collegial dialogue with their fellow officers. Moreover, the portal helps them to broaden their perspective and gain insights from diverse and varied sources of legal wisdom.
4. Justice Clock is an innovative display that was introduced in December 2019, aiming to provide lawyers and litigants with pertinent information about District Judiciary matters when they visit the High Court. However, the advent of COVID-19 necessitated a shift in approach, as physical visits became restricted. To ensure stakeholders could access this valuable information remotely, the concept of a web version of the Justice Clock[41] was born. Launched on 10 February 2021, this digital rendition mirrors the physical Justice Clock installed within the High Court building. Now seamlessly integrated into the High Court's official website, the web version of the Justice Clock offers easy accessibility from the comfort of one's home or office. The web version of the Justice Clock displays various judicial statistics, such as the number of cases filed, disposed of, and pending in the District Judiciary, the number of cases under the National Judicial Data Grid (NJDG), the number of cases under the e-Courts Project, and the number of cases under the Lok Adalat and Mediation. The web version of the Justice Clock also provides a graphical representation of the data, making it easier to comprehend and compare. The web version of the Justice Clock serves as a useful resource for monitoring and evaluating the performance and efficiency of the District Judiciary, and for identifying the areas of improvement and intervention. Additionally, it serves as a transparent and accountable mechanism for informing and educating

the public about the functioning and progress of the District Judiciary, and for enhancing their trust and confidence in the judicial system.[42]

5. Public Interest Litigation (PIL) is a form of litigation that seeks to protect and promote the public interest, especially the rights and interests of the marginalised and disadvantaged sections of society. The PIL Portal,[43] launched in August 2021, serves as a valuable resource for disseminating information about significant pending PILs that are currently under consideration by the High Court of Orissa. In addition to providing a concise description of each case, the portal offers comprehensive access to all the orders issued in a particular PIL. Notably, since August 2021, some of these proceedings have been live-streamed, and the portal includes links to these hearings.[44] The PIL Portal serves multiple purposes, such as:
   - For individuals contemplating the initiation of a fresh PIL in the High Court of Odisha, the portal offers the convenience of checking whether any related matters are already pending. This serves as a helpful measure to prevent the duplication of petitions.
   - For the Bench responsible for hearing PILs, the portal aids them in staying informed about ongoing cases and related developments, and in ensuring the speedy and effective disposal of PILs.
   - For the public, the portal provides an opportunity to learn about the various issues of public interest and importance that are being addressed by the High Court and to witness the judicial process and deliberation in action. This fosters a greater awareness and appreciation of the role and contribution of the High Court in advancing the cause of social justice and public welfare in Odisha.

D. TRAINING PROGRAMMES, MODULES, AND SAFEGUARDING LEGAL HERITAGE

The journey towards integrating technology into the legal landscape of Odisha has been both transformational and enlightening.

To equip legal practitioners with the necessary skills, the High Court of Orissa initiated 'Hands-On Training' programmes focused on e-Filing and e-Services. These practical sessions provide advocates with firsthand experience in utilising technology within their legal practice. Complementing these programmes, the court also developed video tutorials, available in English and local languages. These resources serve as self-help guides, empowering advocates to enhance their technological proficiency independently, covering various aspects of e-filing, e-payment and other essential e-services provided by the High Court and District Courts.

Amidst this technological change, a remarkable discovery was made during the establishment of the Record Room Digitization Centre in April and May 2021. Fragile records dating back to the nineteenth century were uncovered, showcasing the rich legal heritage of the region. Recognising their historical significance, steps were immediately taken to preserve these invaluable records. Expert conservationists were engaged to ensure their safe-keeping, and efforts are underway to digitise them for posterity. Among these records, dating as far back as 1813, are tangible artefacts that offer insights into the region's legal history.

Building upon this preservation effort, the Centre for Judicial Archives was established on 1 May 2022. This initiative seeks to delve deeper into Odisha's judicial history by conducting research on centuries-old records. With a vast repository of Fragile Case Records dating from 1950 and earlier, efforts are underway to catalogue and digitise these records for accessibility and preservation. Led by a Director-cum-OSD, the Centre serves as a beacon of judicial history, offering insights into the evolution of the legal system and judiciary in Odisha.

E. CHALLENGES

The integration of technology into the judicial system, while beneficial, also presents several challenges.

Digitisation of court proceedings and records brings the risk of unauthorised access and potential exposure of sensitive information. The Data Protection and Privacy (DPP) Act plays a crucial role in regulating the collection, storage, processing and sharing of personal data. Compliance with these regulations involves implementing robust encryption, access controls and secure storage methods. Regular security audits and assessments are essential to identify and rectify vulnerabilities.

As technology evolves, software and hardware components become outdated, leading to redundancy. Regular updates and replacements are necessary but come with increased costs and potential downtime. To address this, adopting a modular and scalable infrastructure allows for easier integration of new technologies and reduces the impact of obsolescence. Cloud-based solutions can offer flexibility and automatic updates, mitigating the need for manual interventions.

The traditional judicial systems may be resistant to change due to scepticism, lack of understanding, or trust issues related to digital platforms. Overcoming this requires comprehensive training programmes to educate stakeholders about the advantages of technology. A phased approach to implementation can build confidence gradually. Demonstrating successful pilot projects and highlighting the efficiency gains can contribute to overcoming reluctance.

Allocating resources for technological advancements while balancing other needs is a complex challenge. Prioritisation based on the impact on efficiency, accessibility and overall judicial effectiveness is crucial. Conducting thorough cost–benefit analyses helps in making informed decisions. Collaboration with experts in both technology and law can optimise resource allocation.

Shifting to digital platforms requires a mindset change and dedicated resources for training. Training programmes should be tailored to the needs of different stakeholders, addressing their specific roles and concerns. Ongoing support, workshops and user-friendly interfaces can facilitate the transition and help individuals adapt to new technologies gradually.

AI in judicial functions can introduce bias and lack transparency, raising ethical concerns. Addressing this involves establishing ethical guidelines for AI use, ensuring transparency in algorithmic decision-making, and regularly auditing AI systems for bias. Striking a balance between automation and human oversight is crucial to maintaining fairness and justice.

Clear protocols and governance frameworks are essential for controlling the use of technological tools. Establishing accountability mechanisms for errors or misuse ensures responsible implementation. Transparency in processes, decisions and the functioning of technology is vital for maintaining public trust and confidence in the judicial system's integrity.

F. CONCLUSION

In conclusion, the High Court of Orissa's journey towards digitalisation can be seen as a pilot test of the transformative power of technology in the judicial system. The court's use of Information and Communication Technology (ICT) initiatives, ranging from the National Judicial Data Grid (NJDG) to the High Court of Orissa eServices Mobile App, has significantly enhanced the efficiency, transparency and accessibility of its services. These initiatives have not only empowered stakeholders but also paved the way for a more modern and user-friendly judiciary.

However, this digital transformation is not without its challenges. Issues such as privacy concerns, data security, redundancy, reluctance to change, and the effective utilisation of funds pose significant hurdles. Moreover, the training of staff and changing the mindset of judicial officers, high court judges, lawyers and law clerks to adapt to new technologies requires considerable effort.

While significant strides have been made in integrating technology into judicial processes, it is important to recognise that there is still a long way to go to achieve complete transformation; and in the journey towards eCourts Project Phase III, the High Court of Orissa strides ahead compared to other courts in India, showing significant advancements in technology adoption and judicial effectiveness.

NOTES

1. 'National Policy and Action Plan for Implementation of Information and Communication Technology in the Indian Judiciary' (E-Committee of Supreme Court of India, New Delhi, 1 August 2005) <https://cdnbbsr.s3waas.gov.in/s388ef51f0bf911e452e8dbb1d807a81ab/uploads/2020/05/2020053162.pdf> (accessed 15 February 2024).
2. The terms 'digitalisation' and 'digitisation' are often used interchangeably, but they have slightly different meanings. Digitisation is the conversion of analogue information into digital format, like scanning paper documents into PDFs, enabling electronic processing, storage and transmission, whereas digitalisation is a broader concept involving the use of digital technologies to transform business models, operations and customer interactions, leveraging tools like cloud computing, big data analytics, AI, and Internet of Things (IoT).
3. Caveat matching is a legal process introduced in India in 1989, primarily utilised in appellate courts. When one party anticipates litigation against them, they can lodge a caveat in the court, notifying the court not to pass any order without hearing them if the opposing party appeals. This ensures that both parties are given an opportunity to present their arguments before a decision is made.
4. National Informatics Centre (NIC) under the Ministry of Electronics and Information Technology (MeitY) is the technology partner of the Government of India. NIC was established in 1976 with the objective to provide technology-driven solutions to Central and State Governments: National Informatics Centre, Govt of India <www.nic.in> (accessed 15 February 2024).
5. 'E-Courts' (*Ministry of Electronics and Information Technology*) <www.meity.gov.in/content/e-courts> (accessed 15 February 2024).
6. *Official website of e-Committee, Supreme Court of India* <https://ecommitteesci.gov.in/> accessed 15 February 2024.
7. E-Committee, Supreme Court of India (n. 2).
8. 'Policy and Action Plan Document Phase II of the eCourts Project' (e-Committee of Supreme Court of India, New Delhi, 2014) <https://cdnbbsr.s3waas.gov.in/s388ef51f0bf911e452e8dbb1d807a81ab/uploads/2020/05/2020053169.pdf> (accessed 15 February 2024).
9. 'Digital Courts Vision & Roadmap e-Courts Project Phase III' (e-Committee of Supreme Court of India, New Delhi, 2022) <https://cdnbbsr.s3waas.gov.in/s388ef51f0bf911e452e8dbb1d807a81ab/uploads/2023/04/2023042088.pdf> (accessed 15 February 2024).
10. The author took over as the Chief Justice of the High Court of Orissa on 4 January 2021 and continued as such until his retirement on 7 August 2023.
11. High Court of Orissa, *Circular Order 03 of 2022* (2022) <https://districts.ecourts.gov.in/sites/default/files/circular%20order%206.pdf> (accessed 28 October 2023). It stipulated that 'every disposed of Case Record of applications under sections 438 and 439 of the Code of Criminal Procedure, 1973 would be destroyed after one year and three years, respectively, from the date of the final order. For all other case records, destruction would occur after five years from the date of the final order. Importantly, no record would be destroyed unless it had been digitised and verified. In cases where any part of the file was too

fragile for digitization, that portion would be preserved permanently in the Fragile Records Section.'

12. A video explaining RRDC – High Court of Orissa, 'One Year of The High Court Record Room Digitization Centre' (10 September 2022) is available at <www.youtube.com/watch?v=Uhlv4vCpWzY> (accessed 15 February 2024).
13. High Court of Orissa, *Cumulative RRDC* <https://orissahighcourt.nic.in/Cumulative_RRDC.pdf> (accessed 15 February 2024).
14. High Court of Orissa, *Annual Report 2021* (2022), 43 <www.orissahighcourt.nic.in/annual_report_2021.pdf> (accessed 28 October, 2023).
15. High Court of Orissa, *Annual Report 2022* (2023), 48 <www.orissahighcourt.nic.in/annual_report_2022.pdf> (accessed 28 October 2023).
16. High Court of Orissa, *Cumulative DCDC* <https://orissahighcourt.nic.in/Cumulative_DCDC.pdf> (accessed 15 February 2024).
17. High Court of Orissa, *Souvenir 1948–2023* (2023), 125 <www.orissahighcourt.nic.in/souvenir.pdf> (accessed 28 October 2023).
18. *Annual Report 2022* (n. 16), 47.
19. High Court of Orissa, 'Inauguration of the Paperless Courts in the Districts and Release of Special Postal Cover' (17 September 2022) <www.youtube.com/watch?v=Gu8C6IaZe0s&t=1044s> (accessed 15 February 2024).
20. *Annual Report 2021* (n. 15), 51–2.
21. *Annual Report 2021* (n. 15), 47–8.
22. *Annual Report 2022* (n. 16), 46.
23. *Annual Report 2021* (n. 15), 56.
24. High Court of Orissa, YouTube channel <www.youtube.com/@highcourtoforissa6196> (accessed 28 October 2023).
25. 'e-Filing 3.0' (High Court of Orissa) <https://orissahighcourt.nic.in> (accessed 15 February 2024).
26. *Annual Report 2022* (n. 16), 50.
27. *e-Inspection – Official Website* <http://112.133.226.244/einspection/appl_form.php> (accessed 15 February 2024).
28. 'e-Court Fees' (*Orissa High Court*) <https://orissahighcourt.nic.in/ecourtfees/> (accessed 15 February 2024).
29. *Annual Report 2021* (n. 15), 54–5.
30. Ibid., 51.
31. Ibid., 50.
32. Ibid., 57.
33. 'eServices Mobile App' (*Orissa High Court*) <https://orissahighcourt.nic.in/mobile-app/> (accessed 15 February 2024).
34. *Annual Report 2021* (n. 15), 57.
35. 'eSeva' (*Orissa High Court*) <https://orissahighcourt.nic.in/esewa/> accessed 15 February 2024).
36. *Annual Report 2021* (n. 15), 54.
37. 'VWDC Scheme PDF View' (*Orissa High Court*) <https://orissahighcourt.nic.in/rules/vwdc-scheme/vwdc-scheme-pdf-view/2/> (accessed 15 February 2024).
38. *Annual Report 2022* (n. 16), 46.
39. *Annual Report 2022* (n. 16), 50.
40. Ibid.

41. 'Justice Clock' (*Orissa High Court*) <https://orissahighcourt.nic.in/justice-clock/> (accessed 15 February 2024).
42. *Annual Report 2021* (n. 15), 58.
43. 'PIL Portal' (*Orissa High Court*) <https://orissahighcourt.nic.in/pil-portal/> (accessed 15 February 2024).
44. Ibid.

REFERENCES

'Digital Courts Vision & Roadmap e-Courts Project Phase III' (E-Committee of Supreme Court of India, New Delhi, 2022) <https://cdnbbsr.s3waas.gov.in/s388ef51f0bf911e452e8dbb1d807a81ab/uploads/2023/04/2023042088.pdf> (accessed 15 February 2024).

'National Policy and Action Plan for Implementation of Information and Communication Technology in the Indian Judiciary' (E-Committee of Supreme Court of India, New Delhi, 1 August 2005) <https://cdnbbsr.s3waas.gov.in/s388ef51f0bf911e452e8dbb1d807a81ab/uploads/2020/05/2020053162.pdf> (accessed 15 February 2024).

'Policy and Action Plan Document Phase II of the Ecourts Project' (E-Committee of Supreme Court of India, New Delhi, 2014) <https://cdnbbsr.s3waas.gov.in/s388ef51f0bf911e452e8dbb1d807a81ab/uploads/2020/05/2020053169.pdf> (accessed 15 February 2024).

'PIL Portal' (Orissa High Court) <https://orissahighcourt.nic.in/pil-portal/> (accessed 15 February 2024).

'VWDC Scheme PDF View' (Orissa High Court) <https://orissahighcourt.nic.in/rules/vwdc-scheme/vwdc-scheme-pdf-view/2/> (accessed 15 February 2024).

High Court of Orissa, *Annual Report 2021* (2022), 43 <www.orissahighcourt.nic.in/annual_report_2021.pdf> (accessed 28 October 2023).

High Court of Orissa, *Annual Report 2022* (2023), 48 <www.orissahighcourt.nic.in/annual_report_2022.pdf> (accessed 28 October 2023).

High Court of Orissa, Circular Order 03 of 2022 (2022) <https://districts.ecourts.gov.in/sites/default/files/circular%20order%206.pdf> (accessed 28 October 2023).

High Court of Orissa, *Souvenir 1948–2023* (2023) 125 <www.orissahighcourt.nic.in/souvenir.pdf> (accessed 28 October 2023).

Chapter 4

Access to Justice and Digitalisation of Courts in South Korea

Nam-Chul Chung

A. INTRODUCTION

Innovation and breakthroughs in information and communication technology (ICT) are accelerating digital transformation in many fields. Digital transformation is an unavoidable fateful task of the future society, and Digitalisation has become the megatrend of the times.[1] Digitalisation and the advent of artificial intelligence (AI) systems have made it possible to collect vast amounts of data and make rapid decisions based on them. The processing of Big Data by digitalisation has brought benefits to human society, but it may also lead to the leakage of personal data or invasion of privacy. Also, artificial intelligence and digitalisation based on algorithms can threaten democracy.[2] Digitalisation may lead to prejudice or discrimination, limiting access to justice.

Lately, computerisation and digitalisation of the judiciary have made remarkable progress in South Korea. Digital transformation is underway in all areas of public administration, and judicial administration is no exception. In Korea, a computerised information system was introduced to judicial affairs, enabling efficient court affairs and improving the quality of judicial services to the people. The Korean judiciary has provided diverse legal information, case search information, Internet real estate registration information, and auction information through the high-speed Internet network. In particular, a 'Comprehensive Legal Information System' provides precedents, legal information, etc. Through this digitalisation, the Korean judiciary has been making significant changes in the trial system and the court's work style beyond simple computerisation of judicial information or computer system support.

In South Korea, the public demand for the disclosure of judicial information has gradually increased. The Korean judiciary approach to expanding people's access to justice through computerisation and digitalisation is essential regarding the rule of law. The imbalance and monopoly of information in the field of the judiciary can make it challenging to seek individual rights relief. It is indispensable to supplement democratic elements in the judicial area, where democratic legitimacy is relatively weak. The Korean court website provides a communication space to expand public participation. These efforts show that the Korean judiciary has been trying to strengthen democratic elements. Furthermore, the Korean judiciary established an 'Electronic Litigation System' due to information and communication technology.

Recently, the Korean judiciary has been discussing ways to use artificial intelligence for trial work. In the field of criminal justice, artificial intelligence technology will be applied soon. These changes and attempts will bring about the efficiency of judicial administration. But they can cause various problems regarding protecting privacy or personal information, democracy, and the rule of law. The following discussion will consider some issues of informatisation and digitalisation of the court, democracy, access to justice, and the rule of law in South Korea.

B. INFORMATISATION AND DIGITALISATION OF COURTS IN SOUTH KOREA

I. Background and progress of an informatisation project

(a) Stage 1

Due to information and communication technology changes, the Korean judiciary has also promoted a so-called 'Informatisation Project' in a social atmosphere to improve services to the people. The concept of 'informatisation', as espoused by the Korean judiciary, is comprehensive in scope and primarily encompasses the computerisation of judicial processes and the establishment of a network of judicial (trial) information. This informatisation laid the foundation for the subsequent digitalisation of the judicial system. The informatisation of the Korean judiciary can be divided into three stages. The first step is as follows. In 1979, the Supreme Court of Korea commissioned the Korea Institute of Science and Technology (KIST) to research the feasibility of computerising judicial affairs. Besides, in the 1980s, the people's enthusiasm for democratisation increased in South Korea. As the people's demand for the right to know also grew, they wanted to know about documents and materials of lawsuits related to them or social issues. Above all, the workload of judges at that time increased rapidly, so there was a need to reform the judiciary's information system to improve work efficiency.[3] The National Court Administration under the Korean Supreme Court established a precedent database between 1980 and 1982. In 1986, it developed the 'Civil Small Claims Trials Management Program' and started operating it. Civil small claim trials mean simple cases with a low value of lawsuits in the civil field, so this programme was the first to be created.[4]

(b) Stage 2

In the second stage, informatisation of the Korean judiciary was promoted through specific plans, and computerisation of the trial affairs was the actual content. In 1992, the Korean National Court Administration established the *'5-year Basic Plan for Computerisation of Judicial Affairs'*. It prepared a comprehensive plan for computerising real estate registration in 1994. The Judicial Affairs Computerisation Promotion Committee was established as an advisory body to the head of the National Court Administration to promote the computerisation of judicial affairs. The Supreme Court of Korea announced the informatisation of the judiciary to systematise judicial works, informatisation of all judiciary staff, and service of judicial information to the public. In addition, the Informatisation Project of the Judiciary was to provide various computerisation means to personal computers supplied to the personnel of the Judiciary under the name of the so-called JURIST (Judiciary Users Requirements for Integrated Systems Technology).[5] It devised the *'Long-term Development Plan for Informatisation of the Judiciary'* and opened the Supreme Court website in 1998.[6] In 1999, the information system of the Korean judiciary began to develop in earnest. As the informatisation project was progressively promoted, the Korean judiciary developed the civil case system in 1999 and created the criminal case system in 2000.

(c) Stage 3

The Korean judiciary established a web-based information system and computerisation network in the third stage. In 2001, the Supreme Court of Korea established a master plan for the judiciary's information communication network and the electronic court. As the computerisation of the judiciary was promoted, a large-scale nationwide network was built. As some problems, such as network failure, old equipment and slow internet speed, were revealed, it became necessary to establish a master plan for building an independent network within the judiciary. This included the development direction of the judicial information network building of courts across the country, uninterrupted service plan, and network access by external users. It completed the so-called *'Case Management System (CMS)'* and set up the electronic court. And the Korean judiciary made a filing master plan in 2002. At that time, the court auction information website was also opened,[7] and the real estate registration internet browsing service was also launched, completing the computerisation of 212 registry offices nationwide. Electronic registration was conducted for paper registers of 45 million lots of land. Entering 2003, the level of information system services began to rise considerably. The *CMS* was improved to be web-based. In 2007, the Korean judiciary established a customised trial support system called 'JUSTICE' to support judges' trial work. This system made it possible to provide systematic and comprehensive support for managing trial schedules, case progress, and the preparation of electronic judgments.[8]

II. The judiciary's working organisation for informatisation and digitalisation

Since 2000, the Korean judiciary has established a working organisation to promote efficient and systematic informatisation and digitalisation. In this regard, the Assistant Minister of the Planning and Coordination Office under the Korean National Court Administration was appointed as the CIO (Chief Information Officer) to take responsibility for the informatisation of the Korean judiciary. The Korean National Court Administration oversees the administrative affairs of courts across the country. The *Deputy Director General for Judicial Information Technology* supervised and assisted the divisional officers. The main task was to establish and coordinate the comprehensive plan for the computerisation and digitalisation of the judiciary.

Currently, the Korean National Court Administration installed the *Judicial Information Technology Bureau* (Judicial IT Bureau) separately. It placed a Deputy Director for Judicial Information Technology under the Judicial IT Bureau. The Judicial IT Bureau has some Departments of Judicial IT facilities, IT support, cyber-safety, and a Judicial Archives Center. In addition, the Korean National Court Administration established the 'Judicial Procedure Office', with a *Deputy Director General for Judicial Procedure* under it. It is preparing a next-generation electronic litigation strategy.[9] As the proportion of electronic litigation gradually strengthens, it is entrusted to the *Judicial Procedure Office*. However, general judicial informatisation tasks and e-lawsuit promotion tasks are distributed, so it may be, in the present writer's opinion, difficult to uniformly carry out tasks related to judicial digitisation.

III. Current status of the Informatisation and Digitalisation

(a) Establishment of a judicial computer network

In 1995, the Korean judiciary installed a judicial computer network only for 28 courts out of 166 nationwide. In 2004, it established and operated a dual high-speed network in all courts. Nowadays, all courts, including city and county courts, are connected and form a large-scale network supported by data centres in Bundang and Daejeon. In 2008, the Korean judiciary established under the Supreme Court the Computer Information Center, the infrastructure for the integrated operation of the judicial information system. The Korean judicial computer network uses a LAN and Internetwork exclusively.

In 1998, the Korean judiciary made, as already mentioned, an integrated menu called the '*Case Management System.*' The Supreme Court of Korea utilises this system that supports cases in all fields, such as civil, family, criminal, administrative, and bankruptcy. Through this system, the Korean judiciary created a standard procedure for case reception, distribution, document arrangement, delivery, preservation, etc. In particular, it built a *'Criminal Justice Information System'* to exchange electronic information on criminal cases with the police, prosecutors and the Ministry of Justice. The Ministry of Justice operates a criminal justice website for citizens.[10] Through this, citizens can know their case progress information and check the payment of fines. However, it should be ensured that these systems do not infringe on an individual's privacy or personal data. Recently, the Ministry of Justice plans to use artificial intelligence to digitally convert the document preparation process. That is, it recognises the contents of the investigation between the investigator and the examinee as voice and converts it into text.

(b) Judicial Information Service for the People

The Korean judiciary provides various judicial information services to facilitate communication with the public. It operates the Korean court website (www.scourt.go.kr) to publicise the court and offer trial materials through the Internet, and an average of 100,000 users view it daily. The Korean court website includes menus such as an introduction to the judiciary, the Supreme Court, courts of all levels, and the judicial information service for the people. The websites of the Supreme Court and courts of all levels provide services such as court introductions, significant decisions and announcements. In particular, the *Judicial Information Service for the People* offers various services such as case search, judgment publicity, comprehensive legal information, various public notices, and access to information. These contribute to communication with people. Besides, the Supreme Court of Korea operates a *Comprehensive Legal Information System.*[11] This System provides free-charge precedents (including Supreme Court and lower courts), statutes, treaties and legal documents.[12]

The Korean judiciary operates an *'Internet Access to Decision Documents System'*, which allows anyone to search and browse civil/administrative/patent/criminal final rulings.[13] The Korean Courts have provided the public with written decisions anonymised to protect the personal data or the privacy of persons involved in the case. From 1 January 2013, the Korean judiciary began disclosing rulings of criminal cases electronically and non-electronically. Also, from 1 January 2014, the list of evidence and criminal justice records was made public. Civil judgments began to be made public on 1 January 2015. On 1 January 2019, the Korean judiciary opened an 'integrated Internet browsing and searching service for the decision'. In addition, from 1 January 2023, unconfirmed civil judgments are also being released.

In 2002, the Korean judiciary completed computerising all registries and established the real estate registration system. In the registration departments and registration offices of courts across the country, all people could obtain certified copies and abridged copies of real estate registries through computerised systems. In parallel with the computerisation of registration, courts and registry offices across the country have installed automatic dispensers to issue certified copies and abstracts of real estate registers, enabling anyone to receive and view necessary documents conveniently. In addition, in 2007, the Internet Registry Office service was launched, allowing easy access to real estate registration information through the Internet. Since 2006, applying for online electronic real estate registration has been possible.[14]

Since January 2008, the Korean judiciary has implemented a new *Family Relation Registration System* to replace the former patriarchal family system following the improvement of the family relation system. In the past, all members' data within the same family register could be revealed, leading to personal data and privacy infringement. Accordingly, it has prepared a system that minimises the disclosure of personal data by classifying certificates into five types of certifications, including family relation certificates, essential certificates, marital relation certificates, etc., according to the purpose of proof. Through the family relation registration information system, local governments (Si/Gun/Gu offices) can receive applications for cases related to birth, death, marriage, divorce, etc., at all family relation registration offices and issue certificates for them. From 4 March 2013, the electronic family relation registration system has issued certificates for each registration item, such as a family relation certificate, basic certificate and marital relation certificate, through the Internet service. People can conveniently obtain a certificate at home or work.

(c) Construction of an electronic litigation system

The era of electronic litigation has come, in which citizens can file lawsuits online without visiting the court in person. Accordingly, the Korean judiciary implemented electronic litigation services for intellectual property rights cases filed at the Patent Court in April 2010, followed by electronic civil litigation in May 2011, electronic family and administrative litigation in January 2013, and electronic litigation for temporary relief applications in September 2013. In April 2014, the Korean judiciary also implemented electronic litigation for rehabilitation and bankruptcy. Furthermore, it established an electronic litigation system for enforcement (civil enforcement, non-litigation cases) in March 2015. Currently, electronic litigation is possible in all cases except for criminal cases.

The Korean judiciary has made an electronic litigation website and operated the *Korean Electronic Case Filing System* (ECFS).[15] It is the Korean Judiciary's electronic litigation system.[16] The use of electronic litigation is now gradually increasing. As of the end of 2016, approximately 95 per cent of patent cases and 66 per cent of civil cases are filed electronically. About 450 electronic courts are being built nationwide in high, district and civil branch courts. A total of 892,607 civil claims were filed through electronic lawsuits in 2021. Among the civil cases on merits, electronic lawsuits at the first instance accounted for 792,702 (97.3 per cent).

Regarding electronic litigation, the 'Act on the Use of Electronic Documents in Civil Litigations, etc.' has been enacted in South Korea. Electronic litigation is operated by conveniently receiving electronic documents on the Internet without paper documents and disclosing trial information, such as the receipt and delivery of documents and the progress of procedures, in real-time through the Internet. In this respect, electronic litigation is more efficient than paper litigation (offline) because it takes less time and money from the standpoint of the litigation parties, and judiciary members can simultaneously view records through a computer. In the electronic court, real-time access to electronic records using computers is possible, and electronic media such as beam projectors, working imagers and large monitors are provided. Through this, the Korean judiciary is working to increase trial procedures' efficiency and transparency and expand judicial information sharing.

C. DIGITALISATION OF THE JUDICIARY AND DEMOCRACY

I. Democratic legitimacy of the judiciary

Since the 1990s, people have strongly demanded the judiciary's democratisation in South Korea. It is challenging to secure democratic legitimacy in the judicial branch compared to the legislative or the executive. Since the independence of judges is protected from the executive or public opinion, so is public participation relatively limited. In 2017, through the impeachment case of a former president in South Korea, many citizens began to recognise the importance of democracy and the people's sovereignty more desperately than ever.[17] As participatory democracy was emphasised, the judiciary reform request has also risen. The guarantee of human rights and the transparency of the litigation process were crucial elements of judicial reform.

In South Korea, appointing Justices and judges is significant for democratising the judiciary. The South Korean President appoints the Chief Justice of the Supreme Court with the approval of the National Assembly. Also, the Korean President appoints the Justices of the Supreme Court with the consent of the National Assembly upon the recommendation of the Chief Justice (Article 104, Paragraphs 1 and 2 of the Constitution of the Republic of Korea). Article 104, Paragraph 3 of the Constitution stipulates that the Chief Justice appoints general judges with the consent of the Supreme Court Justices' Conference. For securing the democratic legitimacy of the judiciary, the participation of the National Assembly or the Judiciary Selection Committee is essential.[18] In the Korean judiciary, personal democratic legitimacy is fundamental. Although the Supreme Court Justice Candidate Recommendation Committee is established to select Supreme Court Justice candidates, the final recommendation of Supreme Court Justice candidates ultimately depends on the Chief Justice's decision.

In addition, as the President finally appoints the Supreme Court Justice, the political orientation of the Supreme Court judges may change according to the change of government, which may be a crucial problem in light of the principle of separation of powers. To strengthen the democratic legitimacy of the Korean judiciary, it is essential to improve the process of appointing Supreme Court justices. At least the person recommended by the National Assembly should be the Supreme Court Justice candidate. The authority on judicial administration concentrates on the Korean National Court Administration. It is a fundamental cause of the judicial bureaucracy. The decentralisation of the judicial administration authority in South Korea will be the starting point for judicial reform in the future.

In Germany, various theories of democratic legitimacy have been proposed, including the German sociologist *Max Weber*'s theory of democratic orthodoxy.[19] And former German Federal Constitutional Court Justice E.-W. Böckenförde established the classical theory of democratic legitimacy.[20] Recently, there has been a new discussion about democratic legitimacy in South Korea. In particular, E. Schmidt-Aßmann, a German jurist, emphasised procedural legitimacy, such as acceptance, participation, and making public.[21] Among them, *making public* is related to access to documents or information.

II. Digitalisation and procedural vulnerability

Digitalisation and automated administrative decisions are vulnerable regarding procedural requirements, such as prior notice, hearing, signature, etc. Even in judicial administration, prejudice or discrimination can arise due to insufficient data or information distortion by digitalisation. Digitalisation in the judicial sector can also seriously infringe on personal data and privacy, so it is essential to supplement the procedural element. In particular, automated administrative decisions by artificial intelligence are becoming a significant legal problem. The rise of artificial intelligence systems and digitalisation can make it challenging to secure democratic legitimacy, especially from a procedural point of view. Domination or control by algorithms may threaten meaningful constitutional values like democracy and the rule of law. The formation of free political opinion is a crucial element of democracy. But political decision-making can be distorted by fake news or artificial intelligence algorithms, and the emergence of so-called *algocracy* can endanger the foundation of democracy.[22]

III. Democratic control over judicial administration

Democratic control must be strengthened to secure procedural legitimacy in the judicial sector. In this regard, procedural elements like public participation must be supplemented in a trial or judicial administration. And access to judicial information and fair and transparent procedures must be fully guaranteed. The Korean judiciary has made a menu on *public participation* on the court website, where people can report irregularities, corruption and budget waste. Besides, some improvements to the website can be suggested via the Internet.[23] This shows that the Korean judiciary has tried to communicate with the public. The *Act on Citizens' Participation in Criminal Trials* in South Korea has been enacted to introduce a participatory trial system similar to a jury system. It means that democratic legitimacy is supplemented to some degree through this system.[24]

Even though it sounds paradoxical, judicial digitalisation can complement procedural democratic legitimacy. Expanding access to judicial information can strengthen democratic control by public opinion or the media. The Korean judiciary should reinforce publicity for the digital transformation and inform the public so they can easily access information about it. It also contributes to enlarging communication and public participation in digital transformation. In addition to the democratisation of judicial administration, transparency and fairness of trial procedures should be secured in judicial digitalisation. In the Korean Electronic Case Filing System (ECFS), litigants and their attorneys can file cases and access electronic case records, procedural information, etc. Protecting personal information is still crucial for a fair trial. Thus, it should be strengthened in the digital transformation of litigation data. In this regard, the Korean judiciary should prepare procedures for notifying the parties or obtaining consent about processing personal information. It can help to increase transparency and fairness in electronic litigation.

D. ACCESS TO JUSTICE AND THE RULE OF LAW

I. Emergence of artificial intelligence and access to justice

Ensuring access to justice is a core element of the rule of law. The protection of equal access to justice for all is also essential. The digitalisation of the judiciary should not result in trial discrimination. Discrimination and restricted access to justice can seriously violate the right to a fair trial. The Korean judiciary must guarantee equitable access to justice to ensure litigants' rights in a court. AI systems based on algorithms may cause problems of discrimination or prejudice, and a trial operated by an AI system may threaten the independence of judges.[25] Discrimination in access to justice can seriously violate the rule of law, so the Korean judiciary must sufficiently guarantee access to justice for the socially underprivileged or information-vulnerable.

Artificial intelligence has already been used in the United States and the United Kingdom criminal justice.[26] In particular, the Wisconsin Supreme Court of the United States ruled that using artificial intelligence (e.g. COMPAS) for the decision did not violate constitutional due process.[27] Also, along with the computerisation and digitalisation of trials, some Korean legal scholars actively argue for introducing artificial intelligence in South Korea.[28] In recent years, the Korean National Court Administration entrusted research on 'Artificial Intelligence Utilisation Plans in Damage Compensation Cases'. This research examines calculating the percentage of negligence or the amount of damage automatically through learning judgment data of courts. If this research is realised, it will reduce the judge's work and save time. However, it may be highly controversial whether introducing artificial intelligence into trials violates the right to a trial by judges under the Constitution and laws. To what extent the judges will be involved in this regard is essential. Utilising Chat GPT to find the facts of the case or related issues will help the efficiency of the trial work. But it is a constitutionally significant challenge if artificial intelligence makes the final decision beyond this role.

Recently, there has been a lively discussion in South Korea that so-called Generative AI like Chat GPT 4.0 should be used to open up a new legal service market. There is also a positive evaluation that it will automate about 50 per cent of the work of associate judges in courts.[29] On the other hand, there are concerns that this use of generative artificial intelligence may infringe on personal information, trade secrets, and copyrights. In the future, the appearance of Chat GPT will have a significant impact on the judicial field. The recently revised Korean Privacy Act stipulates the right to reject automatic administrative decisions, including artificial intelligence, if they significantly impact individual rights or obligations (Article 37-2).

II. Access to justice and disclosure of court rulings

Disclosing court rulings is essential regarding access to justice in South Korea. Criminal trial suspects can also effectively defend themselves using judgments and judicial data. The Korean judiciary has expanded the scope of precedents disclosure through a Comprehensive Legal Information Service. This service dramatically helps ordinary citizens, lawyers, law school students and law scholars. However, not all courts' rulings are public. In particular, information for unconfirmed rulings was not provided, and the contents could only be known simply from the court's press release. As the disclosure of judgments may violate privacy rights or personal information, anonymising the decision is essential. Due to this anonymisation work, disclosing the written judgments of courts was limited.

In particular, non-finalised courts' decisions were not announced, and it was not easy for the parties to the lawsuit or interested parties to grasp and understand the contents of the judgment. A fee for reading and disclosing courts' rulings, except for *Comprehensive Legal Information Service*, must be paid. However, lawyers' organisations (e.g. the Korean Bar Association) have requested improvements in fees and payment methods related to the disclosure of decisions. A particular reading service for judgment information allows people to visit the court library and search for the rulings, but the viewing time is limited. In response, the Supreme Court introduced an integrated Internet browsing and searching service for judgments on 1 January 2019. As criticism of lawyers' organisations for non-confirmed rulings continued, from 1 January 2023, unconfirmed civil court rulings were also made public.

III. Digitalisation and risk-based regulation

The guarantee of access to justice includes the right to a 'speedy and public (open) trial'.[30] Article 27, Paragraph 3 of the Constitution of the Republic of Korea stipulates that all citizens have the right to a speedy trial. The digital transformation of the judiciary can also help people realise the right to a speedy trial. The digitalisation of the Korean judiciary contributes to the efficiency of the court's administration and trial affairs. Judges can quickly obtain reference materials by digitalising litigation data to make draft judgments and efficiently analyse related precedents. It contributes to the writing of courts' decisions by computerising litigation records and converting various data into digital ones. This digitalisation makes it possible to overcome the limitations of time and space. If people can quickly obtain data or information accumulated through digitalisation, it helps to increase the chance of receiving a speedy trial.

It is difficult to predict how the digitisation of justice and the rise of artificial intelligence will affect access to justice and the rule of law. Although the digitisation of the judiciary cannot promise only a rosy future, it should be used to strengthen access to justice. Also, it is necessary to try to find ways in which the digitalisation of the judiciary contributes to fair and non-discriminatory trials. Risk management is essential to prevent problems derived from artificial intelligence and the digitalisation of courts. For example, like the European Union (EU)'s regulation on artificial intelligence, real-time remote biometric identification systems for facial recognition, fingerprints and walking photographs should, in principle, be prohibited.[31] A lifelong risk management system is needed for high-risk artificial intelligence that can harm human health and safety or negatively affect fundamental rights. To this end, transparent information provision, human supervision, regular risk assessment and public participation procedures must be secured.[32] In the era of digitalisation and artificial intelligence, it is also required to introduce a risk-based regulatory method in the judicial field.

E. CONCLUSION

The 'Informatisation Project' pursued by the Korean judiciary was relatively successful. The judiciary's digitalisation has enhanced the efficiency and transparency of court work and expanded citizens' access to justice by providing various judicial information. However, this digitalisation also faces many complex challenges in the future. With the rapid development of digitalisation and the rise of artificial intelligence, there are many concerns about protecting fundamental rights, democracy and the rule of law. The Korean judiciary should try to solve this problem so that digitalisation and artificial intelligence systems do not undermine the rule of law or democracy.

In response to the challenges of digital transformation, some institutional improvements should be prepared systematically. First, democratic control over judicial administration has to be strengthened. Public participation and cooperation are also significant in the judicial system. To reinforce the democratic legitimacy of the judiciary, opportunities for citizens' involvement in judicial reform need to be expanded. Second, access to justice should be fully guaranteed through securing access to judicial information. The emergence of artificial intelligence or electronic courts should not exclude oral trials or infringe on the right to a fair trial. Also, discrimination and bias in access to justice should not limit the chances of substantive remedies for citizens' rights. The Korean judiciary must try to expand access to justice for the socially underprivileged. To obtain citizens' trust, transparent and fair access to digitalised judicial information must be guaranteed. In this regard, discrimination in electronic litigation must not occur.

Finally, risk management is crucial to protect fundamental constitutional rights such as human rights, non-discrimination and privacy rights. The risk that may result from the digitalisation and introduction of artificial intelligence systems should be reduced as much as possible. What is essential is to establish norms or standards that can regulate the use of high-risk digitisation or artificial intelligence systems. To this end, the Korean judiciary should consider introducing the risk-based regulation proposed by the European Union in earnest. At least, it should prohibit behaviours that violate human dignity or fundamental rights or threaten constitutional values. Besides, regulatory strategies for high-risk artificial intelligence should be established. Regarding this, the Korean judiciary should prepare transparent and sufficient access to judicial information, procedural provisions for citizens, human supervision and public participation, and regular risk assessment.

NOTES

1. Meinhard Schröder, 'Neue Grundrechte für ein digitales Zeitalter?' [2019] JZ 953.
2. Utz Schliesky, 'Digitalisierung: Herausforderung für den demokratischen Verfassungsstaat' [2019] NVwZ 696; Meinhard Schröder, 'Rahmenbedingungen der Digitalisierung der Verwaltung' [2019] VerwArch 331.
3. The Korean National Administration Office, *Current Status and Prospect of Informatization of the Judiciary* (2008), 2–3 (in Korean).
4. Supreme Court of Korea, 'Progress of the Judiciary' (in Korean) <http://www.scourt.go.kr/judiciary/information/progress/index.html> (accessed 17 April 2023).

5. Deok-Ryeol Han, 'Current Status and Prospect of Informatization in the Judiciary' in *Informatization and Trial Practice* (1998) 79 *Trial Materials* 16, 17 (in Korean).
6. Deok-Ryeol Han, 'Current Status and Prospect of Informatization in the Judiciary' in *Informatization and Trial Practice* (1998) 79 *Trial Materials* 67 (in Korean).
7. 'Court Auction' (in Korean) <https://www.courtauction.go.kr> (accessed 17 April 2023).
8. 'History of the eCourt' (*Supreme Court of Korea*) <http://eng.scourt.go.kr/eng/judiciary/eCourt/history.jsp> (accessed 17 April 2023).
9. 'Affiliate Organizations' (*Supreme Court of Korea*) (in Korean) <www.scourt.go.kr/judiciary/organization/affiliate/index.html> (accessed 17 April 2023).
10. 'Korea Information & Communication Society' (in Korean) <www.kics.go.kr> (accessed 17 April 2023).
11. 'Korea Legislation Research Institute' (in Korean) <http://glaw.scourt.go.kr> (accessed 17 April 2023).
12. 'Public Information' (*Supreme Court of Korea*) (in Korean) <https://www.scourt.go.kr/judiciary/information/public/index.html> (accessed 17 April 2023).
13. 'Perusal Status' (*Supreme Court of Korea*) (in Korean) <https://www.scourt.go.kr/portal/information/finalruling/peruse/peruse_status.jsp> (accessed 17 April 2023).
14. 'Industrial Property Information Service' (in Korean) <www.iros.go.kr> (accessed 17 April 2023).
15. 'Electronic Case Filing System' (*Supreme Court of Korea*) (in Korean) <https://ecfs.scourt.go.kr> (accessed 17 April 2023).
16. 'Electronic Case Filing System (e-Court)' (*Supreme Court of Korea*) (in Korean) <https://ecfse.scourt.go.kr/ecf/ecfE00/ECFE00.jsp> (accessed 19 April 2023).
17. Nam-Chul Chung, 'Challenges for Securing Democratic Legitimacy of the Executive Branch and the Judiciary from a Public Law Perspective' (2018) 727 *Bopjo (Korean Lawyers Association)* 442 (in Korean).
18. Andreas Voßkuhle and Gernot Sydow, 'Die demokratische Legitimation des Richters' [2002] JZ 677.
19. M. Weber, *Wirtschaft und Gesellschaft* (5th edn, Tübingen, 1972), pp. 122–4.
20. Böckenförde, in Josef Isensee and Paul Kirchhof (eds), *Handbuch des Staatsrechts II* (3rd edn, Heidelberg, 2004), pp. 437–45.
21. Schmidt-Aßmann, *Das allgemeine Verwaltungsrecht als Ordnungsidee* (2nd edn, Heidelberg, 2004), pp. 101–10.
22. Woo-Min Shim, Freedom, 'Democracy, and Legislation in the Age of Artificial Intelligence' in *Artificial and Law* (Bakyoungsa, 2020), pp. 86–7 (in Korean).
23. 'Supreme Court of Korea' (in Korean) <http://www.scourt.go.kr/portal/main.jsp> (accessed 17 April 2023).
24. Nam-Chul Chung, *Constitutional Litigation and Administrative Litigation* (Bobmunsa, 2022), p. 613 (in Korean).
25. Nikolas Graichen, *Die Automatisierung der Justiz* (Baden-Baden, 2022), p. 317.
26. John Buyers, *Artificial Intelligence: the practical issues* (Law Brief Publishing, 2018), p. 85.
27. *State of Wisconsin* v. *Erich Loomis*, 881 NW 2d 749 (Wis. 2016); G. Buchholtz, 'Artificial Intelligence and Legal Tech: Challenges to the Rule of Law' in Wischmeyer and Rademacher (eds), *Regulating Artificial Intelligence* (Springer, 2020), pp. 186–7.

28. Si-Yoon Lee, *New Civil Procedure Law* (12th edn, Pakyoungsa, 2018), p. 55 (in Korean).
29. *Korean Lawtimes* (Seoul, 13 April 2023), 2.
30. Hee-Yol Kay, *Constitutional Law II* (2nd edn, Pakyoungsa, 2007), p. 634 (in Korean).
31. COM (2021) 206 final.
32. Nam-Chul Chung, 'Enactment and characteristics of EU artificial intelligence norms' (2020) 38 *European Constitutional Research* 233 (in Korean).

REFERENCES

Böckenförde, E.-W., in J. Isensee and P. Kirchhoff (eds), *Handbuch des Staatsrechts II* (3rd edn, Heidelberg, 2004).

Buchholtz, G., 'Artificial Intelligence and Legal Tech: Challenges to the Rule of Law' in Thomas Wischmeyer and Timo Rademacher (eds), *Regulating Artificial Intelligence* (Springer, 2020), pp. 175–98.

Buyers, John, *Artificial Intelligence: the practical issues* (Law Brief Publishing, 2018).

Chung, Nam-Chul, *Constitutional Litigation and Administrative Litigation* (Bobmunsa, 2022) (in Korean).

Chung, Nam-Chul, 'Enactment and characteristics of EU artificial intelligence norms' (2020) 38 *European Constitutional Research* 215 (in Korean).

Chung, Nam-Chul, 'Challenges for Securing Democratic Legitimacy of the Executive Branch and the Judiciary from a Public Law Perspective' (2019) 727 *Bopjo (Korean Lawyers Association)* 442 (in Korean).

Graichen, Nikolas, *Die Automatisierung der Justiz* (Baden-Baden, 2022).

Han, Deok-Ryeol, 'Current Status and Prospect of Informatization in the Judiciary' in *Informatization and Trial Practice* (1998) 79 *Trial Materials* 7 (in Korean).

Kay, Hee-Yol, *Constitutional Law II* (2nd edn, Pakyoungsa, 2007) (in Korean).

Korean National Court Administration, The, *2022 Judicial Yearbook* (2023) (in Korean).

Korean National Administration Office, The, *Current Status and Prospect of Informatization of the Judiciary* (2008) (in Korean).

Lee, Si-Yoon, *New Civil Procedure Law* (12th edn, Pakyoungsa, 2018) (in Korean).

Schliesky, U., 'Digitalisierung: Herausforderung für den demokratischen Verfassungsstaat' [2019] NVwZ, 693–701.

Schmidt-Aßmann, E., *Das allgemeine Verwaltungsrecht als Ordnungsidee* (2nd edn, Heidelberg, 2004).

Schröder, M., 'Neue Grundrechte für ein digitales Zeitalter?' [2019] JZ 953–1004.

Schröder, M., 'Rahmenbedingungen der Digitalisierung der Verwaltung' [2019] VerwArch 328–48.

Shim, Woo-Min, 'Freedom, Democracy, and Legislation in the Age of Artificial Intelligence' in *Korean Association for Artificial Intelligence and Law* (Bakyoungsa, 2020), pp. 86–97 (in Korean).

Unger, S., 'Demokratische Herrschaft und künstliche Intelligenz', in Sebastian Unger and Antje von Ungern-Sternberg, *Demokratie und künstliche Intelligenz* (Mohr Siebeck, 2019), pp. 113–28.

Voßkuhle/Sydow, 'Die demokratische Legitimation des Richters' [2002] JZ 673–82.

Weber, M., *Wirtschaft und Gesellschaft* (5th edn, Tübingen, 1972).

Chapter 5

Digital Transformation of the Philippine Judiciary for the Filipino People

Ingrid Rosalie L. Gorre

A. BACKGROUND

According to the United Nations Development Programme (UNDP), access to justice involves a spectrum of actions both from the grievance side (demand side) and the remedy side (supply side). Thus, strengthening access to justice involves improving capacities in terms of legal protection, legal awareness, legal aid and counsel, adjudication, and enforcement. (See Figure 5.1.)

The UNDP framework[1] shows that strengthening adjudication and enforcement is just as important as legal empowerment in addressing the justice gap in the Philippines. 'A strong and impartial judiciary is a cornerstone of access to justice.'[2]

I. The justice gap in the Philippines

In 2021, the European Union–Philippines Justice Sector Reform Programme: Governance in Justice (EU GOJUST) commissioned a National Justice Needs Survey (JNS) conducted by the Social Weather Station that outlines the justice-seeking behaviour of Filipinos.[3] Based on a JNS, 36 per cent or 70.84 million Filipinos have experienced some kind of justiciable issue.[4] Of the 36 per cent that had justiciable issues, 63 per cent took action to resolve the issue and at the time of the survey, 60 per cent of the 63 per cent (or more than half that took action) reported that the issue had already been resolved.[5] When asked how the issue was resolved, only 19 per cent went through the formal justice system in resolving their disputes, either through the barangay (village) justice system (17 per cent), dispute resolution agencies (1 per cent) or the court (1 per cent).[6] According to the JNS, 'plurality to majority of those whose disputes have been resolved are satisfied with how their disputes were ultimately resolved', [7] with the exception of those who went to Small Claims Court; 100 per cent of the respondents said they were satisfied.[8] In terms of those who went to a court trial, '27% are satisfied, 42% are undecided if satisfied or not and 31% are not satisfied'.[9]

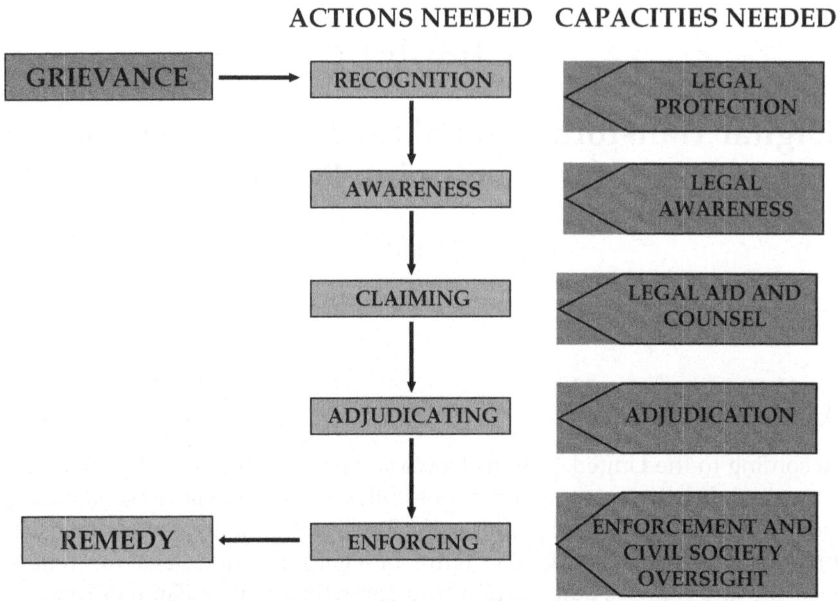

Figure 5.1 Fundamental elements of access to justice

The satisfaction rating for dispute resolution through the courts is also reflected in the relatively low percentile ranking of the Philippines in three selected sub-factors of the World Justice Project Rule of Law Index (see Figure 5.2). In particular, the percentile rank of the Philippines in the timeliness and effectiveness of criminal justice has remained in the lowest 85–90 percentile between 2015 and 2022. The two sub-factors in civil justice are generally much higher in percentile rank and have shown significant improvement since 2015. In particular, the sub-factor relating to 'civil justice not subject to delay' has improved from 92 percentile rank in 2015 to 66 in 2022, an improvement of 22 points. The sub-factor on access to civil justice was at 62 percentile rank in 2022. The improvements in the percentile rank for the two sub-factors in civil justice is reflected in the high satisfaction rating for Small Claims Courts in the Justice Needs Survey.

In the context of the Philippines, issues around efficiency and delay exacerbate challenges in access to justice. To illustrate, one of the main reasons for overcrowded jails in the Philippines and the lengthy pre-trial detention are the delays in criminal cases. 'Jail congestion is a consequence of a defective criminal justice system rather than increasing criminal activity.'[10] According to 2021 data from the Bureau of Jail Management and Penology (BJMP) and the Bureau of Corrections, 63.61 per cent of persons deprived of liberty (PDLs) in Philippine jails are awaiting court trial or final judgment.[11]

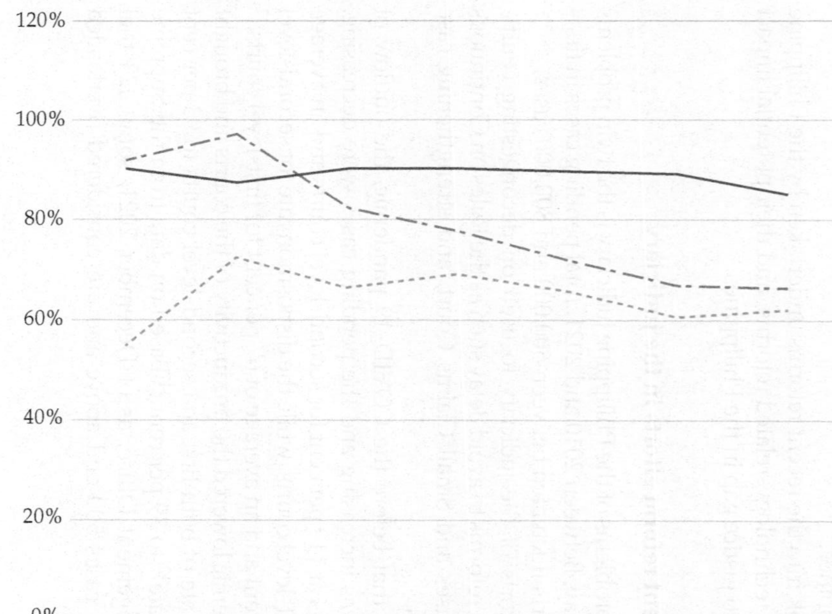

	2015	2016	2017–2018	2019	2020	2021	2022
—— Criminal adjudication is timely and effective	90%	80%	90%	90%	90%	89%	85%
- - - - People can access and afford civil justice	55%	73%	66%	69%	66%	60%	62%
— - — Civil justice is not subject to unreasonable delay	92%	97%	82%	78%	72%	67%	66%

Figure 5.2 Percentile rank of the Philippines in selected sub-factors of the World Justice Project Rule of Law Index (2015–2022)

Notes:

[1] 100 percentile rank reflects the lowest rank in the World Justice Project: Rule of Law Index.

[2] 'Rule of Law Index: Global 2022' (*World Justice Project*, 2022) <https://worldjusticeproject.org/rule-of-law-index/global/2022> (accessed 3 April 2023).

The above data shows why improving efficiency and effectiveness of courts and reducing delay should also be a key strategy in improving access to justice in the Philippines.

This study will look into the recent reforms undertaken by the Philippine Judiciary, particularly technology-related reforms, and their potential impact in closing the access to justice gap in the Philippines.

II. Overview of recent reform efforts in the judiciary

One of the foremost problems of the Philippine judiciary is the twin problems of congestion and delay. Between 2010 and 2021, total pending cases in first- and second-level courts fluctuated between 600,000 and 800,000 cases.

Recent reform efforts of the judiciary focused on decongesting courts, instituting procedural reforms to avoid delay such as the Rules on Continuous Trial for Criminal Cases and Small Claims Court, and strengthening case management systems.

Figure 5.3 shows that before the COVID-19 pandemic, the outflow of cases in the courts was increasing and the pending cases were decreasing. The clearance rate was at 119 per cent for second-level courts and an average of 104 per cent for first-level courts, while the disposition rate for second-level courts was at 43 per cent and an average of 67 per cent for first-level courts.[12] The COVID-19 pandemic lowered the productivity of the courts and brought down the clearance rate of both first and second-level courts to 93 per cent and the disposition rate[13] to 39 per cent.[14] Based on data from the Supreme Court – Court Management Office, as of December 2021, some 423 trial courts have pending cases 500 and above and are considered overloaded

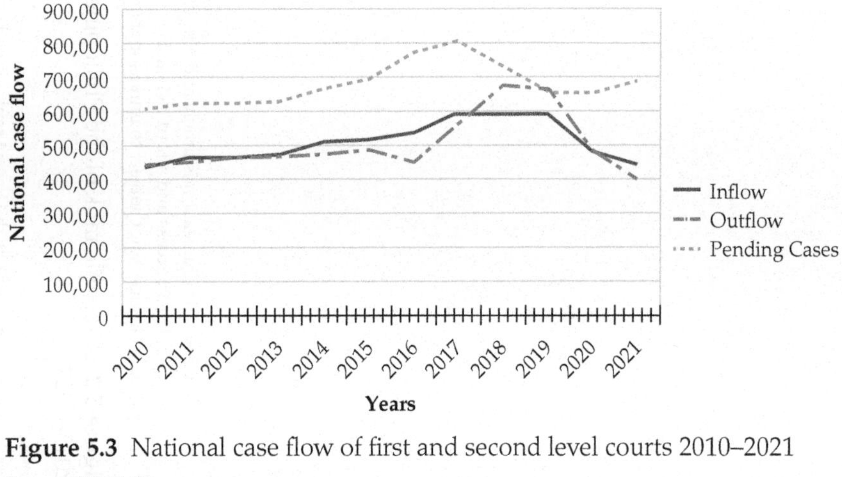

Figure 5.3 National case flow of first and second level courts 2010–2021

Source: SC CMO

courts, and 103 trial courts have pending cases 1,000 and above.[15] Generally, in areas where the courts are overloaded, jails are also often congested.

With the appointment of the current Chief Justice of the Philippines Alexander G. Gesmundo, a new round of reform initiatives is being undertaken. On 14 October 2022, the Philippine Supreme Court launched the Strategic Plan for Judicial Innovations: 2022–2027 (SPJI).[16] The SPJI seeks to address persisting problems of congestion and delay in the judiciary caused by 'scarce resources, poor court-to-population ratio, rules of procedure that allow for protracted litigations, manual processes that engender delay, and incompetence or negligence on the part of some court officials and employees'.[17] The SPJI recognises that the outcome of this persisting problem is 'distrust and lesser confidence in the courts on the part of the general public'[18] as evidenced by the low satisfaction rating indicated by court users in the Justice Needs Survey.

Recognising the need to leverage technologies to address problems besetting the judiciary, the new reform programme puts in the centre the digital transformation of the judiciary. The SPJI is anchored on the principles of timely and fair justice, transparent and accountable justice, equal and inclusive justice, and technologically adaptive management[19] and seeks to have outcomes on efficiency, innovation, and access.

B. HIGHLIGHTS OF ICT REFORM IN THE JUDICIARY

I. Early technology innovations prior to SPJI

The Philippines is in a very nascent stage of digital transformation. At present, most courts are still using antiquated equipment and legacy systems. Some of the technology innovation projects piloted and/or implemented before 2023 include the following.

(a) Electronic service of notice, subpoenas, and warrants

One of the early technology-related reform efforts was in relation to the electronic service of subpoenas to police witnesses.[20] The e-Subpoena is

> an automated web-based notification system that enables the courts to send electronic subpoenas to the police witnesses and the police units where they are assigned. Through the system, receipt of subpoenas is automatically acknowledged by the Philippine National Police, the e-Subpoena is electronically routed to the unit of the concerned police officer, and automatic confirmation of the attendance of said officer is likewise electronically issued to the relevant trial court. The e-Subpoena is deemed served upon receipt of confirmation.[21]

Prior to the pilot and roll-out of the e-Subpoena, judges complained that cases were often postponed because police witnesses were unable to attend hearings. After an initial pilot in the Quezon City court station, anecdotal evidence from judges indicated that the attendance rate of police witnesses increased by 90 per cent. This led to the nationwide roll-out of the programme.

Delays in the service of notices and subpoenas to non-police witnesses because of the postal service also resulted in postponement and delays in cases. The Supreme Court authorised electronic service of notices and subpoenas through A.M. No. 12-11-12-SC and expanded the application to civil cases through A.M. No. 13-04-11-SC on 5 August 2014. The rules allowed for the use of short message service (SMS), phone calls and email for the service of notices and subpoenas. The objective of the reform was 'to expedite the timeline of serving notices and subpoenas to parties, witnesses, and counsel to eventually reduce overall duration of trial court proceedings'.[22]

Based on an unpublished study of EU GOJUST of 59 pilot courts for the E-Notice,

> 80% of 59 participating trial courts in the CALABARZON Region reported using the e-Notice system but to widely varying degrees of usage (25–100%). Findings show the most robust uptake is for SMS/text messaging as an alternative mode of issuing notices, followed by mobile phone calls, and then emails. Empirical data show that 81.3% of trial courts have used SMS/text messaging from some time to all the time (25–100%). Seventy-one percent reported using mobile phone calls from some time to all the time (25–100%), while only 50.9% reported using email notifications. Overall, court personnel are optimistic (84.7%) on the innovations e-Notice brings to the court since 84.7 percent of them also agree that it made the task of informing court litigants much easier.[23]

While both reforms were widely used by the pilot courts, courts also faced a challenge in using e-Notice and e-Subpoena for those with poor internet access. The use of mobile phones and SMS was considered as a useful alternative.[24]

The Supreme Court institutionalised the use of electronic service of pleadings, summons, subpoenas in 2019 Amendments to the 1997 Revised Rules on Civil Procedure.[25]

(b) Pilot of first generation of eCourt system for lower courts

In 2013, the Supreme Court of the Philippines, with support from United States Agency for International Development (USAID), piloted the eCourts, an electronic case management system in Quezon City court station. The pilot was expanded to ten other court stations, with a total of 327 court branches.

> The eCourt system has two main components: (1) court computerization, including a case management system for operational support; and (2) an on-site kiosk allowing public access to basic case information. The core features of the eCourt system include docketing of cases; electronic raffling of cases; monitoring and management via a dashboard of dates important to a case; generating reports and calendars; recording of different actions taken during hearings, including decisions and writs of execution; printing and serving of orders from the bench; and determining and recording fee payments. These measures sought to improve

transparency by linking court kiosks with eCourts, providing supervising judges with easy access to case records, and ensuring fairness in case assignment through e-raffling.[26]

In 2019, the International Initiative for Impact Evaluation conducted an assessment study of the eCourts. Based on qualitative interviews and an online survey, court users were generally supportive of the eCourts. According to the online survey, benefits of the eCourts include the following: 'checking of case status (67%), raffling of cases (61%), safekeeping of records (41%) and setting of hearing dates (32%). They also claimed that eCourt increases the number of cases disposed (23%) and speeds up case disposal (20%).'[27] The study also reported challenges in the implementation of the eCourts such as 'lack of computers and server connections, inadequate training of court personnel and the lack of IT support, and a shortage of human resources to update and maintain the eCourt system'.[28]

While the study found the eCourts generally useful, it also found that only '33% of respondents claimed to have fully integrated eCourts in their workflow' while the rest of respondents used it daily or a few times a week.[29] The study also found that despite the existence of eCourts in their court branch, some courts still have parallel case management systems whether manual or Excel-based.[30]

The study reiterated that for an eCourt system to be successful, court branches should be provided with the basic infrastructure, regularly update old and new cases, transition fully into the eCourts, and mitigate the other inefficient case management practices of the court, among others.[31]

(c) Pilot of videoconferencing hearings

In 2019, the Supreme Court, with support from EU GOJUST, conducted a pilot of videoconferencing hearings between courts and jails in Davao City for the remote appearance or testimony of certain persons deprived of liberties (PDLs).[32] On 27 April 2020, in response to the nationwide quarantine measures due to the COVID-19 pandemic and to address the restriction on movement of people, the Supreme Court expanded the pilot to include more than seventy court stations nationwide.[33] Based on a successful pilot, the Supreme Court issued Guidelines on the Conduct of Videoconferencing Hearings (2020 Guidelines) on 9 December 2020. The 2020 Guidelines now allowed the roll-out of videoconferencing hearings nationwide.[34]

The 2020 Guidelines allowed for continuity of court cases despite the restrictions on mobility posed by the COVID-19 pandemic. According to Associate Justice Midas Marquez, as of 13 October 2022, 'there have been 1,139,720 video conferencing hearings conducted with a success rate of 89.27%. We likewise released 132,916 persons deprived of liberty (PDLs), 2,120 of which are children in conflict with the law (CICL), because of videoconferencing hearings.'[35]

The 2020 Guidelines also allowed for videoconferencing hearings to be conducted in Philippine Embassies and consulates abroad for Overseas Filipino Workers (OFWs), Filipinos Residing Abroad or Temporarily Outside the Philippines, and Non-resident Foreign Nationals.[36] The 2020 Guidelines have the potential to address the justice needs of an estimated 1.83 million OFWs[37] who would otherwise have to go home to the Philippines to attend court hearings.

The 2020 Guidelines also include as a ground for videoconferencing hearings the 'inability or difficulty of litigant, witness or counsel to physically appear in court due to security risks in his or her transport in going to and from the court, real or apparent danger to his or her life, security or safety, serious health concerns, disability, or the fact that he or she is a victim of a sexual offence or domestic violence'.[38] The 2020 Guidelines provide a technology solution not just to address the limited movement during the COVID-19 pandemic but also seek to address access to justice issues faced by some sectors.

According to a study conducted by the EU-GOJUST in 2023,

> One considerable factor of trial courts in determining whether to allow the conduct of VCH is allowing a participant who faces considerable difficulties in accessing the courts to nonetheless take part in the proceeding. Over 60% of courts reported allowing VCH when the participant is inconvenienced by illness, while over 59% allow VCH when the participant is inconvenienced by physical distance. Over 27% of courts also reported that they have authorized VCH proceedings where a participant does not have the financial resources to travel to court. During the FGDs, informants had cited that for several litigants or witnesses, notwithstanding poverty, would have to incur considerable travel expenses to attend court hearings; VCH has reduced their expenses in undertaking litigation. Practicing lawyers, including those representing public interest cases, have also reported that because of VCH, they are able to handle more cases and even schedule hearings on the same day in court stations that are hundreds of kilometers apart.[39]

Videoconferencing hearings also facilitate hearings for those who have already been previously convicted by final judgment and serving sentence in a penal facility. The logistical challenge in attending a court hearing by a convicted PDL has been a repeated problem faced by courts and litigants prior to the adoption of videoconferencing hearings. For example, the completion of the trial and eventual second conviction of an infamous child trafficker/pornographer/child abuser was made possible by videoconferencing hearings held by a court in Misamis Oriental attended by the accused in the Davao Penal Colony where he was serving a prior sentence.[40]

Based on November 2022 unpublished data from the Supreme Court – Court Management Office, 2,510 court branches or an estimated 78 per cent of trial courts nationwide have used videoconferencing for hearings at one point or another. However, frequent users of videoconferencing hearings

(500 videoconferencing hearings and above) are only at 438 trial courts or 14 per cent of total trial courts.

Poor internet connection and lack of equipment not just for the judiciary but for all stakeholders has remained the biggest challenge in the roll-out. The Supreme Court and other justice agencies need to provide further investment in technology, equipment and network infrastructure in order to allow increased adoption of videoconferencing technology for the entire court proceeding.

(d) Deploying Philippine Judiciary Office 365 nationwide

In the early part of the COVID-19 pandemic, the Supreme Court deployed Office 365 to all courts nationwide for video conferencing hearings through Microsoft Teams. Eventually, Philippine Judiciary Office 365 became 'a unified communication and collaboration platform'.[41] On 25 September 2020, the Office of the Court Administrator issued a circular announcing that dissemination of all administrative orders, circulars and other court issuances, as well as court reports, will be done through the official Philippine Judiciary Office 365 accounts.[42] Prior to the deployment of the Judiciary Office 365 accounts, not all courts had official email addresses and courts that had official email addresses were based on a slow legacy email system. The deployment of Judiciary Office 365 accounts also provided for official email addresses to courts facilitated the electronic filing of pleadings by litigants, as well as the electronic service of notices and subpoenas. (See early discussion on electronic service.)

(e) Bar Personal Login Unified System (Bar PLUS)

The Office of the Bar Confidant of the Supreme Court (SC-OBC) has deployed the Bar Personal Login Unified System (Bar PLUS) as the online platform for applicants to the Philippine Bar. Prior to Bar PLUS, applicants had to submit their forms to the SC-OBC in Manila. This meant that applicants from outside Metro Manila needed to travel just to file their application.[43]

(f) Judiciary Electronic Payment Solution (JePS)

After a successful pilot in 2022, the Supreme Court rolled out the Judiciary Electronic Payment Solution (JePS). 'The JePS is a platform that allows the assessment and payment of legal fees and other collections of the Judiciary in a more convenient and accessible manner. It provides litigants, their counsels/representatives, and persons requesting clearances, certifications, and other services from the courts, the option to pay online through major banks and digital wallets.'[44] Prior to the introduction of the JePS, litigants had to go to the courts physically for the assessment and payment of fees. The introduction of the JePS 'aims to streamline the processes of assessment and payment of court fees, increase the accessibility of the public to judicial services, increase transparency and accountability, and provide the Supreme Court with efficient accounting and auditing mechanisms.'[45]

(g) Philippine Judicial Academy (PHILJA) Learning Management System[46]

During the COVID-19 pandemic, the Philippine Judicial Academy (PHILJA) launched a Learning Management System (LMS), an online training platform for judges and judiciary personnel.[47] The online platform will allow distance learning through 'interactive online services, including information, tools, and research materials'.[48] The LMS contains available courses and their schedules. The LMS is still in an early stage of development and PHILJA intends to develop more research materials and asynchronous courses for judges and court personnel.

The COVID-19 pandemic fast-tracked the roll-out and implementation of some of these reforms. The Supreme Court has recently adopted an agile approach in developing and rolling out the ICT applications and microservices so that court users and the general public can quickly benefit from the benefits of the digital transformation of the judiciary.

II. Strategic Plan for Judicial Innovations: 2022–2027 (SPJI)

The new reform agenda of the Philippine Supreme Court seeks to leverage technology to transform the judiciary to meet the justice needs of the Filipino people. The SPJI promotes 'innovation by utilising the most appropriate, secure, and advanced technologies to enhance the efficiency of court services, reduce delays in case processing and disposition, and increase justice system-wide collaboration'[49] with the end goal of 'seamless access to justice for all'.[50]

Some of the initiatives identified in the SPJI have already been implemented as discussed in the previous section. However, there are other initiatives that are still going to be undertaken over the next few years. Some of these initiatives include the following.

Exploring the use of AI applications

Initiatives include exploring the use of artificial intelligence (AI) applications such as the following:

1. AI-enabled voice-to-text transcription application in the production of court stenographic notes.[51]

   Currently, the mode of producing stenographic notes in the judiciary is still largely a manual process. In recent years, it has been more difficult to recruit qualified stenographers. The limited number of stenographers deployed in trial courts sometimes causes delay in cases especially when stenographers are unable to deliver the transcript of stenographic notes (TSN) in a timely manner to aid the litigants and the courts in preparing their pleadings, orders, resolutions and decisions. An AI-enabled voice-to-text transcription application can speed up the process of producing TSNs and hopefully also reduce delays in cases.

In June 2024, the Philippine Supreme Court with support from the EU GOJUST programme completed the successful pilot of the use of a voice-to-text transcription solution for the production of court TSNs. With the use of machine learning, a Tagalog-English language model was developed allowing the solution to accurately transcribe English with Filipino accent, as well as mix of Tagalog and English language. By the end of the pilot, the solution was able to transcribe audio recordings of court hearings using a mix of Filipino and English with an accuracy rate of 90 per cent. The solution effectively reduced the time to produce the court TSNs by 50 per cent. Some users even indicated a reduction of time by 80 per cent. The Philippine Supreme Court will be rolling out the transcription solution to other courts. In addition, the Philippine Supreme Court is also planning to develop additional language models for other local languages such as Ilokano, Waray, Cebuano, and Kapampangan. This innovation is very important to the Philippines because it is estimated that the Philippines has around 130 languages.[52]

2. The SPJI also indicated that the Judiciary E-Library will be re-developed with the use of AI-enabled legal research tools[53] and 'AI-enabled platforms for self-help and public assistance services'[54] will be deployed.

Developing the next generation of eCourts

The SPJI also prioritised the development of the next generation of eCourts (eCourts PH 2.0) that aims to move more court processes into the digital space: e.g. online filing, service of notices, warrants, decisions online. The eCourts PH 2.0 system aims to automate processes such as raffling, computation of overstaying PDLs, and computation of sentences.[55] It will have the following functionalities:

- eCourt Portal – 'single window' for the clients of judiciary institutions
- eFiling via eCourt Portal and through external systems
- fully digitalised *rollo* or case records
- ePayment
- full automation of raffling
- workflow-driven processing
- auto-generation of outgoing documents
- digital signing based on biometric features
- electronic service (mailing)
- personal calendars, court calendar, and hearing room calendars
- system-supported scheduling
- report generator based on query wizard
- extensive tracking with reminders and notifications
- intra-office and/or inter-office messages
- information exchange with external institutions.

Exploring interoperability with systems of other agencies

The Supreme Court also intends to explore interoperability with systems of other agencies.[56] The data will be shared through the National Justice Information System (NJIS) 'based on parameters that will be authorised by the Court'.[57] NJIS is:

> [a] project that involves the development and setup of core agency information management systems and inter-agency exchange mechanisms. The NJIS is composed of two discrete clusters: the Law Enforcement Cluster composed of the DOJ National Prosecution Service, Philippine National Police, National Bureau of Investigation, Philippine Drug Enforcement Agency, Dangerous Drugs Board, and Bureau of Immigration; and the Corrections Cluster involving the Bureau of Jail Management and Penology; Bureau of Corrections; Board of Pardons and Parole; and Parole and Probation Administration.[58]

The Department of Justice has developed a middleware exchange platform whereby case management systems of the different justice agencies can connect through an interoperability layer. Currently, the Supreme Court is not part of the NJIS implementing agencies. However, the Philippine Development Plan: 2023–2028 and the SPJI include the participation of the judiciary in the NJIS as a target.

Real-time exchange of information such as subpoenas, orders, decisions and warrants will not only expedite cases but may also be critical in ensuring the delivery of justice. Real-time delivery of a Hold Departure Order to an immigration officer may prevent an accused from absconding. At the same time, real-time delivery of Judgment of Acquittal to a detention facility may allow a person deprived of liberty to be released immediately.

These initiatives are all in their early development.

C. ACCESS TO JUSTICE CONSIDERATIONS IN TECHNOLOGY TRANSFORMATION IN THE JUDICIARY

I. Technological transformation must include building the capacity of people

Critical to the digital transformation initiative is the strengthening of the Management Information System Office (MISO). In May 2021, the Supreme Court approved the MISO Reorganisation and Development Plan. Under the approved MRDP, the MISO will 'serve as a catalyst of change to enhance and support the Philippine Judiciary in the dispensation of justice and to institutionalise its core functions and competencies on ICT Governance and Planning, Information Security, Project Management, Systems Development, Systems Operations, and Technical Support Services'. For the first time, the chief of the MISO is now designated as a

Chief Technology Officer. The Supreme Court is also currently strengthening the capacity of MISO.

In any digital transformation initiative, it is important that there is no one left behind. In 2022, GOJUST conducted a survey on Information and Communications Technology (ICT) and cybersecurity competency and training for judiciary personnel.[59] An estimated 35 per cent of judiciary personnel responded to the training. Based on the survey, it is confirmed that there is a high percentage of judiciary personnel that can already be considered digital natives: 92% of respondents own mobile phones while 76% own a computer. The majority of judiciary personnel have indicated that they have either basic, sufficient or advanced knowledge/skill on basic ICT concepts. However, there are still gaps in basic ICT and cybersecurity knowledge. The Philippine Judicial Academy, with support from GOJUST, intends to roll out training on basic ICT and cybersecurity for judiciary personnel.

II. Technology and fundamental rights

(a) Balancing needs to improve efficiency with access to justice

According to the 2020 Philippine Digital Economy Report by the World Bank, 'the limited digital infrastructure of the Philippines has generated a digital divide, contributing to an unequal access to services delivered via the internet'. In 2018, about 40 per cent of the Philippines' 103 million total population and 23 million of the households did not have internet access. Digital and technological innovations promise increased efficiency for courts and court users. However, there is a need to ensure that those without access to the internet and technology tools will still be able to access court services. Thus, there is still a need to maintain dual platforms. For example, analogue filing systems need to be retained side-by-side online filing options or there is a need to at least provide accessibility options for those who do not have access to the internet and the technology tools, such as online kiosks similar to what is envisioned in the SPJI. A strategy also needs to be in place to ensure that maintaining dual platforms does not negate the efficiency gains of the technology. Based on lessons from the first roll-out of the eCourts in the Philippines, requiring courts to maintain records both digitally and in an analogue format involved repetitive work for the staff and discouraged them from utilising the eCourts system to the fullest.

(b) Balancing needs to improve efficiency with constitutionally mandated rights

During the COVID-19 pandemic, videoconferencing hearings have been allowed nationwide. This was to ensure business continuity despite on-and-off lockdowns. Challenges to the implementation include the lack of adequate equipment for both the courts and the litigants, and poor internet connection, among others. Judges have learned to balance the need to avoid delay in proceedings and the need to ensure integrity in the proceedings. Based on unpublished Indicative Findings on the Assessment of Court Remote and Videoconferencing Hearings in the Philippines, 59.7 per cent of courts surveyed prefer face-to-face hearings so they can better observe witness demeanour.[60] For persons deprived of liberty (PDLs), access to their lawyers is also sometimes affected when the hearing is through videoconferencing.[61] Safeguards need to be provided to ensure that constitutionally mandated rights are protected.

(c) Need to strengthen security measures and measures to protect the right to privacy

The digital revolution is also a massive transfer of data from analogue format to the digital space. Court data contains sensitive information. Security measures and measures to protect the right of privacy of litigants must be strengthened.

(d) Respect for labour rights and security of tenure

The SC with the support of GOJUST has recently completed a study on reorganisation for lower courts and the Office of the Court Administrator. The study sought to examine the following, among several others:

- Technology tools needed to facilitate the work of the courts and the court administrators.
- Implication of technology on human resources including re-evaluating competency requirements.

The digital transformation initiative can affect those who are not adept and knowledgeable in the new technology. There is a need to ensure that those who have limited capacity in technology are provided with the opportunity to learn new skills required for the new systems.

(e) Opportunities for increased access to justice

Based on the 2021 Justice Needs Survey, aside from legal fees and lawyer's fees, transportation and communication costs are one of the main cost centres for those who have court cases. The digital space can also provide an opportunity for reducing these costs. For example, hearings can be via videoconferencing hearings to avoid the need for travel. This is very important for OFWs who have court cases in the Philippines. Currently, OFWs and other Filipinos overseas can avail of videoconferencing hearings within the premises of Philippine embassies and consulates overseas.

(f) Open justice

The expanding digital space can also be an opportunity for the judiciary to provide information to the general public on the court and its operations. At present, aside from its website, the Supreme Court is also maximising the use of social media platforms to disseminate court information. Oral arguments or hearings on issues of public importance are also streamed live on YouTube. The Supreme Court has also made available to the public the Supreme Court E-Library, which was formerly available to judiciary personnel only.

The information currently available in the various online platforms of the Supreme Court is mostly highly technical and may only be understood by those in the legal field. However, the Supreme Court Public Information Office (SC-PIO) is also now slowly adding content that will make recent SC issuances accessible and understandable for the general public.[62]

D. ELEMENTS FOR A SUCCESSFUL DIGITAL TRANSFORMATION INITIATIVE

Based on the Philippine experience, the following are key elements in a successful digital transformation initiative.

I. Strong leadership and strong consensus within the implementing agency

There should be a strong consensus among the leadership and at all levels in the judiciary. All of the ICT reforms discussed were authorised by the Supreme Court *en banc*. In addition, a change management strategy is in place that includes having champions at the local level and providing information and education materials for each reform introduced. A communication strategy for the SPJI is also currently being developed.

In 2009, an Enterprise Information System Plan (EISP) was adopted by the Philippine Supreme Court. In 2013, the EISP was reviewed and an updated work plan and budget for the EISP was approved.[63] More than a decade has passed since the first version of the EISP was drafted. New technologies have been developed in the interim and some technologies that have been identified in the original EISP may have become obsolete. 'The EISP failed to guide the judiciary in managing these projects. These problems range from having failed biddings, misinterpreted requirements during implementation, ineffective or lack of use of up-to-date technologies, to fragmented information systems developed from within and outside the judiciary.'[64] The Supreme Court is currently developing an ICT Governance Framework, a Five-Year Strategic Plan, and a Judiciary MIS Operations Manual to leapfrog the technological transformation of the judiciary.[65]

II. Financing must be available

The adoption of the EISP has provided the Supreme Court with an accompanying budget to implement the plan. Over the years, the Supreme Court has used this budget together with parallel funding and/or technical assistance from development agencies and other donors to implement various ICT initiatives. More often than not, budget and planning agencies view ICT initiatives as a capital outlay investment. However, since technology is quickly changing, there should be provision for modifications in the system and a recurring budget for equipment. All of these must be available in a timely manner for ICT reform efforts to succeed.

There should also be a budget for redundancy in equipment and internet facilities. As the judiciary moves into the digital platform, ensuring the availability of backup equipment is important for business continuity. At present, some judges have subscribed to multiple internet providers to ensure continued access to online court systems.

III. Strong technical capacity must be present in the organisation

One of the lessons from the early implementation of the eCourts is that for the roll-out of ICT projects to be successful, there must be strong technical support internally. Even if the software is developed externally, technical personnel of the Supreme Court must be able to determine whether the software delivered is sufficient and acceptable. They should also be able to troubleshoot and maintain the system. Currently, the Supreme Court is striving to develop some of its software internally with the hope of ensuring the sustainability of the systems.

IV. Proof of concept

Technological innovations usually require a huge investment by the government. Conducting pilot testing of a technological reform initiative and showing proof of concept will justify the investment and also convince both decision-makers and other stakeholders on the effectiveness of the reform.

V. Enabling rules

In the past, certain technological reforms have been hindered by the absence or by conflicting rules. In recent years, successful initiatives such as the e-Subpoena, e-Warrant, Videoconferencing Hearings and the like have been successful because the Supreme Court was quick to adopt enabling rules to allow for ICT reform.

VI. Technological transformation must be an iterative process

Finally, technological transformation is an iterative process. The development of software is not completed in its first iteration. There should be room for improvement and re-development based on stakeholder feedback.

The agile approach currently adopted by the Supreme Court MISO allows for this strategy. Financing for ICT projects should also take this into account.

E. CONCLUDING REMARKS

In the past two decades, the Philippine Supreme Court has introduced significant ICT solutions to improve the efficiency and effectiveness of the judiciary. As pointed out at the start of this paper, all the substantive, procedural and technological reforms that have taken place have led to some significant improvement especially in terms of civil justice sub-factors on delay.

As the Supreme Court rolls out more reforms, it is hoped that improved effectiveness and efficiency of the courts will lead to greater access to justice for Filipinos. At the end of the day, however, technology solutions should never be a monolithic solution but should only be part of a plethora of reform options for the court. Technology should not be the end but the means to achieve the goal of providing for the justice needs of the Filipino people.

NOTES

1. United Nations Development Programme (UNDP), 'Justice for All' (Practice Note, UNDP March 2004) <https://www.undp.org/sites/g/files/zskgke326/files/publications/Justice_PN_En.pdf> (accessed 2 December 2022).
2. Ibid., 3.
3. Social Weather Station, 'Final Survey Report: Justice Needs Survey (August 29–September 4, 2021) conducted for the European Union Justice Sector Reform Programme: Governance in Justice II, Quezon City, December 2021' (Unpublished).
4. Ibid., p. vii. The 2021 survey confirms the 2018 World Justice Forum Survey in the Philippines indicating that 35% of respondents experienced a legal problem in the last two years. 'Global Insights on Access to Justice: Philippines' (*World Justice Project,* 2018) <https://worldjusticeproject.org/access-to-justice-data/#/country/PHL> (accessed 2 April 2023).
5. Ibid., 128.
6. Ibid., 157.
7. Ibid., 172.
8. Ibid., 172.
9. Ibid., 172.
10. Rochelle D. Curiba, 'Trapped in a Broken Bail System: Re-thinking Pre-trial Detention Practices in the Philippines' (2021) 65 UST Law Review 59 <https://lawreview.ust.edu.ph/trapped-in-a-broken-bail-system/> (accessed 13 March 2023).
11. BJMP Annual Report 2021, p. 8 and Bureau of Correction Statistics 1990–2022.
12. Supreme Court of Philippines, *Judiciary Annual Report 2019* (2020) <https://sc.judiciary.gov.ph/3d-flip-book/2019-judiciary-annual-report/> (accessed 1 March 2023).
13. Clearance rate is total case disposal divided case inflow multiplied by 100, while disposition rate is case disposal divided by total case input multiplied by 100.

14. Supreme Court of Philippines, *Judiciary Annual Report 2021* (2022), 103 <https://sc.judiciary.gov.ph/3d-flip-book/2021-judiciary-annual-report/> (accessed 1 March 2023).
15. Supreme Court – Court Management Office (Unpublished).
16. Supreme Court of Philippines, 'Supreme Court Launches the Strategic Plan for Judicial Innovations: 2022–2027' (2022) <https://sc.judiciary.gov.ph/supreme-court-launches-the-strategic-plan-for-judicial-innovations-2022-2027/#:~:text=The%20SPJI%20is%20the%20High,and%20(4)%20technology%20adaptive.> (accessed 3 March 2023).
17. Ibid., 8.
18. Ibid., 8.
19. Supreme Court of Philippines (n. 17).
20. Office of the Court Administrator Manila, 'OCA Circular No. 244-2017' (December 2017) <https://oca.judiciary.gov.ph/wp-content/uploads/2018/01/OCA-Circular-No.-244-2017.pdf> (accessed 2 March 2023).
21. 'Evaluation Report: E-Notice and E-Subpoena Projects' (EU GOJUST (Unpublished) 2019), 2.
22. Ibid., 2.
23. Ibid., 3.
24. Ibid., 15.
25. Supreme Court of the Philippines, '2019 Amendments to the Rules of Civil Procedure (A.M. No. 19-10-20-SC) (2020)' <https://sc.judiciary.gov.ph/wp-content/uploads/2022/08/2019-rules-of-civil-procedure.pdf> (accessed 3 March 2023).
26. Aniceto C. Orbeta, Jr, Vicente B. Paqueo and Bilal Siddiqi, 'Impacts of Electronic Case Management Systems on Court Congestion in the Philippines' (2021) 3ie Impact Evaluation Report 133 <https://doi.org/10.23846/PWPIE133> (accessed 16 February 2024).
27. Ibid., 35.
28. Ibid., 36.
29. Orbeta, Jr and others (n. 27).
30. Ibid.
31. Orbeta, Jr and others (n. 27), 38.
32. Supreme Court of the Philippines, 'Notice of Resolution Regarding Videoconferencing' (A.M. 19-05-05-SC, August 2019) <https://oca.judiciary.gov.ph/wp–content/uploads/2019/08/AM–Videoconferencing–Pilot.pdf> (accessed 5 January 2024).
33. Supreme Court of the Philippines, 'Administrative Circular No. 37-2020' (April 2020) <https://www.pwja.org/sites/www.pwja.org/files/2020-04/AC-37-2020.pdf> (accessed 5 January 2024).
34. Office of the Court Administrator Manila, 'OCA Circular No. 209-2020' (A.M. No. 20-12-01-SC, January 2021) <https://oca.judiciary.gov.ph/wp-content/uploads/2021/01/OCA-Circular-No.-209-2020.pdf> (accessed 5 January 2024).
35. Supreme Court Public Information Office, 'JSCC Holds Justice Zone Dialogue in Davao City' <https://sc.judiciary.gov.ph/jscc-holds-justice-zone-dialogue-in-davao/> (accessed 5 April 2023).
36. A.M. No. 20-12-01-SC (n. 35), Section 3(b)(vii) and (viii).

37. Philippine Statistics Authority, '2021 Overseas Filipino Workers' (2 December 2022), <https://psa.gov.ph/content/2021-overseas-filipino-workers-final-results> (accessed 6 April 2023).
38. A.M. No. 20-12-01-SC (n. 35), Section 3(b)(iii).
39. Jose Jesus Disini, Jr and Michael A. Dizon, 'Report and Recommendations on the Implementation of Videoconferencing Hearings in Philippine Trial Courts', Non-Key Expert Mission No. 3, EU GOJUST Programme (Manila, 2023), p. 17, unpublished study.
40. Marlon Alexander Luistro, 'Australian man gets 129 years imprisonment for qualified trafficking in person, child pornography, rape and abuse', *Hong Kong News* (Hong Kong, 10 November 2022) <https://hongkongnews.com.hk/balita/australian-man-gets-129-years-imprisonment-for-qualified-trafficking-in-person-child-pornography-rape-and-abuse/#:~:text=Back%20in%202018%2C%20Peter%20Scully,fleeing%20from%20Australia%20in%202011> (accessed 25 March 2023).
41. Microsoft Philippines Communications Team, 'Supreme Court of the Philippines Institutionalizes Videoconferencing Hearings to Ensure Continuation of Justice Throughout COVID-19 and Beyond', *Microsoft News* (16 March 2021) <https://news.microsoft.com/en-ph/2021/03/16/supreme-court-of-the-philippines-institutionalizes-videoconferencing-hearings-to-ensure-continuation-of-justice-throughout-covid-19-and-beyond/> (accessed 15 March 2023).
42. Office of the Court Administrator Manila, 'OCA Circular No. 162-2020' (25 September 2020) <https://sc.judiciary.gov.ph/to-all-judges-and-personnel-of-first-and-second-level-courts-re-use-of-official-philippine-judiciary-office-365-accounts-for-dissemination-of-administrative-orders-circulars-and-other-court-issuanc/> (accessed on 30 March 2023).
43. In addition to online filing, the Supreme Court also deployed local testing centres to make the bar exams accessible to those who live outside Metro Manila. Prior to the COVID-19 pandemic, the bar examinations only took place in one site in Metro Manila, requiring all applicants to travel to Metro Manila for the exam.
44. 'What is JePS?' (*Judiciary E-Payment Solution Center*) <https://help-epayment.judiciary.gov.ph/result.html?search=What%20is%20JePS?> (accessed 15 March 2023).
45. Benjamin Pulta, 'SC taps GCash, GrabPay for online court payment', *Philippines News Agency* (11 January 2023) <https://www.pna.gov.ph/articles/1192491> (accessed 15 March 2023).
46. *Philippine Judicial Academy (PHILJA)* <https://philja.lms.ph/> (accessed 5 January 2024).
47. Supreme Court of the Philippines, 'Strategic Plans for Judicial Interventions 2022–2027' <https://sc.judiciary.gov.ph/3d-flip-book/spji/> (accessed 5 March 2023).
48. Ibid.
49. SC of the Philippines, 'Strategic Plan' (n. 48), 17.
50. Ibid.
51. SC of the Philippines, 'Strategic Plan' (n. 48), 18.
52. 'Mga Wika ng Pilipinas' <https://kwfwikaatkultura.ph/mga-wika-ng-pilipinas/> (accessed 26 August 2024).

53. SC of the Philippines, 'Strategic Plan' (n. 48).
54. Ibid., 24.
55. Ibid., 18–19.
56. SC of the Philippines, 'Strategic Plan' (n. 48), 23.
57. Ibid.
58. National Government Portal (NGP), *Philippine Development Plan 2023–2028* <https://pdp.neda.gov.ph/wp-content/uploads/2023/01/PDP-2023-2028.pdf> (accessed 16 February 2024), 310.
59. Emily Manuel, 'Survey on ICT and Cybersecurity Competency and Training' (GOJUST (Unpublished)), 5–6.
60. Non-Key Expert Mission No. 3, 'Indicative Findings on the Assessment of Court Remote and Videoconferencing Hearings in the Philippines' (Presented to Supreme Court Associate Justice Midas Marquez (Chair of the Committee on Videoconferencing Hearing), p. 10, GOJUST, 21 April 2023).
61. Non-Key Expert Mission No. 3 (n. 61).
62. Supreme Court of Philippines, 'The 2019 Amendments to the 1989 Revised Rules on Evidence' (6 July 2021) <https://www.youtube.com/watch?v=xzd92JX_3UE> (accessed 12 March 2023); 'The 2019 Amendments to the 1997 Rules of Civil Procedure' (6 July 2021) <https://www.youtube.com/watch?v=W9cC8nRqpNM> (accessed 12 March 2023); '2019 Amendments to the 1997 Rules of Civil Procedure and to the Revised Rules on Evidence' (2 July 2021) <https://www.youtube.com/watch?v=FowUE9J05yA> (accessed 12 March 2023); 'Judiciary ePayment System (JePS)' (30 March 2022) <https://www.youtube.com/watch?v=eBHjJ6nPIyg> (accessed 12 March 2023).
63. Supreme Court of the Philippines, 'Approval of Updated Electronic Information Security Plan (EISP) A.M. No. 14-09-06-SC' (*Competitive.org.ph*, September 2014) <https://www.competitive.org.ph/doingbusiness/reference/downloads/Summit/forupload/RDEC/EC_REFERENCE2b_Approval_of_Updated_EISP_A.M._no._14-09--06-sc.pdf> (accessed 20 March 2023).
64. Supreme Court of the Philippines Bids and Awards Committee (BAC SC), 'Contract No. 2022-02, Contract for the Consulting Services for the Development of the Judiciary ICT Governance Framework, Five-Year Strategic Plan, and Judiciary MIS Operations Manual' (13 December 2022) <https://sc.judiciary.gov.ph/wp-content/uploads/2023/04/BAC-CS-04-04-2023-2.pdf> (accessed 20 March 2023).
65. SPJI (n. 48), 20–1.

REFERENCES

Bureau of Corrections Statistics of the Philippines (1990–2022).

Bureau of Jail and Penology of the Philippines (2021), *Annual Report.*

Curiba, R., (2021), 'Trapped in a Broken Bail System: Re-thinking Pre-trial Detention Practices in the Philippines', 65 UST Law Review 59 <https://lawreview.ust.edu.ph/trapped-in-a-broken-bail-system/>

Disini, Jr, J. and Dizon, M. (2023), 'Indicative Findings on the Assessment of Court Remote and Videoconferencing Hearings in the Philippines', Non-Key Expert Mission No. 3, EU-GOJUST Programme, Presented to

Supreme Court Associate Justice Midas Marquez (Chair of the Committee on Videoconferencing Hearing).

Disini, Jr, J. and Dizon, M. (2023), 'Report and Recommendations on the Implementation of Videoconferencing Hearings in Philippine Trial Courts', Non-Key Expert Mission No. 3, EU-GOJUST Programme (Unpublished study).

EU-GOJUST Programme (2019), 'Evaluation Report: E-Notice and E-Subpoena Projects' (Unpublished).

Komisyon sa Wikang Filipino,'Mga Wika ng Pilipinas' <https://kwfwikaatkultura.ph/mga-wika-ng-pilipinas/>

Luistro, M. A. (2022), 'Australian man gets 129 years imprisonment for qualified trafficking in person, child pornography, rape and abuse', *Hong Kong News*, <https://hongkongnews.com.hk/balita/australian-man-gets-129-years-imprisonment-for-qualified-trafficking-in-person-child-pornography-rape-and-abuse/#:~:text=Back%20in%202018%2C%20Peter%20Scully,fleeing%20from%20Australia%20in%202011>

Manuel, E. (2023), 'Survey on ICT and Cybersecurity Competency and Training', EU-GOJUST Programme (Unpublished).

Microsoft Philippines Communications Team (2021), 'Supreme Court of the Philippines Institutionalizes Videoconferencing Hearings to Ensure Continuation of Justice Throughout COVID-19 and Beyond', *Microsoft News* <https://news.microsoft.com/en-ph/2021/03/16/supreme-court-of-the-philippines-institutionalizes-videoconferencing-hearings-to-ensure-continuation-of-justice-throughout-covid-19-and-beyond/>

Office of the Court Administrator of the Philippines (2017), 'OCA Circular No. 244-2017' <https://oca.judiciary.gov.ph/wp-content/uploads/2018/01/OCA-Circular-No.-244-2017.pdf>

Office of the Court Administrator of the Philippines (2020), 'OCA Circular No. 162-2020' <https://sc.judiciary.gov.ph/to-all-judges-and-personnel-of-first-and-second-level-courts-re-use-of-official-philippine-judiciary-office-365-accounts-for-dissemination-of-administrative-orders-circulars-and-other-court-issuanc/>

Office of the Court Administrator of the Philippines (2020), OCA Circular No. 209-2020' (A.M. No. 20-12-01-SC) <https://oca.judiciary.gov.ph/wp-content/uploads/2021/01/OCA-Circular-No.-209-2020.pdf>

Orbeta, Jr, A. C., Paqueo, B. and Siddiqi, B. (2021), 'Impacts of Electronic Case Management Systems on Court Congestion in the Philippines', 3ie Impact Evaluation Report 133 <https://doi.org/10.23846/PWPIE133>

Philippine Development Plan 2023–2028 <https://pdp.neda.gov.ph/wp-content/uploads/2023/01/PDP-2023-2028.pdf> (accessed 16 February 2024), 310.

Philippine Judicial Academy *(PHILJA)* <https://philja.lms.ph/>

Philippine Statistics Authority (2022), '2021 Overseas Filipino Workers' <https://psa.gov.ph/content/2021-overseas-filipino-workers-final-results>

Pulta, B., (2023), 'SC taps GCash, GrabPay for online court payment', *Philippines News Agency* <https://www.pna.gov.ph/articles/1192491>

Social Weather Station (2021) 'Final Survey Report: Justice Needs Survey', conducted for the EU-GOJUST Programme, <https://www.gojust.org/_files/ugd/c1dcc8_15897e67df914cb6833128dbdd548734.pdf>

Supreme Court of the Philippines, 'What is JePS?' (*Judiciary E-Payment Solution Center*) <https://help-epayment.judiciary.gov.ph/result.html?search=What%20is%20JePS?>

Supreme Court of the Philippines (2014), 'Approval of Updated Electronic Information Security Plan (EISP) A.M. No. 14-09-06-SC' (*Competitive.org.ph*) <https://www.competitive.org.ph/doingbusiness/reference/downloads/Summit/forupload/RDEC/EC_REFERENCE2b_Approval_of_Updated_EISP_A.M._no._14-09--06-sc.pdf>

Supreme Court of the Philippines (2019), 'Notice of Resolution Regarding Video-conferencing' (A.M. 19-05-05-SC, August 2019) <https://oca.judiciary.gov.ph/wp–content/uploads/2019/08/AM–Videoconferencing–Pilot.pdf>

Supreme Court of Philippines (2020), *Judiciary Annual Report 2019* <https://sc.judiciary.gov.ph/3d-flip-book/2019-judiciary-annual-report/>

Supreme Court of the Philippines (2020), '2019 Amendments to the Rules of Civil Procedure (A.M. No. 19-10-20-SC)' <https://sc.judiciary.gov.ph/wp-content/uploads/2022/08/2019-rules-of-civil-procedure.pdf>

Supreme Court of the Philippines (2020), 'Administrative Circular No. 37-2020' <https://www.pwja.org/sites/www.pwja.org/files/2020-04/AC-37-2020.pdf>

Supreme Court of the Philippines (2020), A.M. No. 20-12-01-SC.

Supreme Court of the Philippines (2021), 'The 2019 Amendments to the 1989 Revised Rules on Evidence' <https://www.youtube.com/watch?v=xzd92JX_3UE>

Supreme Court of the Philippines (2021), Rules of Civil Procedure, <https://www.youtube.com/watch?v=W9cC8nRqpNM>

Supreme Court of the Philippines (2021), '2019 Amendments to the 1997 Rules of Civil Procedure and to the Revised Rules on Evidence' <https://www.youtube.com/watch?v=FowUE9J05yA>

Supreme Court of Philippines (2022), *Judiciary Annual Report 2021* <https://sc.judiciary.gov.ph/3d-flip-book/2021-judiciary-annual-report/>

Supreme Court of Philippines (2022), 'Supreme Court Launches the Strategic Plan for Judicial Innovations: 2022–2027' <https://sc.judiciary.gov.ph/supreme-court-launches-the-strategic-plan-for-judicial-innovations-2022-2027/#:~:text=The%20SPJI%20is%20the%20High,and%20(4)%20technology%20adaptive>

Supreme Court of the Philippines (2022), 'Strategic Plans for Judicial Interventions 2022–2027' <https://sc.judiciary.gov.ph/3d-flip-book/spji/>

Supreme Court of the Philippines (2022), 'Judiciary ePayment System (JePS)' <https://www.youtube.com/watch?v=eBHjJ6nPIyg>

Supreme Court of the Philippines Bids and Awards Committee (BAC SC) (2022), 'Contract No. 2022-02, Contract for the Consulting Services for the Development of the Judiciary ICT Governance Framework, Five-Year Strategic Plan, and Judiciary MIS Operations Manual' <https://sc.judiciary.gov.ph/wp-content/uploads/2023/04/BAC-CS-04-04-2023-2.pdf>

Supreme Court Public Information Office (2022), 'JSCC Holds Justice Zone Dialogue in Davao City' <https://sc.judiciary.gov.ph/jscc-holds-justice-zone-dialogue-in-davao/>

Supreme Court – Court Management Office (2010–2021), 'National Caseflow of First and Second Level Courts' (Unpublished).

United Nations Development Programme (UNDP), 'Justice for All' (Practice Note, UNDP March 2004) <https://www.undp.org/sites/g/files/zskgke326/files/publications/Justice_PN_En.pdf> (accessed 2 December 2022).

World Justice Project (2018), 'Global Insights on Access to Justice: Philippines' <https://worldjusticeproject.org/access-to-justice-data/#/country/PHL>

World Justice Project (2022), 'Rule of Law Index: Global 2022' <https://worldjusticeproject.org/rule-of-law-index/global/2022>

Chapter 6

Empowering Judiciaries to Protect People's Rights in the Design of Court Technologies in ASEAN

Diana Torres, Tomas Kvedaras and Sarah McCoubrey

Technology is transforming justice services. People relying on courts expect greater transparency, faster data processing and access to court documents and decisions. Technology is also changing the administration of justice, streamlining case management, facilitating electronic evidence and virtual hearings and other data-driven possibilities.

The transformation from a paper-based, analogue system to a digital, integrated system has been somewhat slower than the disruptions evident in other sectors. However, the pace of technological change in justice accelerated considerably because of the widespread lockdowns during the COVID-19 pandemic. In some courts judges and court staff scrambled to run virtual trials, using software previously designed for meetings or academic institutions. Other courts invested in purpose-built video platforms. As temporary solutions to keep courts functioning transition into permanent changes in justice services, courts and legal professionals are addressing long-standing knowledge and capacity deficits when it comes to technology. The historic reluctance or refusal of justice systems to adopt automated or digital services has given way to a new recognition of the vulnerability of analogue, paper-based, justice systems. There is a new appetite for digitalisation and e-justice. New technologies are now being seen as tools not just for efficient operations but also as strategies for resilient and secure administration of justice.

Human rights scrutiny and Rule of Law protections remain critical as courts navigate these changes, both planned and crisis-based. Judges are the independent, neutral guardians of fundamental rights. Their leadership is necessary to maintain fair trials and cultivate public confidence in digital court processes. Situations of crisis and fragility, whether caused by climate crises, war and violence, or political instability, make judicial involvement in new technologies essential for stable, healthy democracies. The Bangalore Principles of Judicial Conduct (Figure 6.1), which emphasise integrity, independence, impartiality and competence, must continue to guide the judiciary as it adapts to these technological changes. Ensuring these principles are

> The Bangalore Principles of Judicial Conduct, adopted in 2002, are a set of six core values that serve as an international standard for ethical behaviour in the judiciary. These principles – independence, impartiality, integrity, propriety, equality, and competence and diligence – provide a framework for judges to uphold and promote the independence of the judiciary, ensure fair treatment of all parties, and maintain the dignity of the court.

Figure 6.1 Bangalore Principles of Judicial Conduct

upheld in the digital era is essential to preserving public trust and upholding the rule of law.

In the Asia Pacific region, there is wide variation in the adoption of court technologies. Some courts have adopted robust plans for digital transformation responsive to data security needs while others made ad hoc adaptations to the pandemic-era lockdowns. Judges, court staff and lawyers have participated in training, hired external IT support, and looked into best practices in court technology to accelerate the digital transformation in justice.

Not only does technology make it easier to maintain court files or store evidence, but it also results in improved outcomes for the public. Digital case management reduces human errors, speeds up court processes and allows people to monitor the progress of their cases, resulting in faster processes that are easier to understand. Technology can be used to track the pace of cases, streamline scheduling, assign human resources and reduce the opportunities for corruption. Adaptive technologies make it easier for people with disabilities to participate in court processes. Virtual appearances can protect vulnerable victims, child witnesses, and allow people in rural and remote areas to attend court. Technologies like these allow for increased access to justice, cultivate public confidence and allow for media and public scrutiny of justice institutions. Any discussion that treats technology simply as an efficiency tool, while confining judicial leadership to the courtroom, misses a critical opportunity to integrate justice outcomes with administrative priorities.

To ensure a meaningful judicial voice in the technological evolution of courts, individual judges and judiciaries need to be empowered to participate fully. Judges are not simply users of court technologies but are also experts in the range of rights issues that arise in the courtroom, the impact of the digital divide on litigants, and the rigorous, rights-based scrutiny required of emerging court technologies. Yet, too often, digital technology projects are planned by IT departments, technology providers and court administrators without the expertise of judges in the design of digital transformation. Sidelining judicial perspectives runs the risk of wholescale denial of rights, increasing the vulnerability of minority communities and exposing people to data and privacy risks. Integrating judicial leadership in the implementation of new technologies can embed critical rights protections in the evolution of digital justice services.

A. CHANGING JUSTICE NEEDS

The COVID-19 pandemic revealed the vulnerability of justice systems across the globe as courthouses closed, files were inaccessible, prisons and police restricted access, and judges and lawyers had to use personal devices to connect. It also revealed the extent of inequality and injustice.[1] Beyond the initial health crisis, economic instability and disruptions in global trade have resulted in recession, protracted conflicts, and a rise in authoritarianism. Climate emergencies have put pressure on local communities and national and regional decision-makers.[2] Justice and injustice are threads that weave through each of these crises. In times of instability and transition, people rely on stable democratic structures to protect rights, guarantee stability and uphold the rule of law. A strong functioning justice system is more important than ever – and gaps in the administration of justice have more dramatic impacts than ever.

Courts are being asked to address individual rights and to protect citizens and consumers against the increasing, globalised power of corporations. They are navigating competing and overlapping pluralistic rights protection mechanisms. The global economy and the accumulation of wealth by a small proportion of society are increasing disparities. When combating these challenges, technology can be an effective tool for defending human rights, enabling access to justice, and increasing the transparency and accountability of institutions.

However, not everyone has had equal access to justice. In 2019 it was estimated that 5.1 billion people globally have unmet legal needs.[3] The promise to Leave No One Behind[4] creates an overarching obligation to continually raise questions about how to close this justice gap.

Women and minority communities have less access to justice and feel the impacts of economic and political inequalities more dramatically. When excluded from decision-making, systems miss the opportunity to build on women's perspectives or address their needs. This is even more evident in conflict situations, where women and girls are disproportionately impacted. Gender injustices must not be treated as less urgent or less significant than wider human rights issues.[5] There are corresponding opportunities to promote women's leadership and access to justice when emerging from periods of conflict and crisis.

In 2020, when Dr Ngozi Okonjo-Iweala assumed the role of director general of the World Trade Organization (WTO) she noted that 'women face a glass cliff: they are given leadership roles only when things are going really badly'.[6] Justice sector reform has the opportunity to proactively engage with women leaders before reaching that metaphorical cliff and invite women's leadership for meaningful, sustainable solutions.

Failing to meaningfully address gender inequality as we transform fundamental democratic systems misses the opportunity to address these inequalities. Ignoring gender equality and treating justice sector reform as a neutral, administrative task will further entrench gender biases that heighten grievances, destabilise societies, and contribute to conflict and violence.

When introducing justice reforms and new technologies, there is a risk of perpetuating and reinforcing the power imbalances and inequalities that have both caused discrimination and led to conflict.[7] If digital processes require expensive devices, data or infrastructure, these system improvements will only be available to those with financial resources. Without attention to linguistic and literacy barriers, technology will further exclude people. Artificial intelligence can entrench discrimination if not designed to eliminate, rather than replicate bias and assumptions evident in past decisions.[8] Justice reform must be based on an examination of the power imbalances entrenched in the system. As we enter a period of accelerated change, there is an opportunity to examine and address the range of power relationships reflected in justice situations.

B. E-JUSTICE AS A TRANSFORMATIVE STRATEGY

Often dismissed as simply an infrastructure concern, e-justice has the potential to advance sustainable, rights-respecting development. To meet these goals, it must be planned and implemented with a nuanced understanding of the positive and negative implications of these new digital tools.

Table 6.1 illustrates the multifaceted nature of technological integration in the legal process. At each stage, from avoiding legal issues to appeals, there is a range of technologies being employed to address specific needs, such as ease of use, affordability (user needs) and transparency, discretion, cost efficiency (judicial needs) as well as security for both users.

New court technologies can replicate or entrench sexism, racism and systemic discrimination or they can provide solutions to these systemic issues. They can increase access to justice for those in remote areas or using adaptive technologies, or they can exclude those without reliable internet and access to devices. Digital tools designed to simply replicate existing court processes will embed the biases and inequalities of the old system, rather than uprooting them.

E-justice projects often promise greater efficiency and cost savings, yet primarily benefit the justice system itself and those who can afford lawyers to navigate complex systems. Bringing judicial understandings of inequality into the design of digital solutions offers a chance to introduce reforms that harness technology not just to make the system more efficient, but to make

Table 6.1 Technologies in the legal process and associated needs

Stage in a Legal Process	Technologies in Use	Public User Needs	Judicial Needs
Avoid legal issues	Automated contract reviewers Blockchain	Easy access Affordable	
Learning about legal issues	Legal education Apps WhatsApp and other communication platforms	Multi-lingual Free	
Reporting legal issues	Apps to record experiences Police reporting tools Portals	Private Secure Trauma-informed Admissible in court	Secure Admissible in court Compatible with evidentiary standards
Starting a legal case	e-filing Forms wizards Guided pathways	Easy to use Secure	Secure Different levels of access
Progression of the case	Online Dispute Resolutions Case management platforms AI predictions of case progress	Quick Secure Transparent	Secure Transparent Allow for judicial discretion
Disclosure, discovery, evidence submission	Police reporting apps Case management platforms e-filing	Secure Admissible in court Simple	Secure Admissible in court Different levels of access

Hearings	Video platforms Language interpretation Accessibility tools	Secure Free	Secure Free
Decision writing	AI recommendations on decisions Auto-generated decisions	Transparent algorithms	Allow for judicial discretion Transparent algorithms
Delivery of decisions	Video platforms Automated media distribution WhatsApp and other direct-to-public platforms	Secure Free	Secure Free
Enforcement	Blockchain and e-garnishment tools	Secure Effective	Secure Different levels of access
Appeals	Case Management platforms	Quick Secure Transparent	Secure Transparent Allow for judicial discretion

it fundamentally more equitable. The role of judges in this process of transformation is critical.

Informed by the voices of judges in the region and based on its strategic commitment to digital transformation to advance development goals, UNDP is advancing a vision for judicial leadership in digital transformation in the Asia Pacific.

C. JIN ASEAN

The Judicial Integrity Network ASEAN, a UNDP initiative, has been working to amplify judicial leadership in the digital transformation of courts. It connects judges and judiciaries across the ASEAN region to share resources and amplify the discussion about judicial excellence. JIN ASEAN's model of peer-to-peer support and capacity building is designed to support judges, as an independent voice, able to balance the drive for efficiency with careful attention to human rights and the rule of law. JIN ASEAN produced two publications designed to build a regional understanding of the impacts of emerging technologies and to support judges participating in e-justice initiatives.

In 2020–21, JIN ASEAN researched international best practices and emerging trends in court technologies. It then surveyed ASEAN region judges about their own experiences with technology. Gender equality and issues of digital privacy were key concerns, while the use of data collection, algorithmic monitoring and electronic case management all raised questions and opportunities to protect human rights and amplify the needs of vulnerable communities. Technology was cited as making courts more accessible, and faster, with particular benefits for women and people with disabilities.[9]

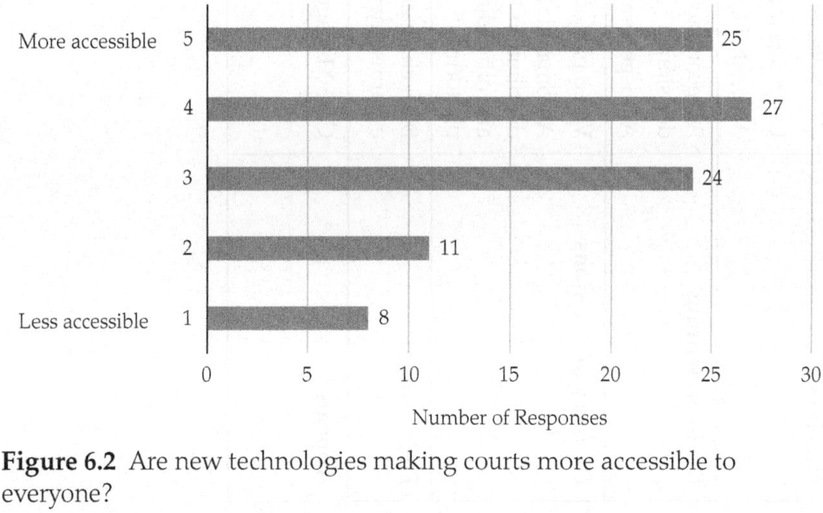

Figure 6.2 Are new technologies making courts more accessible to everyone?

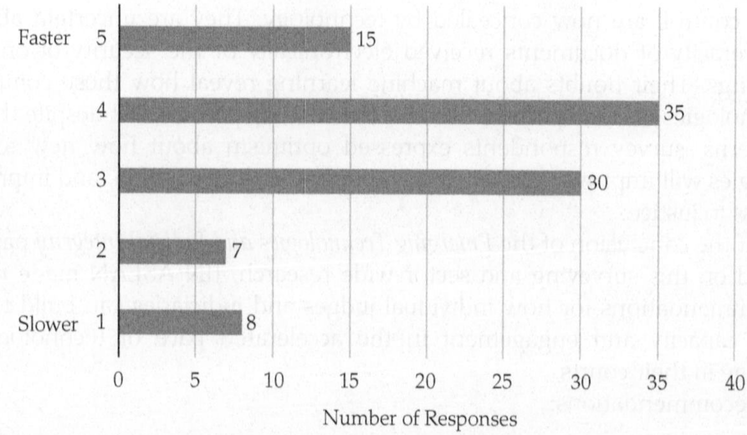

Figure 6.3 How are technologies affecting the speed of trials?

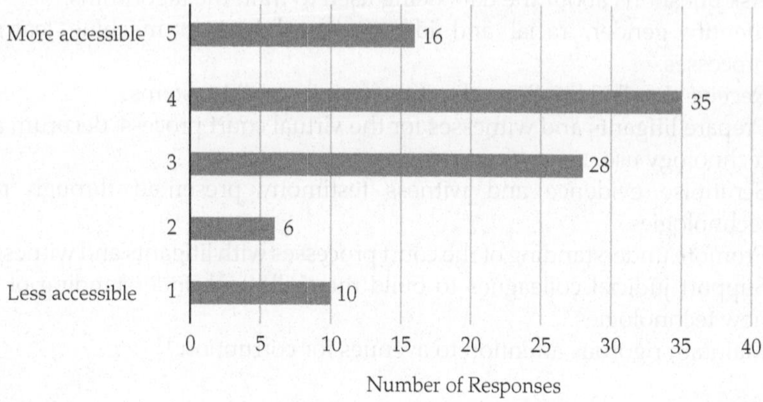

Figure 6.4 How are technologies affecting the ability to participate from home or from their communities?

The survey of ASEAN region judges revealed the urgency of judicial participation in decisions about the technologies in use in their courts. Technologies were already in use, or at stages of development in each country. Without active judicial input, these technologies may perpetuate inequality, erode public confidence in the judiciary, and obscure critical information that judges require to make independent, transparent decisions.

The research also revealed that emerging technologies are often developed by an external technology company, or a ministry department focused on court efficiency, but not led by judges. Judges are not always engaged in the design, selection or implementation of new technologies. Judges in the region expressed concerns that aspects of the trial process, previously within their control, are now concealed by technology. They are uncertain about the veracity of documents received electronically or the security of online hearings. Their doubts about machine learning reveal how these complex technologies obscure parts of the decision-making process. Yet despite these concerns, survey respondents expressed optimism about how new technologies will improve transparency, protect against corruption, and improve access to justice.

At the conclusion of the *Emerging Technologies and Judicial Integrity* paper, based on this surveying and sector-wide research, JIN ASEAN made nine recommendations for how individual judges and judiciaries can build their own capacity and engagement in the accelerated pace of technological change in their courts.

Recommendations:

1. Raise the rule of law and trial fairness criteria when new technology is proposed.
2. Ask questions about the data being used to train the algorithms.
3. Identify gender, racial and identity-based bias in machine learning processes.
4. Receive detailed briefings about the training of AI systems.
5. Prepare litigants and witnesses for the virtual court process, decorum and technology use.
6. Scrutinise evidence and witness testimony presented through new technologies.
7. Promote understanding of the court processes with litigants and witnesses.
8. Support judicial colleagues to build the skills and understanding of the new technologies.
9. Maintain rigorous attention to avenues for corruption.[10]

A complementary Toolkit[11] was designed to build the capacity of judges and judiciaries to engage in the design of e-justice to address their specific regional needs. It includes a range of tools that can be used by individual judges to better understand the technologies in their courts, or by the judiciary as a whole when designing digital technologies. The toolkit includes:

- Understanding Emerging Technologies
- Understanding Artificial Intelligence/Machine Learning
- Understanding Online Dispute Resolution
- Understanding Blockchain
- Understanding Virtual or Remote Courts
- Understanding Electronic Case Management
- Understanding E-Filing and Online Forms
- Understanding Guided Pathways and Public Education Apps
- Judicial Role in Design and Procurement Criteria

- Judicial Excellence Procurement Checklist
- Evaluating New Technologies
- A2J and the Rule of Law Implications of Courtroom Technologies: Judicial Excellence Checklist.

The two JIN ASEAN publications have been the basis for virtual training and strategic foresight activities.

JIN ASEAN also supports efforts by judiciaries to conduct self-assessments and adopt action plans to address judicial excellence and strengthen the independence of the judiciary. The Judicial Integrity Checklist, developed by JIN ASEAN, has been integrated into the International Framework for Court Excellence.[12] It outlines key areas of transparency and judicial independence and assesses the level of training and institutional protections within the judiciary. Based on the results, judiciaries develop action plans to address self-identified deficiencies and to protect areas of strength.

Currently, four ASEAN countries are using the Emerging Technologies publications as a component of developing Action Plans for assessing and protecting judicial excellence in the ongoing evolution of national courts. Courts in Vietnam, Thailand, Laos PDR and Indonesia are each engaging with new technologies in different ways, examining gender equality and trial fairness in the process of technological change.[13]

Starting in 2022, Lao PDR started workshops for its judges on the Self-Assessment process and worked with UNDP to develop an action plan focused on public user engagement. Indonesia is strengthening its anti-corruption efforts and protecting whistleblowers through a new online anti-corruption platform that also monitors gender equality and the services provided to people with disabilities. Vietnam's Supreme People's Court has introduced the Self-Assessment process through a two-day workshop and is implementing the process in the court. Thailand developed a Judicial Service Design workshop and is preparing the court in one region to develop an Action Plan.

UNDP supports these projects through the JIN ASEAN initiative to cultivate independent, robust judiciaries.

D. ADVOCATING FOR AN EQUITABLE FUTURE

UNDP's work to empower judiciaries to actively participate in digitalisation is premised on the view that the judiciary can work to ensure that digital transformation does not exacerbate the digital divide or further exclude those already marginalised. Instead, judges can use their position as protectors of individual rights to actively promote digital transformation that protects the most vulnerable and focuses innovation on the needs of those most excluded.

To do this, gender equality must continue to underpin these reforms. Women's legal rights to property, safety and autonomy must be protected by legal institutions if women and children are going to benefit from the digitalisation of justice systems. Access to justice must not only be maintained in digital platforms but must be expanded to rectify gaps created by geography, economic status and discrimination.

At each stage of digital transformation, privacy rights and individual data protection are a high priority for judges leading this change. Most people who do not understand how technology operates will rely on decision-makers to protect their interests. Judges are uniquely situated to combine their understanding of people's needs and the impacts of rights violations on the most vulnerable with their justice system expertise. Judges, as a community of professionals with shared obligations, can support each other to build capacity and continue to collectively raise concerns about the impact of technologies, while still advocating for digital transformation. This model of independent, principled leadership will set high expectations for other legal professionals to embrace technology as a tool for advancing rights and protecting the rule of law.

NOTES

1. World Justice Project, 'The COVID-19 Pandemic and the Global Justice Gap' (October 2020) <https://worldjusticeproject.org/our-work/publications/policy-briefs/covid-19-pandemic-and-global-justice-gap> (accessed 13 February 2024).
2. Aditi Mukherji, Abdul Wajid Rana and Devesh Roy, 'The Pakistan floods, COP27, and prospects for recovery and climate justice' (International Food Policy Research Institute, 4 November 2022) <www.ifpri.org/blog/pakistan-floods-cop27-and-prospects-recovery-and-climate-justice> (accessed 13 February 2024).
3. Task Force on Justice Innovating Working Group, 'Innovating Justice: Needed and Possible' (2019) <www.hiil.org/wp-content/uploads/2019/02/Task-Force-on-Justice-Innovating-Working-Group-Report.pdf> (accessed 13 February 2024).
4. UNDP, 'What Does it Mean to Leave No One Behind?' (2022) <www.undp.org/sites/g/files/zskgke326/files/publications/Brochure_LNOB_web.pdf> (accessed 13 February 2024).
5. UNDP, 'Beyond the Pandemic: The Justice Emergency Paper' (2022) <www.undp.org/publications/beyond-pandemic-justice-emergency> (accessed 13 February 2024).
6. Larry Elliott, '"It can't be business as usual": the Nigerian frontrunner to be next WTO head', *The Guardian* (London, 10 September 2020) <www.theguardian.com/world/2020/sep/10/nigerian-frontrunner-to-be-next-wto-head-ngozi-okonjo-iweala-trade-covid-19?CMP=Share_AndroidApp_Other> (accessed 13 February 2024).
7. Tom Yun, 'Zoom hearing abruptly ends when court realizes suspect is in same home as victim of alleged assault', *CTV News* (9 March 2021) <www.ctvnews.ca/world/zoom-hearing-abruptly-ends-when-court-realizes-suspect-is-in-same-home-as-victim-of-alleged-assault-1.5340677> (accessed 13 February 2024).
8. 'Algorithmic Accountability for the Public Sector: Learning from the First Wave of Policy Implementation' (Open Government Partnership, 2021) <www.

opengovpartnership.org/stories/algorithmic-accountability-for-the-public-sector-learning-from-the-first-wave-of-policy-implementation/> (accessed 13 February 2024).

9. JIN ASEAN, 'Emerging Technologies and Judicial Integrity in ASEAN' (UNDP, 2023) <www.undp.org/asia-pacific/judicial-integrity/publications/emerging-technologies-and-judicial-integrity-asean> (accessed 13 February 2024).
10. JIN ASEAN, 'Emerging Technologies and Judicial Integrity in ASEAN' (UNDP, 2023) <www.undp.org/asia-pacific/judicial-integrity/publications/emerging-technologies-and-judicial-integrity-asean> (accessed 13 February 2024).
11. JIN ASEAN, 'Emerging Technologies and Judicial Integrity Toolkit for Judges' (UNDP, 2023) <www.undp.org/asia-pacific/judicial-integrity/publications/emerging-technologies-and-judicial-integrity-toolkit-judges> (accessed 13 February 2024).
12. International Consortium for Court Excellence, 'Court Excellence Self-Assessment Questionnaire' <www.courtexcellence.com/resources/self-assessment> (accessed 13 February 2024).
13. Judicial Integrity Network ASEAN, 'Country-Specific Projects Building Judicial Excellence Through Self-Assessment and Action Planning' (UNDP) <www.undp.org/judicial-integrity-network-asean-country-specific-projects-building-judicial-excellence-through-self-assessment-and-action-planning> (accessed 13 February 2024).

REFERENCES

'Algorithmic Accountability for the Public Sector: Learning from the First Wave of Policy Implementation' (Open Government Partnership, 2021) <www.opengovpartnership.org/stories/algorithmic-accountability-for-the-public-sector-learning-from-the-first-wave-of-policy-implementation/> (accessed 13 February 2024).

'Beyond the Pandemic: The Justice Emergency Paper' (UNDP, 2022) <www.undp.org/publications/beyond-pandemic-justice-emergency> (accessed 13 February 2024).

'Court Excellence Self-Assessment Questionnaire' (International Consortium for Court Excellence) <www.courtexcellence.com/resources/self-assessment> (accessed 13 February 2024).

'Emerging Technologies and Judicial Integrity in ASEAN' (UNDP, 2023) <www.undp.org/asia-pacific/judicial-integrity/publications/emerging-technologies-and-judicial-integrity-asean> (accessed 13 February 2024).

'What Does it Mean to Leave No One Behind?' (UNDP, 2022) <www.undp.org/sites/g/files/zskgke326/files/publications/Brochure_LNOB_web.pdf> (accessed 13 February 2024).

Elliott L, '"It can't be business as usual": the Nigerian frontrunner to be next WTO head', *The Guardian* (London, 10 September 2020) <www.theguardian.com/world/2020/sep/10/nigerian-frontrunner-to-be-next-wto-head-ngozi-okonjo-iweala-trade-covid-19?CMP=Share_AndroidApp_Other> (accessed 13 February 2024).

JIN ASEAN, 'Country-Specific Projects Building Judicial Excellence Through Self-Assessment and Action Planning' (UNDP) <www.undp.org/judicial-integrity-network-asean-country-specific-projects-building-judicial-excellence-through-self-assessment-and-action-planning> (accessed 13 February 2024).

Mukherji, A., Rana, A. W. and Roy, D., 'The Pakistan floods, COP27, and prospects for recovery and climate justice' (International Food Policy Research Institute, 4 November 2022) <www.ifpri.org/blog/pakistan-floods-cop27-and-prospects-recovery-and-climate-justice> (accessed 13 February 2024).

Task Force on Justice Innovating Working Group, 'Innovating Justice: Needed and Possible' (2019) <www.hiil.org/wp-content/uploads/2019/02/Task-Force-on-Justice-Innovating-Working-Group-Report.pdf> (accessed 13 February 2024).

World Justice Project, 'The COVID-19 Pandemic and the Global Justice Gap' (October 2020) https://worldjusticeproject.org/our-work/publications/policy-briefs/covid-19-pandemic-and-global-justice-gap (accessed 13 February 2024).

Yun, T., 'Zoom hearing abruptly ends when court realizes suspect is in same home as victim of alleged assault', *CTV News* (9 March 2021) <www.ctvnews.ca/world/zoom-hearing-abruptly-ends-when-court-realizes-suspect-is-in-same-home-as-victim-of-alleged-assault-1.5340677> (accessed 13 February 2024).

Part II

Adjudicating Technology

Chapter 7

The Division of Adjudicative Tasks in the Age of AI Adjudication in Thailand

Kraiphol Aranyarat

A. THE RISE OF THE MACHINE AND THE CHALLENGE OF SUPERSESSION

Artificial Intelligence (AI)[1] is becoming increasingly integrated into our daily lives, powering a wide range of real-world applications, from facial recognition and language translation tools to virtual assistants such as Siri, Alexa and Chat GPT. In 2020, the global AI market was valued at USD 62.35 billion, and it is expected to grow at a rate of 40.2 per cent annually from 2021 to 2028.[2] This rapid pace of growth and the widespread adoption of AI is having a profound impact on the labour market. Experts predict that AI will replace many professional jobs in the next decade, with some going as far as to say that half of all jobs will be automated by AI within the next fifteen years. This raises the question of how the legal profession will withstand this challenge of supersession.

In the past, people in the legal profession believed that they were immune to the threat of automation through AI. However, the reality is that AI is becoming increasingly prevalent in the legal industry, with the ability to improve efficiency, accuracy, consistency and productivity. This includes the use of AI for contract review and analysis, contract drafting, legal research, and legal chatbots. The same trend can be seen in the law enforcement sector, where AI-based tools are being utilised to support decision-making, implementation, and interaction in various tasks. Today's software already plays a role in detecting and punishing speeding drivers, monitoring prohibited speech on social media platforms, forecasting criminal activities to allocate police resources, and predicting the risk of recidivism in bail determination and the sentencing process.

Apparently, the challenge of supersession is also threatening the state agencies, and the courts, as a crucial state organ responsible for administering justice to the public in an efficient manner, will not be exempt from this pervasive, profound and permanent transformation.[3] Therefore, it is necessary to accept the fact that AI is now knocking at the courtroom's door and judges need to be ready to adapt to changes AI would bring to their role and task.

Next, this chapter will explore how AI could contribute to the current judicial decision-making process at a global level, and discuss how the concept of 'put the right man on the right job' is important to the task allocation in the hybrid human-AI decision-making process. Finally, this discussion will examine whether Thailand is on the right track in adopting AI in the judiciary.

B. HOW COULD AI CONTRIBUTE TO THE CURRENT JUDICIAL DECISION-MAKING PROCESS IN THAILAND AND IN OTHER COUNTRIES?

Contrary to popular belief, the implementation of AI by the judiciary around the world has significantly increased over the last couple of years. In fact, there are some examples of using AI as supporting tools, meaning that AI is used to provide decision support for human judges, or even as a decision-making tool in different jurisdictions around the world. A brief survey of judicial use cases will separate them into two categories: (I) Artificial intelligence in the courts: global use cases; and (II) The adoption of the risk assessment program in Thailand.

I. Artificial intelligence in the courts: global use cases

There are several arguments about a promising future of AI in the courtroom, but our findings show that the current AI use cases in the courts are mostly limited to supporting roles. The following paragraphs will confirm this.

In the United States, the best example and the most widely used AI tool in the judicial sector is the risk assessment tool called 'COMPAS', which is able to assess the likelihood of the defendant becoming a recidivist. This program could help judges make pre-trial bail and sentencing determinations.[4] In Latin America, the judicial decision-support system called *'Expertius'* was introduced to advise judges and law clerks in Mexico upon the determination of whether someone is or is not entitled to claim for a financial pension, and upon the amount of such pension.[5] Also in Argentina, the *'Prometea'* system can analyse the text of the appeal and the prior decisions, predict the most appropriate response to the request, develop the first draft of the judicial determination, and ask the judges some questions to modify the draft.[6] Moreover, in Brazil, the Supreme Court launched the *'Victor'* program that assists in the classification and identification of claims and appeals.[7]

Turning to another example in different parts of the world, in China, some local courts have adopted AI technology in their judicial decision-making process. For example, Beijing High People's Court has developed the 'Wise Judge' *(Rui Fa Guan)* system, which draws on nationwide judgment data to generate first-draft judgments and ensure consistency in treating similar cases.[8] In Shanghai, the High People's Court also uses an AI system called the 'Intelligent Auxiliary System of Criminal Case Handling' that collects mass judicial data to guide judges in ensuring their decisions align with those made elsewhere in the country.[9] Obviously, Chinese courts moved significantly fast to implement AI in judicial adjudication.

The last example that deserves special mention is Estonia. Notably, Estonia's integration of a machine learning system into its small claims court processes has set a new benchmark for other countries. The Ministry of Justice launched a program for a robot judge to handle straightforward small claim disputes of less than EUR 7,000 to clear a backlog of cases.[10] Technically, the software will analyse all relevant documents and render a decision based on pre-programmed algorithms and previous training. The software's decision is legally binding but could be appealed to a human judge.[11] The government is considering granting legal status to robot judges, which would be the first project to entrust decision-making authority solely to algorithms.[12]

II The adoption of risk assessment program in Thailand

In Thailand, the court has been using the 'Risk Assessment' program to help judges predict the likelihood of the defendants breaching a bail condition during a pre-trial release since 2018. Based on a variety of information drawn from a set of questions that the defendant fills out, this program will classify defendants into several groups and rate a particular defendant, ranging from low risk to high risk, using a rule-based technique. The use of the Risk Assessment program in Thailand is considered the first small step in a long journey and the judges in Thai courts are now becoming accustomed to utilising the Risk Assessment program as a supplementary tool when making a decision on a pre-trial release.

According to the 2022–2025 Digital Strategy for the Court of Justice of Thailand, the Thai court needs to advance the development of AI so that it can effectively analyse large amounts of data within its system, thereby supporting the judicial adjudication and case management process. This digital strategy has prompted the Thai court to plan for a wider adoption of Risk Assessment programs in various contexts, including the evaluation of recidivism risk and the optimisation of the criminal sentencing process, and even developing AI-driven systems in the years ahead to assist with the handling of simple, straightforward civil cases.

While the AI use cases explored in this part are mostly supportive tools, Estonia's robot judge project has the potential to revolutionise the field. With this exponential pace of AI development, it will become even more sophisticated and effective than a human judge when making judicial decisions. Therefore, it is reasonable to predict that the extent to which AI will act as a decision-making authority will become gradually larger within the next decade. Nevertheless, it is important to have a plan in place for implementing

AI in the judicial decision-making process to ensure that potential risks such as job displacement, and rigidity in the interface of law and code[13] are carefully considered and addressed. In addition, it is essential to have human oversight and involvement in the decision-making process to prevent potential pitfalls and preserve the integrity of the judicial process. Therefore, before we rely on AI for more advanced tasks in judicial proceedings, we must thoughtfully consider the degree of its involvement to develop a comprehensive model for human judges and AI collaboration in the court. This issue will be discussed in the following part.

C. 'LET'S PUT THE RIGHT MAN ON THE RIGHT JOB'

As the capabilities of AI are continuously expanding and its use in the courts is significantly becoming more widespread, it is important to look ahead and be proactive in developing the model for the hybrid adjudication system by examining the allocation of tasks between the human judges and AI. Here, the concept of 'putting the right man on the right job' applies just as much in the courtroom as it does in any other field. In order for the AI integration to be successful, it is crucial to understand the strengths and limitations of both humans and AI, as well as the distinct features of each judicial task. This part will discuss: (I) the strengths and limitations of humans and AI; (II) the division of adjudicative tasks; and (III) a proposed model of task allocation in hybrid human-AI adjudication.

I. The strengths and limitations of human and AI

This chapter posits that the most effective hybrid human-AI adjudication model is achieved when each of them plays to their strengths. This is the key to avoiding the worst of both worlds.

Typically, concerns about human judges can relate to their ineffectiveness, inconsistency and inaccuracy. However, in terms of tasks performed in the courtroom, AI has yet to surpass human judges in a number of aspects.

First, human judges have the ability to understand contexts and create new knowledge, while AI can only utilise existing data.[14] This makes human judges better suited for perceiving the moral foundations of their community, and increases their connection to social legitimacy and procedural fairness. From this view, the legitimacy of judicial decisions requires human judgement.[15]

Second, human judges are better equipped to handle complex legal disputes, known as 'hard cases', which present complicated facts and require extensive use of judicial discretion to evaluate the evidence and witnesses presented by the parties. This view is supported by *Tim Wu,* who argues that humans are more reliable in these situations because (i) AI lacks context and nuance understanding; (ii) AI lacks the ability to balance conflicting values and avoid the absurd consequence; and (iii) the stakes in some hard cases are high enough to merit human involvement.[16]

Third, human judges can provide a wide range of contributions to society as a whole. There are some responsive roles that only human judges can play within the adjudicative framework: for example, the ability of human judges to more effectively enable litigants to determine outcomes through the judge demonstrating curiosity, emotional understanding, agile questioning and exploration of issues.[17]

Last but not least, the ability to explain the outcome of judicial decisions, based on today's technology, exclusively remains with human judges. Obviously, when the judiciary exercises its coercive power, the principle of due process requires that the judiciary explains its own decision because people are entitled to at least some understanding of what is happening to them.[18] The inability of the algorithms to provide an explanation for their outcomes can undermine people's perception of fairness and trust in the judicial system. This is particularly problematic in the context of criminal justice, where the use of algorithms can potentially weaken the defendant's ability to present a defence.[19] For example, in the case of *State* v. *Loomis*,[20] the defendant in the case contended that his due process rights were violated by the court's implementation of the risk assessment software COMPAS, citing his inability to evaluate the accuracy of the program as one of the reasons for his argument.

Even though AI still lacks the capabilities to understand context and nuance, as well as the ability to explain and adjust itself to novel situations, the commentators that prefer AI would argue that AI has its own advantages that should not be overlooked, as follows.

First, AI contributes to efficient judicial adjudication.[21] Unlike human judges, AI provides 24/7 services with no rest needed. Consistent performance and accurate outcomes improve the overall efficiency of the judicial system, leading to timely proceedings and predictable judgment.

Second, AI-based tools use machine learning techniques to generalise patterns from training data and solve new problems.[22] This leads to a significant increase in consistency and standards within the judicial system, as AI consistently evaluates problems using the same set of algorithms every time.

Third, AI can improve transparency and impartiality within the judicial system, increasing public confidence in courts. Pressure from various sources can alter a judge's decision, but AI is immune to these influences, free from the possibility of manipulation or bribery. This enhances the integrity of the judicial process.[23]

Lastly, AI can bring predictability to court judgment by ensuring decisions align with the law and past cases. Lack of stability will have a chilling effect on public trust in the court system, but AI can enhance predictability and bring a more dependable decision-making process.[24]

In this context, we gain insight into the respective strengths of human judges and AI in the scope of judicial adjudication. Next, we need to classify adjudicative tasks in order to properly assign each specific task to the most appropriate decision-maker within the domain of judicial decision-making. This approach to classifying adjudicative tasks would be particularly useful in situations when the chief judge is assigning decision-making tasks to a human judge or AI as it provides a framework for understanding the nature and characteristics of different cases. By categorising adjudicative tasks based on factors such as the demand for judicial discretion or the seriousness of the case, which will be proposed in the following part, the chief judge would be better equipped to make informed decisions about which tasks are best suited for human intelligence or AI. This can help ensure that each case is assigned to the most appropriate decision-maker, ultimately leading to a more efficient and effective judicial process.

II. The division of adjudicative tasks

Even with our understanding of the strengths and limitations of human judges and AI, a perfect task allocation between them requires a comprehensive understanding of adjudicative tasks.[25] With regards to alternative ways of task classification, this chapter proposes that two determining factors – (a) the demand for judicial discretion and (b) the seriousness of the case – can aid in classifying adjudicative tasks in the hybrid human-AI adjudication system. The following paragraphs will elaborate on this issue.

(a) The demand for judicial discretion

'The demand for judicial discretion' could divide adjudicative tasks into two different groups, the discretionary decision-making tasks, and the non-discretionary decision-making tasks.

'Discretionary decision-making task' or 'strong discretion task' refers to the judicial decision that requires the exercise of judicial discretion or the making of an evaluative judgement. On a case-by-case basis, judges have to consider relevant social values, parties' subjective features, and surrounding circumstances before reaching a final decision.[26] Therefore, these strong discretion tasks cannot be rationalised by imposing guidelines or standards.

In criminal or civil cases that go through a full and formal witness trial because the parties could not agree upon the facts, the parties usually assert new and case-specific facts during the trial. This situation requires the exercise of judicial discretion to evaluate the evidence and determine the facts. Also, these strong discretion tasks might include the issuance of court orders in response to some complex legal motions.

Turning to a 'non-discretionary decision-making task' or 'weak discretion task', this kind of task refers to a decision that prioritises consistency over individual circumstances. This type of decision is often guided by pre-existing standards or guidelines, allowing for more predictability in the decision-making process. When dealing with these tasks, judges have limited discretion, following prescribed alternatives in their ruling. This approach emphasises uniformity in decision-making and minimises individualised judgement.[27]

Summary proceedings, whether criminal or civil, are a good example of weak discretionary tasks as they are perceived as low in complexity, discretion and variation. When dealing with these tasks, judges may make a decision based on written submissions and oral arguments, rather than a full witness trial because parties generally do not raise new factual disputes or arguments. Another instance is the issuance of court orders in response to repetitive routine motions such as a motion for an extension of time to file the answer or appellant's brief, a motion for execution of judgment, etc.

By relying on the demand of judicial discretion as a determining factor, we have thus far classified adjudicatory tasks into 'discretionary decision-making' and 'non-discretionary decision-making'. However, in order to gain a deeper insight into the nature and characteristics of court cases, this next section proposes a different approach based on the 'seriousness of the case'. This approach offers a more nuanced perspective that can help us better understand the diverse challenges that judges face when presiding over different types of cases.

(b) The seriousness of the case

While perceptions of a case's seriousness can be subjective and vary among individuals, this chapter asserts that the degree to which a case impacts the freedom and liberty of the parties involved can serve as an objective measure of its seriousness.

Society expects equal treatment of all cases, but real court practice shows this may not always be the case as judges tend to treat cases that exceptionally impact freedom and liberty more seriously than others. Cases with 'a high degree of seriousness' involve decisions that have the potential to significantly restrict the freedom and liberty of the parties involved. For example, criminal cases or high-profile civil cases can cause far-reaching impacts on the defendant.

On the other side of the spectrum where 'the seriousness of the case is low', judicial decisions typically do not impact freedom and liberty for individuals. Rather, it leads to other kinds of legal remedies such as damages, restitution and coercive remedies. This kind of decision-making is often found in civil cases. However, it is noteworthy that some civil cases may hold a higher degree of seriousness than others, such as divorce and family disputes, property disputes, or high-value cases.

In Thailand, the classification of court cases based on the seriousness of the case is not explicitly stated. However, such classification can be deduced by examining the standard of proof required in each case as provided by the Criminal Procedural Code and the precedent of the Supreme Court of Thailand. For instance, Section 227 of the Criminal Procedural Code provides that the court should not find the defendant guilty unless the guilt is established beyond reasonable doubt.[28] This signifies that in criminal cases that could significantly impact the freedom and liberty of individuals, the law requires the highest standard of proof from the judges. On the other hand, in civil cases, Supreme Court Decision No. 3353/2552 established that:[29]

> Unlike criminal cases that require the prosecutor to prove the case beyond a reasonable doubt, the parties in civil cases are required to prove by the standard of preponderance of evidence. If the evidence presented by one side is more convincing and has greater weight than the evidence presented by the other side, the judge will decide the case in favour of that side based on the preponderance of evidence standard.

This means that the law only requires a low standard of proof from the judges in cases where the outcome will not significantly affect the freedom and liberty of people. This serves as an illustration of the law's classification of court cases based on their seriousness. Although this classification cannot be directly observed, it is reflected in the provisions of the law and the precedent set by the Supreme Court of Thailand.

To sum up, this discussion proposes that the division of adjudicative tasks in human-AI adjudication could be classified by the demand for judicial discretion and the seriousness of the case. The following will outline a plan to match human judges and AI with adjudicative tasks that are most aligned with their strengths.

III. A three-tier categorisation of tasks in the hybrid human-AI adjudication

Based on an assessment of the strengths and weaknesses of human judges and AI, as well as the characteristics of adjudicative tasks, we conclude that adjudicative tasks such as rendering court judgment or issuing court orders are generally more suitable for AI if they involve repetitive, non-discretionary and less serious issues. However, if the issues are complicated, discretionary and high-stakes, they are typically better suited for human intelligence. Therefore, a three-tier categorisation of tasks for hybrid human-AI adjudication is proposed as follows.

(a) Tier 1: discretionary decision-making tasks

Tasks that fall under the scope of Tier 1 are alternatively referred to as 'discretionary decision-making' or 'strong discretion' tasks. These tasks often require flexible responses to a wide range of problems and need capabilities other than applying a set of rules to a routine problem. Regardless of the seriousness of the task, the demand for judicial discretion in these tasks makes it a tough nut to crack for AI-based decision-making tools, leaving it as the sole responsibility of human judges.

Examples of these tasks include rendering a court judgment in criminal and civil cases that went through full and formal proceedings because the parties could not agree upon the facts. These cases require the exercise of human discretion in order to assess the evidence and determine the case-specific facts. Moreover, it is worth noting that Tier 1 tasks also include issuing a court order relating to the complex legal motions.

(b) Tier 2: non-discretionary, high-stakes tasks

There are certain adjudicative tasks categorised as Tier 2, which can be performed by solely applying a set of rules to routine repetitive problems. These 'non-discretionary' or 'weak discretion' tasks are ideal for automation. However, despite their suitability for AI, these Tier 2 tasks cannot be fully delegated due to their high level of seriousness. Some experts argue that relying on AI tools for these critical decisions shows a lack of respect for humanity.[30] Thus, the most appropriate approach in this Tier 2 scenario is to preserve human dignity by maintaining humans 'in the loop' and allowing them to work in tandem with AI.[31]

Generally, Tier 2 tasks might include rendering a court judgment after the summary proceedings in high-profile civil cases, family disputes or property disputes where both sides of the parties agreed upon the facts or the summary proceeding in criminal cases that usually takes place after the defendant pleads guilty, as well as issuing a court order in response to the legal motion in these cases.

(c) Tier 3: non-discretionary, low-stakes tasks

In addition to the first two categories that require human interactions to some degree, the highest level of automation or so-called 'full automation', in which the AI is responsible for the whole process of judicial determination, is a key element in a human-machine hybrid adjudication that will unprecedently increase an overall efficiency level of the judicial system. Nevertheless, the types of cases that were tailor-made for the algorithmic decision-making tool are quite narrowed because of the inherent limitations of AI.

To be specific, the adjudicative tasks in Tier 3 that would be handled by the fully automated system must consist of at least two specific characteristics: first, they must be a non-discretionary case that presents a routine, low variation problem so that the AI can create effective generalisation and use such pattern to deal with repetitive cases. Second, the seriousness of these cases is supposed to be low enough in a way that the final decision of the case will not affect people's freedom and liberty, or that it will not significantly impact an individual's right or property. The adjudicative tasks in Tier 3 include rendering a court judgment in summary civil proceedings such as collecting a small amount of debt or enforcing a contract, as well as issuing a court order relating to these cases.

After all, it is noteworthy that the new task allocation in the age of AI adjudication, as this chapter proposes, is built on the combination of two main factors: the 'demand for judicial discretion' and the 'seriousness of the case'. A certain degree of each factor in a particular case will determine the area in which such a case should be allocated, as illustrated in Figure 7.1.

In this chart, the determination of which decision-making tasks should be assigned to human judges or AI is represented. The X-axis denotes the degree of seriousness of the case, whereas the Y-axis represents the level of demand for judicial discretion. The chart proposes that for cases that demand a high level of judicial discretion (Tier 1 tasks), regardless of the seriousness of the case, the decision-making task must be reserved for human judges. As previously discussed, human judges possess the capability to comprehend the social context, values and nuances that are typically essential in cases involving strong discretion or complex issues. Moreover, hard cases usually entail complicated issues that require a detailed explanation, which is an inherent limitation of AI and the exclusive skill of human judges.

In contrast, the judicial decision-making tasks with a low demand for judicial discretion and a low degree of seriousness (Tier 3 tasks) may be suitable for assignment to AI. The efficiency and consistency of AI in dealing with routine and weak discretion tasks have already been highlighted in

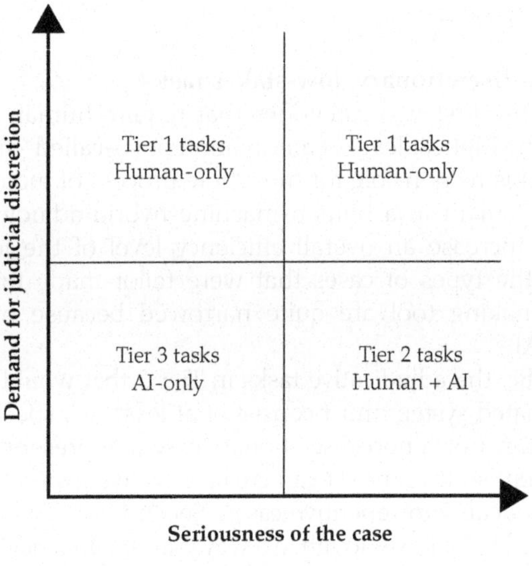

Figure 7.1 Chart illustrating the model of task allocation in hybrid human-AI adjudication

this discussion. Through the creation of generalisations and patterns from routine, easy cases, AI can ensure that these cases are evaluated in the same manner every time, with consistent performance and speed throughout the day.

Nevertheless, if a case has a high degree of seriousness but a low demand for judicial discretion, it may be assigned to AI with the oversight of human judges (Tier 2 tasks). As mentioned earlier, AI is ideal for cases with low demand for judicial discretion due to its consistency and efficiency. However, the challenge with assigning these cases to AI is that they present a high degree of case seriousness that often requires an understanding of social context and nuance, which only human judges can provide. Furthermore, for some people, the idea of fully delegating such serious cases to AI could be seen as a total disrespect to humanity and human dignity. As a result, policymakers must combine the advantages of both human judges and AI to handle such cases. This approach will ensure that the cases are handled efficiently and consistently, while also taking into account the complexity and seriousness of the issues involved.

This chapter aims to put the chart to the test by examining the Thai court's use of the Risk Assessment program and the possible future AI use case in Thai court in the following discussion.

D. IS THE THAI COURT ON THE RIGHT TRACK?

This chapter has investigated the application of AI in courts globally, with a particular emphasis on the court in Thailand. Also, the study took a moment to reflect and reconsider the plan and finally proposed a model for task allocation between the human judges and AI. Without determining if this model is right or wrong, the discussion will now examine whether the use of the Risk Assessment program in Thailand and the possible future use of AI in Thai courts align with the model's direction.

I. The use of the risk assessment program in Thailand

Considering that the Risk Assessment program is used to evaluate the likelihood of breaching bail in criminal cases, the degree of seriousness of this task is unquestionably high. However, the demand for judicial discretion in making bail decisions is varied. In 'routine petty offences', a demand for discretion is low since there are clear and certain factors that judges have to take into account, and judges usually follow the court guideline or previous decision to maintain a single standard. Due to low discretion but high seriousness, this task is clearly a Tier 2 task, which requires human judge–AI collaboration. Under this context, the use of the Risk Assessment program as a supporting tool for judges in Thailand is aligned with the proposed model.

Nevertheless, a bail decision in 'serious or complex offences' requires judges to consider a number of circumstantial factors such as age, criminal record, employment status, the seriousness of the crime, and danger to society. Thus, the extensive use of human discretion is required, which makes this task fall within a unique territory of human judges (Tier 1 task). Under this situation, the Thai court's use of the Risk Assessment program might not fully align with the proposed model.

II. The possible future AI use case in the Thai court

According to the 2022–2025 Digital Strategy for the Court of Justice of Thailand, there is a growing interest in integrating AI technologies to support judicial adjudication. While the precise nature of the future AI use cases within the Thai court remains unclear, this chapter hypothesises that low-discretion and low-seriousness cases are likely candidates for integration with AI technology. Accordingly, it is postulated that the Thai court may develop an AI-powered software solution, similar to the robot judge utilised in Estonia, for handling simple and straightforward civil cases, such as debt collection and the enforcement of basic contracts.

Given the assumption that the use of robot judges is limited to small civil disputes, such cases may be considered as having a relatively low degree of seriousness. In cases where the defendant does not respond to the claim and a summary proceeding is initiated, there is typically a low demand for judicial discretion. As such, these cases may be categorised as Tier-3 tasks, which could be fully handled by AI due to their low degree of seriousness and limited demand for judicial discretion.

However, in small-claim civil cases that involve complicated issues, such as when the defendant challenges the claim and the case proceeds to a witness trial, the demand for judicial discretion increases significantly. This is due to the fact that such cases often involve new factual disputes, and the decision-maker must analyse and evaluate various forms of evidence, including witness testimony, documentary evidence and expert testimony. As a result, such cases are typically classified as Tier-1 tasks, which are exclusively reserved for human intelligence.

In a broad picture, the implementation of AI in the Thai court appears to be advancing in a cautious and gradual manner, which reflects a commendable approach. To further the AI implementation, this study recommends that the Thai court consider the degree of case seriousness and the demand for judicial discretion together when applying AI to more complex tasks. This approach would optimise the collaboration between human judges and AI, ensuring that human judges work harmoniously with AI, rather than being replaced by it.

Although the use of AI in courts across most regions is limited to a supportive role, and the idea of AI as an autonomous decision-making authority appears to be a distant vision, this chapter will not ignore the facts: the AI industry is advancing rapidly and the idea of AI replacing human judges in some specific, limited civil proceedings is already underway. Therefore, it would be totally irresponsible for us to hang on for a few decades until the machine literally exceeds human capabilities without any strategic preparation. Still, the idea of task allocation between human judges and AI requires more in-depth studies and analysis of the details. It is hoped that the finding of this chapter could serve as a broad guideline for task allocation in the soon-to-come AI adjudication and foster further research in this field.

NOTES

1. By 'Artificial Intelligence', this paper covers the traditional forms of rule-based systems and the most recent forms of machine learning, which trains models to learn from existing data and provide predictive outcomes.
2. 'Artificial Intelligence Market Size (2021–2028). Share & Trends Analysis Report' (Grand View Research, 2021) <https://www.grandviewresearch.com/industry-analysis/artificial-intelligence-ai-market> (accessed 15 February 2024).
3. Richard Susskind, *Online Courts and the Future of Justice* (Oxford University Press, 2019), p. 264.
4. Sam Corbett-Davies and others, 'A computer program used for bail and sentencing decisions was labeled biased against blacks. It's actually not that clear', *The Washington Post* (17 October 2016) <https://www.washingtonpost.com/news/monkey-cage/wp/2016/10/17/can-an-algorithm-be-racist-our-analysis-is-more-cautious-than-propublicas/> (accessed 15 February 2024).
5. Caceres Enrique, 'EXPERTIUS: A Mexican Judicial Decision-Support System in the Field of Family Law, The Foundation for Legal Knowledge Based Systems' [2008] JURIX 78 <10.3233/978-1-58603-952-3-78> (accessed 15 February 2024).
6. Enrique (n. 5).
7. Ibid.
8. Changqing Shi and others, 'The Smart Court – A New Pathway to Justice in China?' (2021) 12(1) Int'l. J. Ct. Admin. <https://www.iacajournal.org/articles/10.36745/ijca.367/> (accessed 7 July 2022).
9. Rachel E. Stern and others, 'Automating Fairness? Artificial Intelligence in the Chinese Court' (2021) 59 Colum. J. Transnat'l L. 515, 526.
10. Tania Sourdin, *Judge, Technology and Artificial Intelligence* (Peter K. Yu, ed., 2021), p. 142.
11. Tara Vasdani, 'Estonia Set to Introduce "AI Judge" in Small Claims Court to Clear Court Backlog' (*Law 360 Canada*, 10 April 2019) <https://www.law360.ca/ca/articles/1747943> (accessed 15 February 2024).
12. Franciska Zsófia and others, 'The AI is Now in Session – The Impact of Digitalization on Courts' [2019] *Cybersecurity and Law* 280.
13. Lord Sales, 'Algorithms, Artificial Intelligence and the Law' (The Sir Henry Brooke Lecture for BAILII, London, 12 November 2019).
14. 'The New Division of Labor – Bots and Humans Mix It Up in Industry 4.0' (*Sprocket Express*, 9 April 2019) <https://www.sprocketexpress.com/blog/the-new-division-of-labor> (accessed 15 February 2024).

15. Tania Sourdin and others, *The Responsive Judge: International Perspectives* (Tania Sourdin and Archie Zariski, eds, 2018), p. 99.
16. Tim Wu, 'Will Artificial Intelligence Eat the Law? The Rise of Hybrid Social-Ordering Systems' (2019) 119 Colum. L. Rev. 2001, 2023.
17. Sourdin, *Judge, Technology and Artificial Intelligence* (n. 10), p. 97.
18. Danielle Keats Citron, 'Technological Due Process' (2008) 85 Wash. U. L. Rev. 1249, 1252.
19. Ashley Deeks, 'The Judicial Demand for Explainable Artificial Intelligence' (2019) Colum. L. Rev. 1833.
20. *State* v. *Loomis*, 881 NW 2d 749 (Wis. 2016).
21. Zsófia and others (n. 12), 8.
22. Magnimind, 'What is Generalization in Machine Learning?' (*Machine Learning Blog*, 13 September 2020) <https://magnimindacademy.com/blog/what-is-generalization-in-machine-learning/> (accessed 25 July 2022).
23. Zsófia and others (n. 12), 13.
24. Ibid.
25. By 'adjudicative tasks', this chapter restricts to judicial decision-making responsibilities, including the rendering of court judgments and issuing court orders in civil and criminal adjudications.
26. Sourdin, *Judge, Technology and Artificial Intelligence* (n. 10).
27. Richard M. Re and others, 'Developing Artificially Intelligent Justice' (2019) 22 Stan. Tech. L. Rev. 242, 283.
28. Criminal Procedural Code (Thailand), s. 227.
29. Supreme Court Decision No. 3353/2552.
30. Margot E. Kaminski, 'Binary Governance: Lessons from the GDPR's Approach to Algorithmic Accountability' (2019) 92 S. C. L. Rev. 1529, 1542.
31. Wu (n. 16).

REFERENCES

'Artificial Intelligence Market Size (2021–2028). Share & Trends Analysis Report' (Grand View Research, 2021) <https://www.grandviewresearch.com/industry-analysis/artificial-intelligence-ai-market> (accessed 15 February 2024).

'The New Division of Labor – Bots and Humans Mix It Up in Industry 4.0' (*Sprocket Express*, 9 April 2019) <https://www.sprocketexpress.com/blog/the-new-division-of-labor> (accessed 15 February 2024).

Citron, D. K., 'Technological Due Process' (2008) 85 Wash. U. L. Rev. 1249.

Criminal Procedural Code (Thailand).

Davies, S. C. and others, 'A computer program used for bail and sentencing decisions was labeled biased against blacks. It's actually not that clear', *The Washington Post* (17 October 2016) <https://www.washingtonpost.com/news/monkey-cage/wp/2016/10/17/can-an-algorithm-be-racist-our-analysis-is-more-cautious-than-propublicas/> (accessed 15 February 2024).

Deeks, A., 'The Judicial Demand for Explainable Artificial Intelligence' (2019) Colum. L. Rev 1833.

Enrique, C., 'EXPERITUS: A Mexican Judicial Decision-Support System in the Field of Family Law, The Foundation for Legal Knowledge Based Systems' [2008] JURIX 78 <10.3233/978-1-58603-952-3-78> (accessed 15 February 2024).

Kaminski, M. E., 'Binary Governance: Lessons from the GDPR's Approach to Algorithmic Accountability' (2019) 92 S. C. L. Rev. 1529.

Magnimind, 'What is Generalization in Machine Learning?' (*Machine Learning Blog,* 13 September 2020) <https://magnimindacademy.com/blog/what-is-generalization-in-machine-learning/> (accessed 25 July 2022).

Re, R. M. and others., 'Developing Artificially Intelligent Justice' (2019) 22 Stan. Tech. L. Rev. 242.

Sales, Lord, 'Algorithms, Artificial Intelligence and the Law' (The Sir Henry Brooke Lecture for BAILII, London, 12 November 2019).

Shi, C. and others, 'The Smart Court – A New Pathway to Justice in China?' (2021) 12(1) Int'l. J. Ct. Admin. <https://www.iacajournal.org/articles/10.36745/ijca.367/> (accessed 7 July 2022).

Sourdin, T., *Judge, Technology and Artificial Intelligence* (Peter K. Yu, ed., 2021).

Sourdin, T. and others, *The Responsive Judge: International Perspectives* 99 (Tania Sourdin and Archie Zariski, eds, 2018).

State v. Loomis, 881 NW 2d 749 (Wis. 2016).

Stern, R. E. and others, 'Automating Fairness? Artificial Intelligence in the Chinese Court' (2021) 59 Colum. J. Transnat'l. L. 515.

Supreme Court Decision No. 3353/2552.

Susskind, R., *Online Courts and the Future of Justice* (Oxford University Press, 2019).

Vasdani, T., 'Estonia Set to Introduce "AI Judge" in Small Claims Court to Clear Court Backlog' (*Law 360 Canada,* 10 April 2019) <https://www.law360.ca/ca/articles/1747943> (accessed 15 February 2024).

Wu, T., 'Will Artificial Intelligence Eat the Law? The Rise of Hybrid Social-Ordering Systems' (2019) 119 Colum. L. Rev. 2001.

Zsófia, F. and others, 'The AI is Now in Session – The Impact of Digitalization on Courts' [2019] *Cybersecurity and Law* 280.

Chapter 8

The Past, Present and Future of Technology on Sentencing in Taiwan: Some Constitutional Reflections

Yi-Yi Lee

A. BACKGROUND

Sentencing is a complex decision in which judges must consider factors in multi-dimensions. In Taiwan, the turn to the application of technology in sentencing commenced with the White Rose movement in 2011, the large-scale public movement triggered by a judgment that pronounced three-years-and-two-months' imprisonment, whereas the prosecutor had asked for seven-years-and-ten-months' imprisonment for a person who was convicted of sexually assaulting a six-year-old girl.[1] Such considerable discrepancy between the requested and handed down sentencing invoked the public's questioning whether sentencing decisions were consistent, transparent and reasonable. Responding to the public's call for reform, the highest administration – the Judicial Yuan – committed to the public that it would endeavour to enhance the transparency and consistency of sentencing decisions.[2] However, sentencing decisions pertain to the discretion enjoyed by judges, who are obliged only to follow the law,[3] especially not any orders from the government and the judicial administration. To carry out the judicial administration's commitment without jeopardising judicial independence, the Judicial Yuan began the procurement of a series of tools, with different levels of reliance on technology, to enhance the transparency of sentencing.

This chapter introduces three generations of the above-mentioned tools, their methodologies, and their practice (see 'B. The Past, Present and Future'). To assess the constitutional implications contextually, it also introduces two changes in the law – the Constitutional Court Procedure Act and the Citizen Judges regime, which entered into force respectively in 2022 and 2023 – and their relevance to the application of sentencing technologies (see 'C. Sentencing Legal Techs amid Changes'). Finally, it analyses the accompanying constitutional issues amid changes (see 'D. Constitutional Issues').

B. THE PAST, PRESENT AND FUTURE – PROCUREMENT AND PRACTICE THROUGHOUT THREE GENERATIONS

The procurement of the sentencing tool commenced right after the White Rose movement. The first generation of sentencing tools emerged in 2012 and was publicised in 2016. Whilst still online and accessible to all, the maintenance of its data stopped in 2019. The procurement and open timeline of the second-generation tool overlapped with the first-generation one. The second-generation tool was publicised in 2018 and is still online and accessible.[4] The third-generation tool has been online since February 2023.[5] It is now exclusive to the judiciary. Nevertheless, considering the publicising trajectory of its predecessors, it is likely to be open to all in the future.

I. First generation (the sentencing database)

(a) Motivation for procurement

The motivation for procuring a sentencing tool directly responded to the dilemma between enhancing the transparency of sentencing decisions and avoiding infringing judicial independence. The first proposed solution by the Judicial Yuan was straightforward, to provide a case database with search tools.

(b) Methodology and maintenance

The methodology of providing a case database as the sentencing tool stems from two presumptions: first, like cases should be treated alike; and, second, if how cases which were similar to the present case have been decided by other judges in the past can be easily checked, the average and the distribution of the sentencing decisions in past judgments shape the benchmarks which assist all stakeholders – the judges, the parties and the civil society – to examine the consistency and reasonableness of the sentencing decision for the present case.

In order to realise such a methodology, the Judicial Yuan recruited two sets of people: experienced criminal court judges and law graduates. The former creates the instructions on what factors in the judgments are relevant in defining a 'like case' that must be tagged. Taking sexual assault offence as an example: factors may cover those already stipulated in the law, for example, whether the accused trespassed into the residence of the victim, and circumstantial factors not specified by the law, such as whether the victim suffers from mental illness or was impregnated due to the assault. The latter then follows those instructions, examines all the applicable judgments and tags the factors accordingly.

(c) User interface

Entering by selecting a category of offence, the users may input factors from sets of options; some are single-choice, whereas some are multiple-choice, corresponding to the codebook created by the aforementioned judges. Figures 8.1 to 8.4 display the output. Responding to the input, the page simultaneously shows the number of matches. After clicking search, the next page displays the average distribution of sentencing decisions handed down in those matching judgments.

Once released exclusively to judges in 2012, users soon found the intrinsic limitation of the first-generation tool: the more factors selected, the fewer matches were found. For example, a ten-times gap can be found between Figure 8.1 (2,826 matches of fraud cases where three options were ticked: the specific provision of the aiding fraud offence that was charged, the provision of a deduction of the sentence was applied, and the offender has acquired financial benefit) and Figure 8.2 (246 matches when an additional option, 'motivation for the crime, was due to financial difficulties', was ticked). It is common to find only a handful or zero matches if a user attempts to input all factors, which invokes the pitfall of lacking representativeness.

Figures 8.3 and 8.4 illustrate various aspects of sentencing decisions in judgments based on similar facts in the past. These statistics provide a useful reference for judges. Judges can use this information to quickly acknowledge how their colleagues make decisions and then apply it to the present case, as long as the statistical base is not too small and thus unreliable. Another pitfall is the maintenance cost due to the reliance on human readers to exercise the tagging process.[6] In 2019, the Judicial Yuan ceased further maintenance of the first-generation sentencing system, partly due to the maintenance cost concern.

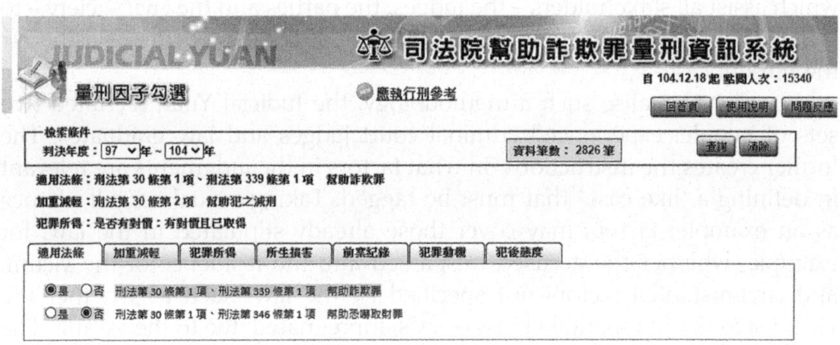

Figure 8.1 A page of the first-generation system displays results (2,826 matches) when the user assigns three factors

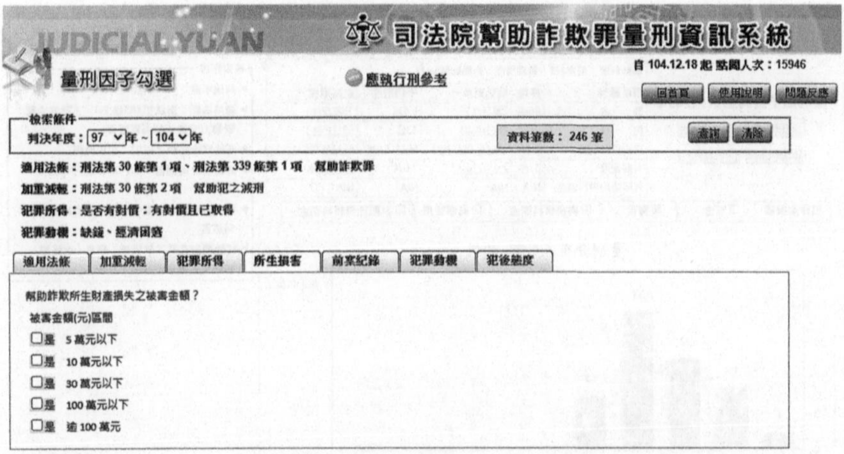

Figure 8.2 A page of the first-generation system displays the number of matches where the user assigns four factors

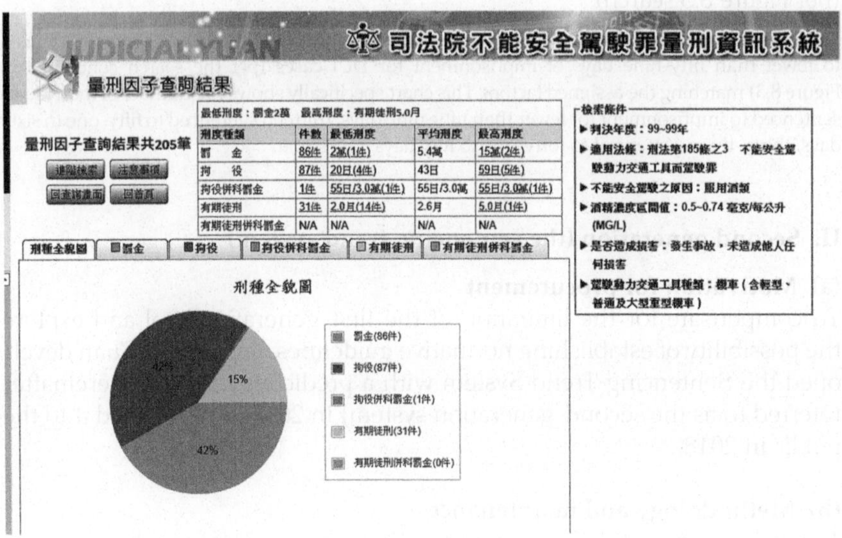

Figure 8.3 A page of the first-generation system displays the distribution of sentences in DUI cases

Note: The box on the right lists the factors assigned in a search result of the distribution of sentences in DUI cases: judgments made in 2010, the specific offence of DUI (Article 185-3 of the Criminal Code), the cause of unsafe driving being alcohol-related, breath alcohol intensity test results of 0.5 to 0.74 mg/L, no harm to others, and the vehicle type being a motorcycle. The table at the top indicates that eighty-six offenders were fined, eighty-seven received a sentence of less than fifty-nine days' imprisonment, one received a combination of both, and thirty-one were sentenced to more than sixty days' imprisonment. The percentages are shown.

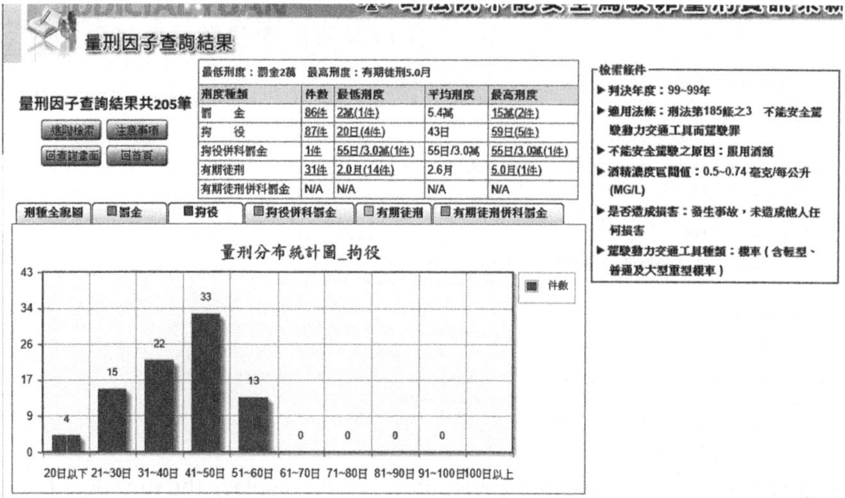

Figure 8.4 The distribution of specific cases in which offenders were sentenced to fewer than 59 days of imprisonment for DUI cases (per Figure 8.3 search)

Note: Figure shows the distribution of the specific cases in which the offenders were sentenced to fewer than fifty-nine days of imprisonment for DUI cases (per the search conducted in Figure 8.3) matching the assigned factors. This chart specifically shows the number of individuals sentenced to imprisonment for fewer than fifty-nine days: thirteen sentenced to fifty-one to sixty days, thirty-three sentenced to forty-one to fifty days, and so on.

II. Second generation (the sentencing trend system)

(a) Motivation for procurement

To compensate for the limitation of the first-generation tool and explore the possibility of establishing normative guidelines, the Judicial Yuan developed the Sentencing Trend System with a predictive function (hereinafter referred to as the second-generation system) in 2014[7] and released it to the public in 2018.

(b) Methodology and maintenance

The methodology of the second-generation system is rooted in the presumption that each criminal conduct corresponds to normatively proportionate sentencing, and the contribution to the sentencing of each factor can be quantified. The methodology of the second-generation system, therefore, goes: a normatively proportionate range of sentencing for any case can be predicted provided the factors involved in the particular case can be ascertained and each applicable factor has been assigned a quantified contribution value to the sentencing.

Similar to the first-generation tool, first, the Judicial Yuan recruited judges to create the codebook and law graduates to execute accordingly. Second, all tagged factors in all applicable judgments undergo regression analysis to find out the contribution, a quantified positive or negative value, of each factor to the sentencing decision. Third, the statistical finding of the contribution of each factor is reviewed by a focus group comprising stakeholders including the sitting judges, prosecutors, practising lawyers, academics and interest groups in civil society.[8] The focus group deliberates over whether the statistical finding coincides with their expectation; if not, the statistical finding would be tendered to reflect a more reasonable contribution.[9]

(c) User interface

The users enter offence from eight categories as presented on the homepage (Figure 8.5). The user may select from lists of applicable factors: for example, in the sexual assault offence, whether the defendant was younger than twenty years old, the number of victims, whether the defendant pleaded guilty, if any instruments other than body parts were used during the criminal conduct, from the left panel (Figure 8.6).

The right panel displays the suggested penalty in the upper box and a range of suggested penalties in the lower box (Figures 8.7 and 8.8 show search results of DUI and Fraud cases, respectively). These values vary simultaneously once the user ticks or unticks different boxes. The users can select

Figure 8.5 The homepage of the second-generation system

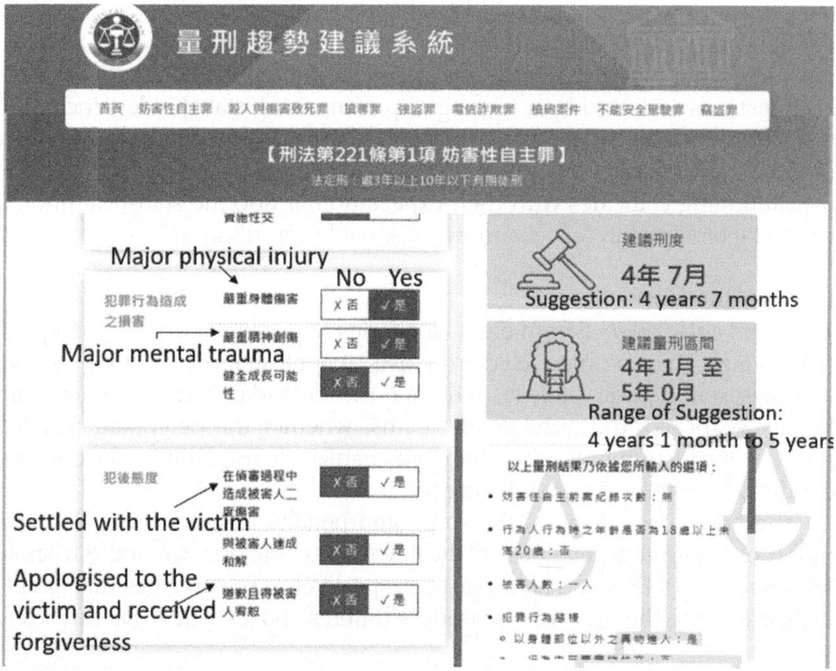

Figure 8.6 Page displayed after selecting one of the eight categories of offences: sexual assault case

from the options in the left panel but cannot insert factors unknown to this system. Subsequently, the adding-up generates the suggested penalty.

III. Third-generation (machine-learning sentencing database)

(a) Motivation for procurement

The loss of law graduates as human resources urged the Judicial Yuan to review the practicality of updating the databases for existing tools. The Judicial Yuan, therefore, began the procurement of artificial intelligence-involved technologies to compensate for the required reading and tagging work previously done by human readers. The third-generation tool, the Sentencing Information Systems, applied semantic labelling and automated tagging to replace the reading and tagging work. It was released to the judges on 6 February 2023.

(b) Methodology and maintenance

The third-generation system comprises two sets of search tools, fact-based and evaluation-based. The former is a renewed first-generation system, in which the human tagging work is replaced by algorithms, semantic

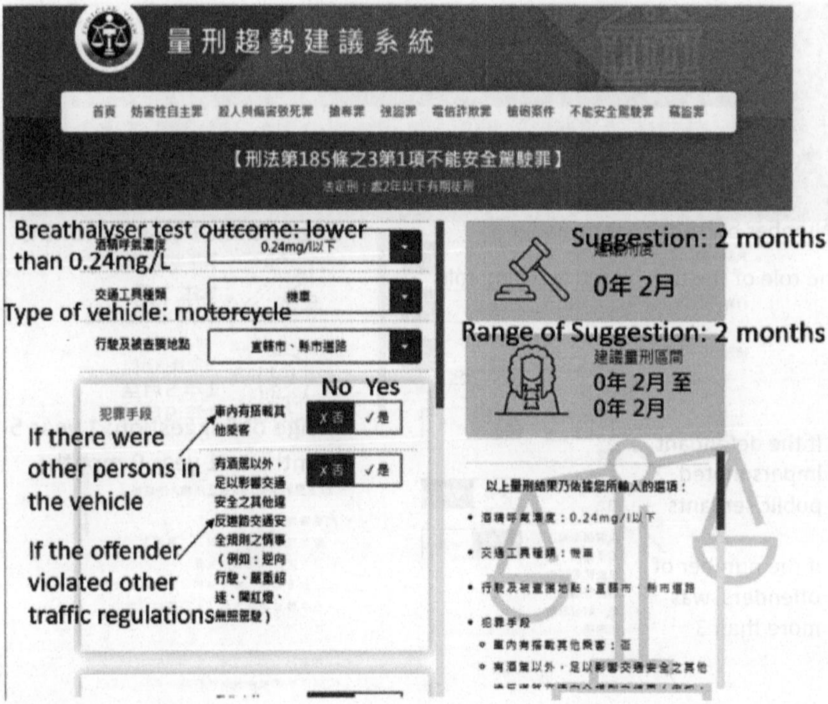

Figure 8.7 Suggestions for DUI cases based on assigned factors (no matching cases)

labelling and automated tagging. The latter is another search tool applying an independent set of search terms. The methodology of the latter shows the user how the positive or negative evaluation of each fact factor in similar cases would impact sentencing decisions in past judgments. For example, a search term might be 'the user gave positive (sympathetic) evaluation to the circumstances under which the accused committed the offence'; whereas the average, range and distribution of the sentencing handed down in the past judgments applying the assigned evaluation factor displays accordingly.

(c) User interface

The UIs for the two search tools are separated. On the fact-based search page, the users may select the offence (Figure 8.9). After entering the second layer, users may designate the fact factors considered in past cases: for example, in DUI cases, the volume of alcohol consumed, whether injuries were incurred, the type of vehicle used, and whether the defendant is a recidivist of the same offence (Figure 8.10). The number of matches may change in response to the user selection. After submission, the next page

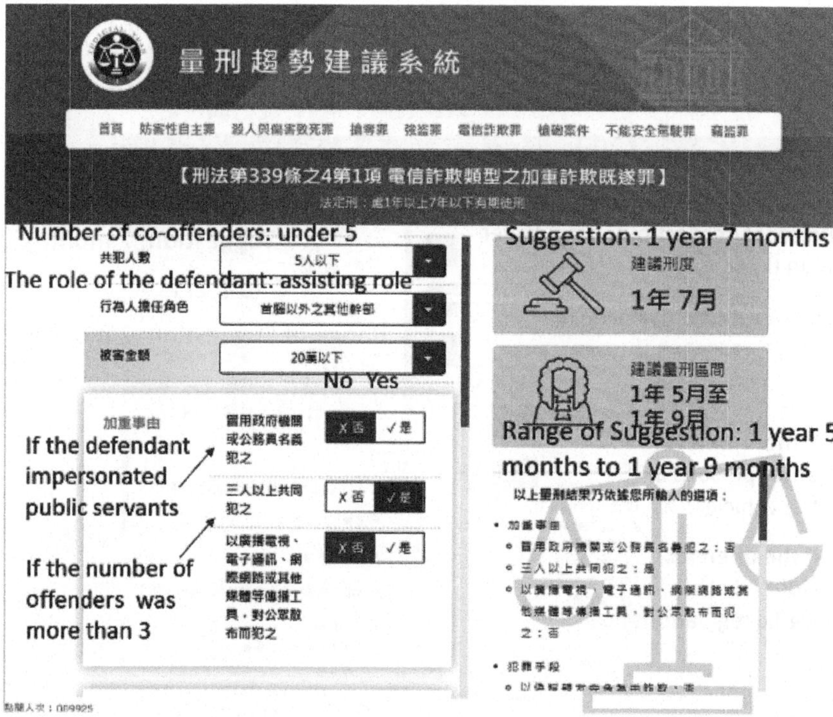

Figure 8.8 Page displaying an instance of fraud

shows the distribution of sentencing decisions matching the designated fact factors in past judgments, by types of punishment or terms of imprisonment (Figures 8.11 and 8.12).

In the evaluation-based system, users enter offences (Figure 8.13). Then, the users may assign their evaluation on each factor as for/against/neutral (on the accused). The factors to which users may assign their evaluation include the post-commission attitude, the damage incurred, the personality of the defendant, the victim's attitude, etc. The number of matches and the distribution of the sentencing decision are displayed simultaneously according to the input (Figures 8.14 and 8.15).

The comparison between Figures 8.14 and 8.15 demonstrates that when more options for 'evaluation for the defendant' were selected, the outcome favours softer sentencing decisions. This is shown from the concentration of the shorter bars on the left side of the distribution chart, given that the total number of cases distribution (curve) remains unchanged.

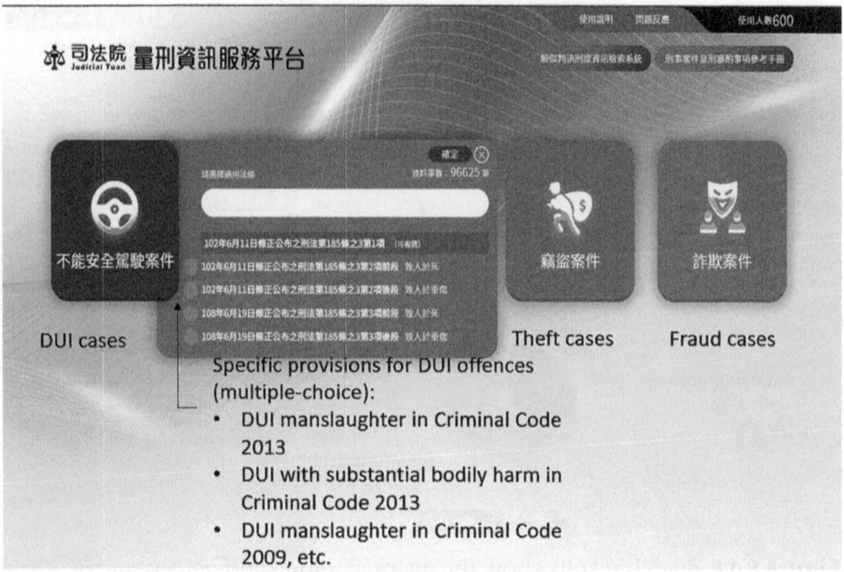

Figure 8.9 Homepage of the third-generation fact-based sentencing information platform

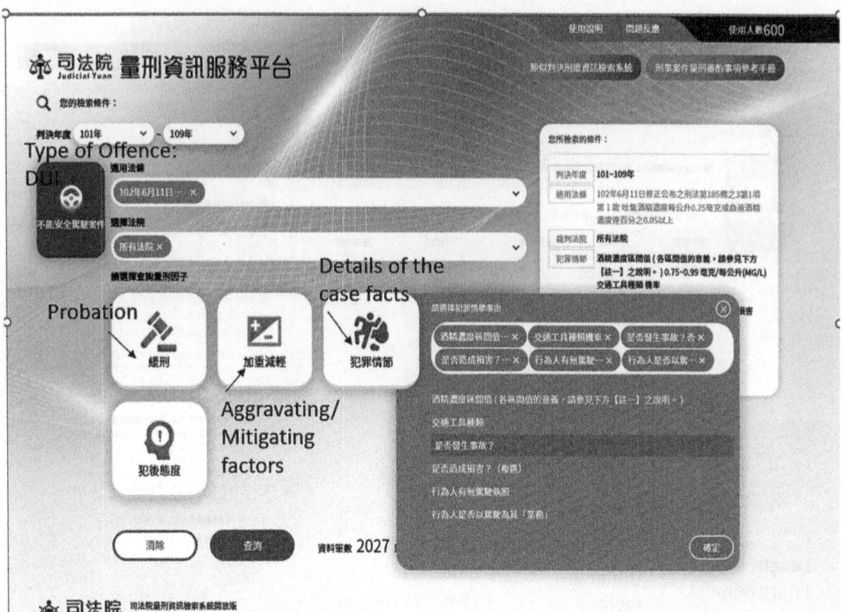

Figure 8.10 Options display: factors stipulated in Criminal Code

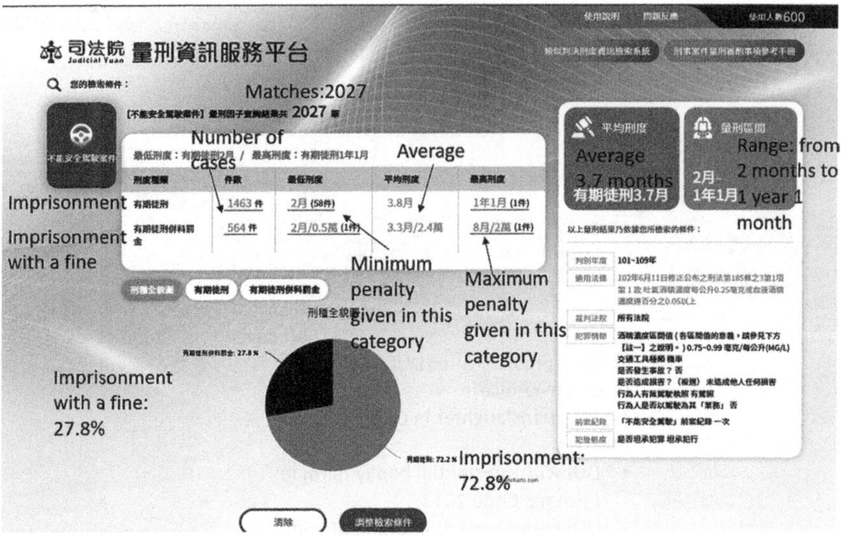

Figure 8.11 Search results show the average, range and percentage of sentencing decisions in the matching judgments

Note: Search result displays DUI judgments for cases involving breathalyser test outcomes between 0.75 and 0.99, the vehicle used being a motorcycle, no harm done to others, the offender having a driving licence, having one DUI record, and pleading guilty.

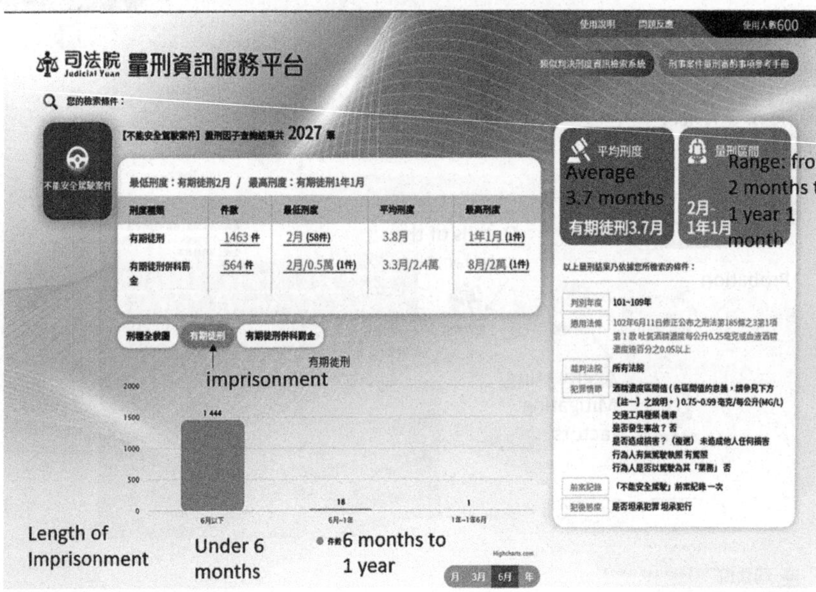

Figure 8.12 Distribution of sentencing decisions in the same matching judgments

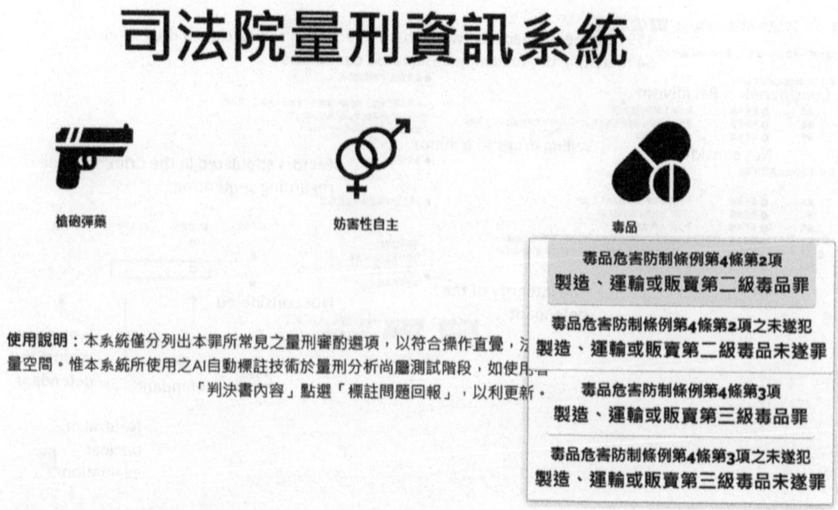

Figure 8.13 Homepage of the third-generation evaluation-based sentencing information system

Note: This system includes three categories of offences: firearms-related, sexual assault, and narcotics-related offences. The Figure uses the narcotics-related category as an example, showing each category can be unfolded into several provisions.

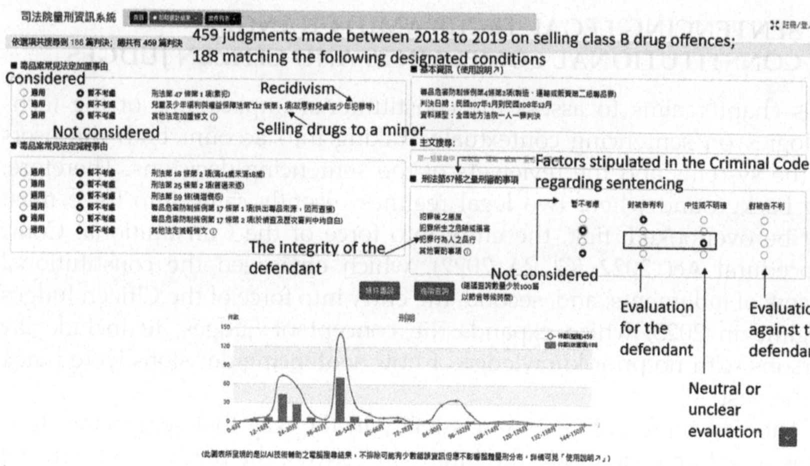

Figure 8.14 The second layer of the evaluation-based system shows the distribution of sentencing decisions handed down in matching judgments

Note: The page displays the total number of judgments in this category within a specific timeframe from 2018 to 2019. The red number shows the number of matching judgments that meet the designated evaluation for each factor: the common aggravating or mitigating factors in drug-related cases and general sentence-related factors.

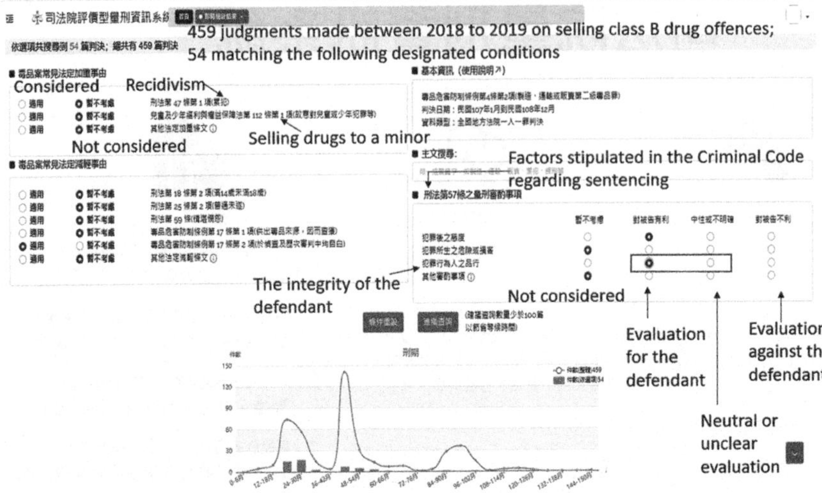

Figure 8.15 Distribution of sentencing decisions handed down in matching judgments

Note: A change that was made (compared to Figure 8.14) was how the factor 'the integrity of the defendant' was evaluated. In Figure 8.14, this factor was not considered, but in Figure 8.15, only judgments that gave a positive evaluation to the integrity of the defendant were counted. As a result, the number of matching cases dropped to 54.

C. SENTENCING LEGAL TECHS AMID CHANGES – CONSTITUTIONAL COMPLAINTS AND CITIZEN JUDGES

This chapter aims to assess the constitutional implications of the technologies on sentencing contextually, taking into account both the users of the systems and the reviewers of the sentencing decisions. Therefore, the background where two legal regimes recently came into force must not be overlooked: first, the entry into force of the Constitutional Court Procedural Act 2022 (CCPA 2022), which envisaged the constitutional review of judgments; and, second, the entry into force of the Citizen Judges Regime in 2023, which expands the concept of 'judges' to include lay persons with no prior knowledge of how sentencing decisions were made in the past.

The first represents a new possibility in the way that sentencing decisions might be reviewed in the future. In Taiwan, the review of sentencing decisions has been exclusive to the superior courts, the High Court and the Supreme Court, whereas the constitutional review of legislative acts is exclusive to the Taiwan Constitutional Court (TCC). The Constitutional Court Procedure Act 2022 bestowed on the TCC an extra jurisdiction to review the constitutionality of how judges interpret and apply those laws.[10] In other words, it now becomes possible for the TCC, if requested by individuals, to review the constitutionality of the judge's interpretation of the laws stipulating sentencing matters, which includes the judge's philosophy and methodology on exercising their discretion on sentencing, with or without technological sentencing tools.

The second represents the emergence of a new group of stakeholders who have access to technological sentencing tools. Although no evidence suggests substantial reliance of the current users, the professional judges, on the existing first-and-second generation systems (details see D.I. 'Conceptualising a fair court – the independent judges and the responsibility to reason'), the status quo is likely to change following the introduction of the Citizen Judges regime, which changes the compositions of the 'judges' backgrounds'. Since the new group of 'judges' will face difficult decisions, it will be worth observing whether this new group tends to refer to or rely on the statistics showing a taxonomy of sentencing decisions made in the past. As a result, after the entry into force of the Citizen Judges Act in 2023, it is not fanciful to expect the practicality of the sentencing system and the judges' willingness to consider referring to the sentencing legal techs to increase.

The following section discusses the constitutional reflections based on precedents regarding the relevant principles of sentencing laid down by the TCC in the past, the practical application of technologies on sentencing and their constitutional issues in the present and the future involving the two new regimes.

D. CONSTITUTIONAL ISSUES – THE CHALLENGE OF DUE PROCESS

The TCC has not yet directly ruled on issues related to the application of technologies on sentencing. However, some case law of the TCC has been established in criminal justice discourse and is worth looking at. It is the TCC's settled case law that punishments must only be imposed by a formally and substantively fair court;[11] to comply with the constitutional safeguard of due process, only admissable evidence verified within an adequate process shall be used against a criminal defendant,[12] who has the right to know and challenge the evidence used against them.[13] It is also the TCC's settled case law that any punishment shall be given by a court whose discretion is intact,[14] in the manner that judges have discretion to apply individualised punishment or treatment responding to the gravity of the conduct and the culpability of the offender (the proportionality of punishment, or the principle of *Nullapoena sine culpa*).[15] Meanwhile, the right not to be discriminated against, or the principle of equality, is explicitly enshrined in the Constitution, which concretises the mandate that 'like cases should be treated alike'. Stemming from these case laws, the following subsections attempt to conceptualise three constitutional mandates in the context of applying technologies on sentencing: the concept of a fair court (D.I); the concept of admissibility of evidence and the right of the defendant to know the evidence used against them (D.II); and the concept of proportionate sentencing will be revisited in the legal tech context (D.III).

I. Conceptualising a fair court – the independent judges and the responsibility to reason

Two dimensions related to the court are worth discussing in the context of the application of technologies to sentencing. First, judicial independence, as a pillar of the rule of law, is enshrined in the Constitution, which stipulates that judges shall only be bound by law and shall not be interfered with internally or externally when carrying out their duties.[16] In this regard, the application of sentencing tools might concern judicial independence if the sentencing suggestions produced by the technological tools gain substantial binding force. One example of the substantial binding force is where the higher court would quash the lower court's sentencing decision if the latter deviated from the suggestions generated by sentencing tools.

Second, this chapter proposes that the constitutional mandate of a fair court encompasses that the judges, to an extent, are obliged to give adequate reasons that support their judgment.[17] However, it must be clarified that there is no case law of the TCC directly affirming this obligation since it concerns the allocation of judicial resources. Such an obligation often hampers judicial efficiency and worsens the workload of judges. The concretisation of such a potential constitutional mandate in the context of the application of sentencing tools may be that judges bear the obligation to state how they applied the sentencing tools, as well as whether and why they adopted or disregarded the suggestions.[18]

Neither did these issues invoke prominent concerns or spark wide discussion in Taiwan. The present writer attributes this to a low reliance on the first-and-second-generation systems in the practice of judges, which coincides with the proclamation of the Judicial Yuan that judges are not bound by the suggestions generated by the systems. The writer observes no obvious impetus suggesting such reliance might increase after the introduction of the third-generation system or the entry into force of the CCPA 2022.

Nevertheless, the entry into force of the Citizen Judges regime in January 2023 is likely to distil such equilibrium. For applicable cases, the Citizen Judges regime changes the background of the judges, from solely professional to partly laypersons and partly professionals. It is arguable that the scientific outlook and methodology of the first-and-second-generation sentencing tools, reflecting that the outputs represent the decisions of experienced professionals, may compensate the layperson's confidence in making the sentencing decision, which subsequently reinforces the layperson's willingness to rely on, or even abide by, the suggestion generated. Moreover, the Judicial Yuan explicitly indicated that facilitating the sentencing procedure in Citizen Judges' involved cases is the main impetus of the third-generation AI-based system.[19] It would be unsurprising if the further 'hi-tech' third-generation system attracts more applications and enhances reliance.

It is therefore suggested that the future challenge is likely to focus on how to ensure the proper technological literacy of the Citizen Judges. Citizen Judges should be informed that factors that contribute to proportionality in sentencing often interrelate with each other;[20] that the function of a trial court includes restoring justice, conflict and achieving social cohesion;[21] and that no legal tech or algorithm can replace the 'independent mind' of a judge.[22]

II. Revisiting the defendant's right to know and challenge the evidence used against them

Under the guarantee of due process and the right to a fair trial, it is the TCC's settled case law that the accused individuals enjoy the constitutional right to know and challenge the evidence used against them. In circumstances where the sentencing suggestion generated by the system is referred to in the judgment, such a suggestion fulfils the widest concept of evidence. The issue then arises as to whether the defendant is entitled to request the disclosure of the algorithms – if any – built into the systems, and the methodology of the systems. A wider out-spill of the issue is whether the defendant is entitled to request the disclosure of what search terms the judge has input to get the output suggestion, as to the methodology inside the judge's mind regarding how they decide to adopt or disregard the suggestions. The latter represents the flip of the coin of the judge's obligation to reason (already addressed in illustrated in D.I).

The issue of disclosure concerns the so-called technological black box. Once requested by the defendant, the relevant information, especially the quantification, formula forming of the system, the date and methodology,[23] and/or algorithm,[24] should be explained to fulfil the defendant's effective opportunity to challenge the reasonableness and admissibility of the evidence.[25] This coincides with the famous umbrella term 'technological due process', proposed by Citron,[26] and the auditability, transparency, and consistency, in the specific context of an algorithm by Villasenor and Foggo[27] and others.[28]

So far, defendants have little motivation to challenge in this regard because of the low reliance of judges on the sentencing systems. However, this aspect of legal challenges might be enriched after the introduction of the AI-based third-generation system by several factors coming into play: the precision of auto-tagging and explainability of the semantic labelling,[29] the neutrality of the evaluation factors is biased,[30] and whether the bias may be corrected.[31]

Moreover, it is worth observing whether the concept of the right to know and challenge evidence used against them would evolve, particularly following the likely increasing reliance on sentencing tools following entry into force of the Citizen Judges regime (as illustrated in Figure 8.4: the defendant's lawyer challenged the black box).

III. Conceptualising fairness in sentencing – between proportionality and equality

It is noteworthy that in a specific case involving a sentencing system, the Supreme Court and the High Court had differing views. The issue of fairness in sentencing was featured in a debate between the two courts. In this case, the High Court was asked to review the fairness of the sentencing decision made by the District Court. The defendant appealed on the ground that the latter's decision was disproportionate. The High Court overturned the District Court's decision. The judgment indicated that, after searching in the first and second-generation systems, it was clear that the District Court's decision departed from the suggestion and average sentencing decision in similar cases. Based on the principle of equality, a justification is required for this discrepancy. As the District Court failed to explain such a discrepancy, its sentencing decision cannot sustain the principle of equality and must be overruled.[32] The Supreme Court was then asked to review the High Court's decision, and it upheld the decision, however, for a contrasting rationale. The Supreme Court emphasised that judges must focus on the specific details of each case when making sentencing decisions[33] to ensure that individuals receive appropriate and tailored punishment. This means judges must not consider irrelevant information from other cases, including decisions of other cases shown in the sentencing systems.[34]

The Supreme Court's view indicates the tension between the legitimacy of any sentencing system and the constitutional principles regarding sentencing. Some even comment that the Supreme Court's ruling, despite not explicitly stating that considering the past data *per se* violates the principle of proportionality and individualised sentencing, has eliminated the practicality of the first-and-second generation systems.[35] A dilemma for judges therefore emerges. Consulting the sentencing tools might help a judge fulfil their task to treat their present case like other 'like cases.' Meanwhile, consulting the sentencing tools might hamper the judge's duty to concentrate on the present case and disregard irrelevant information. The issue then becomes, in the language of criminal procedure, whether the output generated by the first-generation system is admissible;[36] and in the language of the Constitution, whether there is a constitutional space left for the judges to apply sentencing tools in practice. After the expansion of the jurisdiction of the TCC due to the entry into force of CCPA 2022, it is worth observing whether the TCC would elaborate further regarding the nuance between the principle of equality and proportionality.

Another issue is the 'narrowing effect,' which refers to judges' inclination to decide similarly due to consulting the same sentencing system. It is worth observing whether the Courts would elaborate more, after the introduction of the third-generation system and the involvement of layperson judges, on whether fairness is bestowed with dynamic meaning,[37] whether the narrowing effect derived from the application of aggregated data and/or algorithm is desired,[38] or it should be avoided because algorithms do not reflect the degree of severity and might worsen the correctness of the information.[39]

E. CONCLUSION

This chapter introduced three generations of sentencing tools with different methodologies for applying technology. The first-generation search tool and the second-generation (normative) sentencing trend system in Taiwan were the Judicial Yuan's responses to the public's call for transparency and predictability in sentencing. Few constitutional challenges have been raised so far, partly due to awareness of the danger of breaching the principle of individualised sentencing specified by the Supreme Court, and partly due to the professional judges' low reliance on the sentencing tools.

This discussion proposed that the change of users, the change of reviewers of doctrines, and the change of the technology itself are variants of the constitutional implication of sentencing tools. The entry into force of the Citizen Judges regime in January 2023 is likely to put the application of technology on sentencing under the real pressure test by adding a new type of user. If reliance on the sentencing tool increases, the constitutional mandate for a fair court where the judges bear the obligation to reason might be further discussed and defined.

In the same thread, the release of the third-generation systems in February 2023 represents a change in the technology itself. It also increases the likelihood that the accuracy of the technology and the transparency of algorithms would be challenged under the issue of how to carry out the defendant's right to know and challenge the evidence used against them.

The entry into force of the CCPA 2022 adds another variant as a potential competent reviewer of doctrine emerged. The settled doctrine set by the Supreme Court that little space is left for the application of sentencing tools without jeopardising the principle of proportionality, that is, giving individualised sentencing, its intersection with the principle of equality and other applicable doctrines can now possibly be revisited and further elaborated if the TCC decides to admit a complaint regarding the methodology of applying technology on sentencing. The future of these three dimensions remains worth observing.

NOTES

1. Rich Chang, '"White Roses" slam government inertia', *Taipei Times* (July 2011) <www.taipeitimes.com/News/front/archives/2011/07/18/2003508499> (accessed 15 May 2023).
2. '司法院研議建制量刑資訊系統　減少歧異', *Judicial Yuan Weekly* (April 2011) <www.judicial.gov.tw/tw/cp-1429-71505-7757b-1.html> (accessed 15 May 2023).
3. The elements to be considered in sentencing are laid down in Article 57 of the Criminal Code (2006). Ten elements are enumerated, including the motive and purpose of the offence, the stimulation perceived at the moment of committing the offence, the means used for the commission of the offence, the offender's living conditions, the disposition of the offender, the education and intelligence of the offender, the relationship between the offender and the victim, the seriousness of the offender's obligation violation, the danger or damage caused by the offence, and the offender's attitude after committing the offence.
4. 'Sentencing Section' (*Judicial Yuan official website*) <www.judicial.gov.tw/tw/cp-83-57186-1ef46-1.html#%E9%87%8F%E5%88%91%E8%B6%A8%E5%8B%A2%E5%BB%BA%E8%AD%B0%E7%B3%BB%E7%B5%B1> (accessed 15 May 2023).
5. '因應國民法官新制，司法院啟用AI量刑資訊系統--具備二種模式、擁有四大優點' *Judicial Yuan Press Release* (February 2023) <https://www.judicial.gov.tw/tw/cp-1887-806741-d6471-1.html> (accessed 15 May 2023).
6. The recruitment of those law graduates, initially not by the Judicial Yuan, was ceased and led to a gap of timely maintenance. The sentencing, Judicial Yuan website available at <https://www.judicial.gov.tw/tw/cp-83-57186-1ef46-1.html> (accessed 4 Aug 2024).
7. The sentencing trend system <https://sen.judicial.gov.tw/pub_platform/sugg/index.html> (accessed 15 May 2023).
8. '司法院研討肇逃罪量刑資訊系統編碼表內容妥適性' (*Judicial Weekly*, May 2017), <www.judicial.gov.tw/tw/cp-1429-67645-4dc34-1.html> (accessed 15 May 2023).
9. A series of conferences have been held on the inclusion of the sentencing factors responding to different offences, e.g. 'Drug Dealing' (*Judicial Yuan*) <www.judicial.gov.tw/tw/cp-1429-67367-c766e-1.html> (accessed 15 May 2023); 'Trade Secret' (*Judicial Yuan*) <www.judicial.gov.tw/tw/cp-1429-66951-1928d-1.html> (accessed 15 May 2023). '司法院持續建置多項量刑資訊　趨勢建議系統年底開放查詢' (*Judicial Weekly*, September 2018) <www.judicial.gov.tw/tw/cp-1429-66723-c580b-1.html> (accessed 15 May 2023).
10. 'The Constitutional Court Procedure Act entering into force: A New Era of Constitutional Court in Taiwan' (*TCC website*, January 2022) <https://cons.judicial.gov.tw/en/docdata.aspx?fid=2175&id=339891> (accessed 15 May 2023).
11. Interpretation J.Y. No. 436 (1997) <https://cons.judicial.gov.tw/en/docdata.aspx?fid=100&id=310617> (accessed 13 February 2024).
12. Interpretation J.Y. No. 582 (2004) <https://cons.judicial.gov.tw/en/docdata.aspx?fid=100&id=310763> (accessed 13 February 2024); Interpretation J.Y. No.789 (2020). Taiwan Constitutional Court Annual Report 2020 <https://cons.judicial.gov.tw/en/docdata.aspx?fid=5250> (accessed 13 February 2024).

13. Interpretation J.Y. No. 762 (2018) <https://cons.judicial.gov.tw/en/docdata.aspx?fid=100&id=310943> (accessed 13 February 2024); Interpretation J.Y. No.737 (2016) <https://cons.judicial.gov.tw/en/docdata.aspx?fid=100&id=310918> (accessed 13 February 2024).
14. Interpretation J.Y. No. 669 (2009) <https://cons.judicial.gov.tw/en/docdata.aspx?fid=100&id=310850> (accessed 13 February 2024).
15. Interpretation J.Y. No. 775 (2019) <https://cons.judicial.gov.tw/en/docdata.aspx?fid=100&id=310956> (accessed 13 February 2024); Interpretation J.Y. No.792 (2020) <https://cons.judicial.gov.tw/en/docdata.aspx?fid=100&id=310973> (accessed 13 February 2024); Taiwan Constitutional Court Annual Report 2020 <https://cons.judicial.gov.tw/en/docdata.aspx?fid=5250> (accessed 13 February 2024).
16. Article 80 of the Constitution of R.O.C. (Taiwan); Interpretation J.Y. No. 370 (1995) <https://cons.judicial.gov.tw/en/docdata.aspx?fid=100&id=310551> (accessed 13 February 2024).
17. The TCC once affirmed the constitutionality of the legal provision which stipulated that the Administrative Court shall give reason when dismissing a case. Interpretation J.Y. No. 170 (1981) <https://cons.judicial.gov.tw/en/docdata.aspx?fid=100&id=310351> (accessed 13 February 2024).
18. Vincent Chiao, 'Predicting Proportionality: The Case for Algorithmic Sentencing' (2018) 37(3) *Criminal Justice Ethics* 238.
19. 因應國民法官新制，司法院啟用AI量刑資訊系統--具備二種模式、擁有四大優點 (n. 5).
20. Also see 'Holism in the theory of reasons' in Jonathan Dancy, *Ethics Without Principles* (Online edn, Oxford University Press, 2004).
21. 林勤富 '智慧法院之發展與界限（下）—演算法、科技治理與司法韌性' [2022] 324 月旦法學雜誌 109, 112.
22. Ibid., 113.
23. Mark L. Shope, 'Lawyer and Judicial Competency in the Era of Artificial Intelligence: Ethical Requirements for Documenting Datasets and Machine Learning Models' (2021) 34(1) *Georgetown Journal of Legal Ethics* 191-[iv].
24. Danielle Kehl, Priscilla Guo and Samuel Kessler 'Algorithms in the Criminal Justice System: Assessing the Use of Risk Assessments in Sentencing' (2017) Responsive Communities Initiative, Berkman Klein Center for Internet & Society, Harvard Law School; also see ibid.
25. Jonathan Dancy (n. 20); Cyrus Tata, 'The Application of Judicial Intelligence and "Rules" to Systems Supporting Discretionary Judicial Decision-Making' in G. Sartor and K. Branting (eds), *Judicial Applications of Artificial Intelligence* (Springer, Dordrecht 1998).
26. Other values encompass accuracy, accountability, participation and fairness. See Danielle Keats Citron, 'Technological Due Process' (2008) 85 Wash. U. L. Rev. 1249, 1308.
27. John Villasenor and Virginia Foggo, 'Artificial Intelligence, Due Process and Criminal Sentencing' (2020) 2 *Michigan State Law Review* 295–354.
28. Kehl and others (n. 24).
29. Han-Wei Liu, Ching-Fu Lin and Yu-Jie Chen, 'Beyond State v. Loomis: Artificial Intelligence, Government Algorithmization, and Accountability' (2018) 27(2) *International Journal of Law and Information Technology* 122.

30. For example, Kehl and others noted, in the context of risk assessment, the risk of bias and lack of reliability in sentencing could result in revival of discrimination against age, socio-economic status, and gender. See Kehl and others (n. 24).
31. Shope indicated several biases that could contribute in the machine-learning and the suggestion output (see n. 23); Chiao proposed the solution to the worry regarding reinforcement of biases by detecting biased factors and reducing the impact of unjustified consideration: Chiao (n. 18), 253.
32. Taiwan High Court 105-Chiau-Shang-Yi No. 117.
33. Supreme Court 108-Tai-Shan No. 3728 Criminal Judgment. Same rationale, also see Supreme Court 108-Tai-Kang No. 436 Criminal Verdit, 107 Tai-Kang No. 2797 Criminal Judgment.
34. This resonates with the fairness proposed by academics: see Douglas A. Berman, 'Re-balancing Fitness, Fairness, and Finality for Sentences' (2014), 4 Wake Forest J. Law & Policy 151, 157–8.
35. '蘇凱平, '以司法院量刑資訊作為量刑之內部性界限？ ——評最高法院108年度台上字第3728號刑事判決' (August 2020) Court Case Times 85–94.
36. Villasenor and Foggo (n. 27), 314.
37. Comparable ideas are 'dynamic fairness' proposed by Chouldechova and others, Alexandra Chouldechova and Aaron Roth, 'A Snapshot of the Frontiers of Fairness in Machine Learning' (2020) 63 *Communications of the ACM* 82 <https://doi.org/10.1145/3376898> (accessed 13 February 2024); also 'legal concept of fairness' proposed by Kehl and others (n. 24).
38. Proposed by Chiao (n. 18), responded by Jesper Ryberg, 'Sentencing Disparity and Artificial Intelligence' (2023) 57 *The Journal of Value Inquiry* 447.
39. Ibid.

REFERENCES

Chang, Rich, '"White Roses" Slam Government Inertia', *Taipei Times*, July 2011 <www.taipeitimes.com/News/front/archives/2011/07/18/2003508499> (accessed 20 October 2024).

Chiao, Vincent, 'Predicting Proportionality: The Case for Algorithmic Sentencing' (2018) 37(3) *Criminal Justice Ethics* 238.

Chouldechova, Alexandra and Roth, Aaron, 'A Snapshot of the Frontiers of Fairness in Machine Learning' (2020) 63 *Communications of the ACM* 82.

Citron, Danielle Keats, 'Technological Due Process' (2008) Wash. U. L. Rev. 85: 1249, 1308.

Interpretation J.Y. No. 170 (1981).

Interpretation J.Y. No. 370 (1995).

Interpretation J.Y. No. 436 (1997).

Interpretation J.Y. No. 582 (2004).

Interpretation J.Y. No. 669 (2009).

Interpretation J.Y. No. 737 (2016).

Interpretation J.Y. No. 762 (2018).

Interpretation J.Y. No. 775 (2019).

Interpretation J.Y. No. 789 (2020).

Kehl, Danielle, Guo, Priscilla and Kessler, Samuel, 'Algorithms in the Criminal Justice System: Assessing the Use of Risk Assessments in Sentencing' (2017) Responsive Communities Initiative, Berkman Klein Center for Internet & Society, Harvard Law School.

Liu, Han-Wei, Lin, Ching-Fu and Chen, Yu-Jie, 'Beyond State v. Loomis: Artificial Intelligence, Government Algorithmization, and Accountability' (2018) 27(2) *International Journal of Law and Information Technology* 122.

McKeever, Sean and Michael Ridge, 'Holism about Reasons' in *Principled Ethics: Generalism as a Regulative Ideal* (Oxford, 2006; online edn, Oxford Academic, 1 May 2006).

Ryberg, Jesper, 'Sentencing Disparity and Artificial Intelligence' (2023) 57 *The Journal of Value Inquiry* 447.

Shope, Mark L., 'Lawyer and Judicial Competency in the Era of Artificial Intelligence: Ethical Requirements for Documenting Datasets and Machine Learning Models' (2021) 34(1) *Georgetown Journal of Legal Ethics* 191-[iv].

Supreme Court 107-Tai-Kang No. 2797 Criminal Judgment.

Supreme Court 108-Tai8-Tai-Shan No.3728 Criminal Judgment.

Supreme Court 108-Tai-Kang No. 436 Criminal Verdict.

Taiwan High Court 105-Chiau-Shang-Yi No. 117.

Tata, Cyrus, 'The Application of Judicial Intelligence and "Rules" to Systems Supporting Discretionary Judicial Decision-Making' in G. Sartor and K. Branting (eds), *Judicial Applications of Artificial Intelligence* (Springer, Dordrecht, 1998).

Villasenor, John and Foggo, Virginia, 'Artificial Intelligence, Due Process and Criminal Sentencing' (2020) 2 *Michigan State Law Review* 295–354.

林勤富. '智慧法院之發展與界限（下）—演算法、科技治理與司法韌性.' [2022] 324 月旦法學雜誌 109.

蘇凱平, '以司法院量刑資訊作為量刑之內部性界限？——評最高法院108年度台上字第3728號刑事判決' (August 2020) Court Case Times 85–94.

量刑趨勢系統 (The Sentencing Trend System) https://sen.judicial.gov.tw/pub_platform/sugg/index.html.

Chapter 9

AI and Criminal Sentencing in China: Applications, Misgivings and Prospects

Xiaohan Liang

A. INTRODUCTION

The People's Republic of China (PRC) has embarked on the construction of 'smart courts'. First enunciated by the Supreme People's Court of China (SPC) in 2015, the concept of smart courts entails the modernisation of the justice system through informatisation and intelligentisation of judicial processes.[1] The Thirteenth Five-Year National Informatization Plan ("十三五"国家信息化规划) issued by State Council in 2016 fully endorsed the construction of smart courts.[2] Three years later, the President of SPC, Zhou Qiang, stressed once again that

> From the vantage point of serving the construction of a socialist state based on the rule of law, ensuring high-quality economic and social development, and advancing the modernization of the trial system and trial capacity, courts at all levels should take effective measures to comprehensively deepen the construction of smart courts.[3]

Since then, AI and other digital technologies have been applied to various stages of litigation, from case filing and case management to trial proceedings. For instance, courts have outsourced the development of intelligent systems to commercial partners who, among other things, develop applications for retrieving similar cases or recommending custodial sentences.

The application of AI to the criminal domain has attracted both praise and criticism. On the one hand, algorithmic guidance can help maintain consistency across cases, thereby achieving the ideal of having like cases decided alike.[4] On the other hand, AI can also set back the pursuit of substantive justice.[5] Algorithms may propagate bias, especially when they are hidden or not well understood.[6] They may not always be able to balance social and moral values when recommending punishment. Moreover, the intrusion of AI into adjudication, even in an advisory capacity, could blur responsibility for judicial errors due to the separation of legal professional knowledge and technical knowledge. The sophistication of algorithmic systems and the technical expertise required to design them might also result in legal policy being made in the private sphere by technology firms rather than in the public sphere by the political-legal organs.

Despite some extravagant reports on social media and in the popular press about robot judges taking the bench in China,[7] the role of AI in practice remains supportive and auxiliary; decisions are rendered by human judges, not AI systems. Will AI eventually come to replace human judgment and discretion? Prevailing sentiment suggests not. Permitting an algorithm to make decisions on its own exacerbates the accountability and legitimacy concerns touched on above. Moreover, there are persistent worries that automated adjudication might violate a defendant's right to due process.

This chapter will summarise current applications of AI in Chinese criminal sentencing and empirical evidence of the legal community's reception of major functions that have been applied. It will then sketch some misgivings about the use of AI in criminal proceedings before addressing future directions.

B. APPLICATION OF AI IN CHINESE CRIMINAL SENTENCING

The public demand for legality and fairness provides some of the political impetus for technologising the legal system.[8] Secretary-General Xi Jinping has made it a priority that 'people feel fairness and justice in every judicial case'.[9] AI can improve the operational efficiency of the courts, which have been experiencing an explosion in caseloads. AI can also enhance the consistency of adjudicative outcomes and discipline judicial decision-making.[10] In response to the national smart court initiative, local courts have introduced – and advertised – a range of AI solutions. There is not any nationally supplied or approved AI system for criminal sentencing. AI applications vary from region to region and within the judiciary hierarchy. The Shanghai High People's Court, for instance, unveiled the 'Shanghai Intelligent Assist Case Handling System for Criminal Cases' in 2017 to great fanfare. This criminal case management system, also dubbed the '206 System', offers a suite of twenty-four utilities, including review of arrest conditions, electronic file transfer, scheduling of meetings case retrieval, sentencing recommendation, indexing of professional knowledge, document generation, case procedure supervision, audio and video recording, etc.[11]

Although the AI solutions deployed in local courts may be built by different developers and trained on different databases, they tend to share some basic functions. One such function is case retrieval, that is, the task of identifying cases that are close to a given query case. Sentencing disparities for the same crime have, in recent years, provoked public disquiet about the injustice of identical cases being decided un-identically ('同案不同判').[12] The comparison of like cases promotes unity and consistency in the application of the law. Case retrieval has garnered even more importance in 2021 following the SPC's promulgation of the Implementation Measures for the Uniform

Application of Law by the Supreme People's Court.[13] Among other things, these measures require judges to address similar case search in their trial reports or prepare a separate similar case search report.[14]

Since there is no nationally adopted case retrieval system, local courts have acquired their own software and platforms. To illustrate, the High People's Court of Inner Mongolia employs Faxin Zhitui ('法信智推'),[15] a system that automatically extracts and mines the summary and basic facts of an input case to produce a report of similar cases, relevant legal provisions, prior or pending cases involving the same parties, and serial cases.[16] Faxin Zhitui reportedly scours over 120 million judgments, 120 million items of legal scholarship and data on about 230 million cases to generate this information. To take another example, the Yili Kazakh Autonomous Prefecture Branch of the Xinjiang Uygur Autonomous Region High People's Court uses a system featuring three search modalities in the form of a desktop site, a mobile app, and a word processor plug-in.[17] The desktop site allows the judge to specify a number of search criteria, including the pertinent document sections and the logical relationship between keywords. The mobile app, by contrast, automatically extracts key information from an input document; judges do not have to enter any search terms and need only select from the machine-generated tags to obtain relevant results.[18]

Overall, however, due to technical obstacles, data limitations and institutional inertia, case retrieval algorithms have not profoundly changed judicial practice. The glowing publicity about many case retrieval tools is belied by poor functionality and low uptake.[19] Some judges are unaware that their courts have a case retrieval tool,[20] and those who are have complained that the software does not meet their use requirements.[21]

Another common function of AI solutions is recommending sentences. Sentencing recommendations can be made based on legislative interpretations, judicial interpretations and the implementation rules of provincial sentencing guidelines or on previous cases. The application Little Judge Bao, developed by an interdisciplinary team of subject matter experts, combines both approaches to predict sentences.[22] Little Judge Bao is now in service in various courts and is also consulted by other political-legal organs. The Qingyuan Qingcheng District Procuratorate, for one, in Guangdong Province has used Little Judge Bao to prepare sentencing suggestions since October 2022.[23] These suggestions, it is claimed, were all accepted by the courts.[24]

The Shanghai High People's Court's 206 also learns from past cases to give sentencing predictions and recommendations.[25] The 206 System pulls from criminal case documents data about statutory punishment, benchmark punishment, and declared punishment. It also extracts information about sentencing circumstances, discretionary factors, and historical factors to create a training set for machine learning. The statistical model learned by the machine generates sentencing recommendations for the reference of judges and prosecutors.[26] Created by iFLYTEK in 2017, the 206 System is now in its fourth iteration. Analogous criminal case management systems designed by iFLYTEK have been adopted by judicial institutions in Anhui, Shanxi, Guizhou, Xinjiang, Shenzhen, Henan, Qinghai, and other provinces.[27] But not all courts in the country are equivalently equipped.[28]

AI recommendations of sentences are not uncontroversial. There is a worry that algorithmic suggestions, despite their non-binding nature, will distort the independent judgment of the human decision-maker, thereby occasioning mistakes or bias.[29] The heavy caseload confronted by judges may cause them to acquiesce in AI suggestions. Others downplay this threat, arguing to the contrary that algorithmic assistance enhances the precision of sentencing by displacing the multitude of factors that might otherwise bear on the judicial mind.[30] There is also anxiety in some quarters about the lack of transparency into the predictive model used to generate sentence recommendations.[31] To assuage this fear, some have called for AI suggestions to be confined to more simple and clear cases and for suggestions to be accompanied by reasons.[32]

Yet another function of AI solutions is to warn legal decision-makers about dispositions that deviate too far from the norm. The application of a legal rule is an exercise in normative reasoning that calls for social and moral judgment. There can therefore be reasonable disagreement about the results that should follow from any given set of facts.[33] At the same time, gross discrepancies in otherwise undistinguishable cases foster sentiments of unfairness and suspicions of favouritism. The phenomenon of 'identical cases being decided un-identically' can therefore hurt judicial credibility and undermine public trust in the legal system.[34] The monitoring of judicial outcomes by AI can discourage judges from straying too far from some defined standard. In so doing, AI serves as a check on judicial arbitrariness and corruption[35] and furthers the cause of having 'identical cases decided identically'.[36] Indeed, the SPC has promoted intelligent warnings in the adjudicatory phase as a mechanism for regulating judges and guaranteeing a fair outcome.[37]

Jiangsu High People's Court's AI warning platform is illustrative. The platform comprises five functional modules: similar case recommendation, legal knowledge references, intelligent assistance in sentencing, intelligent error correction, and warning of sentencing deviation.[38] The platform automatically captures case file materials and calculates a deviance ratio by comparing the predicted and actual sentences.[39] A warning is triggered when the deviance ratio exceeds a fixed threshold.[40]

Although this cautionary function of AI is, in principle, attractive, establishing the outer limits of sentencing variation is a vexed issue.[41] The difficulty is not merely an empirical one. Implicated in the determination of these limits are questions about the reasonable bounds of judicial discretion and the validity of social or cultural considerations for culpability,[42] and hence whether these factors should be considered by AI in computing sentencing norms. The threshold for deviance ratios like the one described above is often set between 5% and 30% although no rationale has been proffered for the choices made.[43] Some propose that sentencing norms should be derived from the collective experience of criminal judges.[44] Others maintain that procedural regularity, not artificially imposed sentencing ranges, is ultimately the best safeguard against judicial wilfulness and malfeasance.[45]

C. MISGIVINGS ABOUT THE USE OF AI IN CRIMINAL PROCEEDINGS

AI, even when performing an assistive or advisory role, may alter case outcomes.[46] For this reason, even relatively modest applications of AI to the criminal domain have been questioned and criticised. There are several pervasive anxieties about involving AI in criminal proceedings.

First, algorithmic 'black boxes' vitiate the transparency and fairness of criminal proceedings.[47] AI systems can be opaque or uninterpretable, raising doubts about the accuracy and aptness of their suggestions.[48] Algorithms trained on human decisions will learn the biases manifested in those outcomes. This may occur even if algorithms are denied access to protected or special characteristics. The impenetrability of AI shields these biases from public scrutiny, thereby allowing discrimination to be reproduced and even amplified under the guise of scientific objectivity.[49] Although human judges are not free from prejudice and may not be completely forthcoming about their motivations, they are at least constrained by the collegiate panel, the duty to give reasons, and, in China, personal accountability for their reasons.[50] The advent of AI in criminal proceedings can therefore diminish public confidence in the justice system, particularly if judges take algorithmic guidance as justification for their decisions.[51]

Second, AI is thought to be incapable of making the social and moral judgments necessary to reach a fair and reasonable ('合情合理', *heqing heli*) outcome.[52] Criminal sentencing, in particular, calls for a balancing of competing goods, interests, and values. Although the notion of 'public policy and ethics' ('公序良俗', *gongxu liangsu*) is not formally recognised in PRC criminal law, it is a de facto principle of criminal judicial practice to take societal attitudes, practices and discourse into account when passing on a case.[53] AI, it is held, does not have the normative sensibility to articulate the demands of morality for any given set of facts.[54] To the degree, then, that AI influences judicial outcomes, sentencing decisions will fail to give full expression to the requirements of morality and the law.[55]

Third, reliance on AI in criminal proceedings could undermine the adjudicatory and policymaking authority of judicial institutions.[56] PRC courts usually do not have the technical wherewithal to develop their own AI systems; most if not all of the solutions they adopt are procured or commissioned from technology firms.[57] In the course of designing software, these companies make choices that have implications for how the law is interpreted, applied and even made. Take, for example, the threshold for the deviance ratio above which an intended decision is to receive an AI warning. The default parameter for this threshold, if set by the software developer, will shape the sentencing behaviour of judges.[58] The intelligentisation of judicial processes therefore opens a channel for private actors to exercise public prerogatives.[59] Intentional or not, such arrogation of power is all the more disturbing in the sentencing context where the state's agents are invoking its monopoly on force against the individual. Although some might believe the danger to be minimal, these worries are exacerbated when judges repose too much confidence in their algorithmic aides.[60]

Concomitantly, the participation of AI in criminal cases risks blurring the responsibility for judicial mistakes.[61] Under the PRC Criminal Procedure Law, courts have the right to conduct trials and judges are accountable for the cases they try.[62] But the intervention of AI in sentencing raises the difficult issue of who ought to be held responsible if things go awry.[63] Some maintain that a decision-maker can be legally liable only if it can explain its decision.[64] The inexplicability of algorithmic reasoning renders it immune to legal liability; accountability must therefore be borne by the human judge. Or so the argument goes. Others locate the true source of the conflict in the separation of legal professional knowledge and technical knowledge.[65] When AI dominates criminal proceedings, it is the algorithmic designers who are in charge because only they possess the relevant technical expertise. On this line of reasoning, it is they rather than judges who must bear responsibility for AI-induced errors. Still others have insisted that it is judges who must ultimately be answerable for mistakes occasioned by their blind deference to algorithms.[66] But how about situations where the mistake could not have been avoided by judicial diligence or where it surfaced only following advances in the state of the art?[67] In sum, the emerging role of AI in criminal proceedings might render the boundaries of responsibility ambiguous[68] and diminish public trust in judicial authority.[69]

D. FUTURE DIRECTIONS

As technology advances, China continues to explore the integration of justice and technology. In 2024, Suzhou Central Court launched a new generation of artificial intelligence-assisted case handling systems called 'Future Judge Assistant'.[70] In addition to the aforementioned functions, this AI system has autonomous learning capabilities. With the continuous accumulation of case data, the system can continue to learn and iterate on its own, increasingly improving the identification of case characteristics, understanding of legal knowledge, and accuracy of similar case analysis, and continuously improving the overall efficiency of case-handling.[71] As described by Jiangsu Economic News, 'Future Judge Assistant' will give the judicial system the 'strongest intellectual brain'.[72]

AI holds out the promise of faster, cheaper justice and there is no doubt it will find more and greater applications in the Chinese legal system.[73] But will AI ever come to pronounce verdicts and sentences upon criminal defendants?[74] The answer depends on whether ordinary people can accept algorithmic judgment[75] and continue to 'trust the judicial system and feel the concern of the government'.[76]

The prospects so far are not optimistic. Trial by AI appears to compromise fundamental due process rights guaranteed by the PRC Constitution and Criminal Procedural Law. To take a simple example, criminal defendants have a constitutional right to defend themselves. But AI, at present, does not seem capable of affording defendants a meaningful hearing or of responding in a deliberative manner to defendants' claims and arguments.[77] Algorithmically administered justice can therefore erode the legitimacy of the criminal law and legal institutions. Indeed, our own research finds that in the criminal context, human judges are broadly perceived as being procedurally fairer than AI. Additionally, the issue of liability when AI causes risk and damage is also up for debate.[78] The nation's highest court seems to agree. In a December 2022 opinion on the subject, the SPC instructed that:

> AI shall not make judicial decisions substituting for the judge in any case, disregarding technology advancement. The results from AI shall be for supplemental references only, for adjudication or judicial supervision and management. Ensuring all judicial decisions are made by the judicature, all judicial powers are administered by adjudicative authorities, and all judicial accountability ultimately falls on the decision-maker. All users have the right to decide whether or not to use judicial AI assistance and the right to terminate their interface with AI products and services.[79]

It is therefore clear that, for the time being, AI will at most serve as an adjunct to human judgment and decision-making in Chinese criminal sentencing.

NOTES

1. Informatisation refers to the act and process of using information technology such as data platform, internet, big data and artificial intelligence in the trial and management of the court to improve the quality and efficiency of work and intelligent technology is the conversion of available information into knowledge, which in turn guides the achievement of goals in an intelligent manner. Qiang Li, '信息化建设: 全业务网上办理, 全方位智能服务 [Informatization construction: full-service online processing, all-round intelligent services]' *People's Court Daily* (20 March 2018) <http://rmfyb.chinacourt.org/paper/html/2018-03/20/content_136997.htm?div=-1> (accessed 10 May 2023); Xi Zheng, '我国法院信息化建设的未来面向 [The Future Orientation of China's Court Information Construction]' *People's Court Daily* (16 July 2020) <http://rmfyb.chinacourt.org/paper/html/2020-07/16/content_170194.htm?div=-1> (accessed 10 May 2023).

2. State Council, '国务院关于印发十三五国家信息化规划的通知 [The State Council on the Issuance of Notice of the "Thirteenth Five-Year Plan" National Informatization Plan]'.
3. People's Court News and Media Agency, '周强对全国法院网络安全和信息化工作提出要求强调, 深入学习贯彻习近平总书记关于网络强国的重要思想, 全面深化智慧法院建设[Zhou Qiang Stressed on the National Court Network Security and Information Work Requirements, In-depth Study and Implementation of General Secretary Xi Jinping's Important Ideas on Network Power, Deepen the Construction of Intelligent Courts]' <https://www.court.gov.cn/zixun-xiangqing-183782.html> (accessed 10 May 2023).
4. Xinli Yuan and Yuanyuan JI, 'Rengong Zhineng Dui Sifa Lingyu De Zhengfu Shuangchong Gongneng (人工智能对司法领域的"正负"双重功能) [The "positive and negative" dual function of artificial intelligence for the judicial field]' (2018) *Guangxi Social Sciences* 100.
5. Xiaoxiao Wu, 'Rengong Zhineng Falv Yingyong De Lilun Zhengyi Yu Xianshi Kunjing (人工智能法律应用的理论争议与现实困境) [Theoretical Controversies and Practical Dilemmas of Legal Applications of Artificial Intelligence]' (2022) FaZhi BoLan 160.
6. Xiaobin Weng and Shuhui Rao, 'Rengong Zhineng Sifa Juece De Kejieshixing Jiqi Lujing Yanjiu (人工智能司法决策的可解释性及其路径研究) [Research on the Interpretability of Artificial Intelligence Judicial Decision-Making and Its Path]' (2022) *Tribune of Study* 130.
7. Leonard Manson, 'China Uses Robot Judges To Pass Sentences On Various Types Of Misdemeanors' <https://www.somagnews.com/china-uses-robot-judges-to-pass-sentences-on-various-types-of-misdemeanors/> (accessed 10 May 2023); Joshua Park, 'Your Honor, AI' <https://hir.harvard.edu/your-honor-ai/> (accessed 10 May 2023); Chris Pleasance, 'China uses AI to "improve" courts – with computers "correcting perceived human errors in a verdict" and judges forced to submit a written explanation to the machine if they disagree' <https://www.dailymail.co.uk/news/article-11010077/Chinese-courts-allow-AI-make-rulings-charge-people-carry-punishments.html> (accessed 10 May 2023).
8. Benjamin Minhao Chen and Zhiyu Li, 'How Will Technology Change the Face of Chinese Justice?' (2020) 34 Colum. J. Asian L. 1.
9. Bo Peng, '顺应人民对公共安全司法公正权益保障的新期待, 全力推进平安中国法治中国过硬队伍建设' [In line with the people's new expectations for public safety, justice and the protection of rights and interests, and to promote peace and security in China, the rule of law in China to build a strong team]' *People's Daily* (8 January 2013) <http://cpc.people.com.cn/n/2013/0108/c64094-20125182.html> (accessed 10 May 2023).
10. Rachel E. Stern and others, 'Automating Fairness? Artificial Intelligence in the Chinese Courts' (2021) 59 *The Columbia Journal of Transnational Law* 515.
11. Yadong Cui, '司法科技梦: 上海刑事案件智能辅助办案系统的实践与思考 [Judicial Technology Dream: Practice and Reflections on Shanghai's Intelligent Assisted Case Management System for Criminal Cases] (2018) *People·Rule of Law* 92.
12. A prominent example concerns the purchase of replica guns. In 2019, a defendant who had purchased replica guns online was sentenced to seven years and three months in prison on a charge of smuggling firearms. The next year, a

defendant who had purchased replica guns in a toy market was convicted on a charge of illegal possession of firearms but escaped incarceration. In another case, the defendant's daughter said she had never imagined that similar cases could be decided un-identically and the sentence was so serious for her mother who held replica guns only for operating amusement programmes in the park. Fortunately, the sentence has been overturned in the appeal. In this case, the judge had greater discretion of application of law due to ambiguous standards of identifying weapons, making it possible for "identical cases" to be decided "un-identically". The case also aroused public concern and judicial authorities were required to improve the management of replica guns. Yang Wang, '统一裁判标准避免"同案不同判" [Uniform Adjudication Standards to Avoid "Different Judgments in the Same Case"]' *Legal Daily* (2 June 2020) <https://m.yunnan.cn/system/2020/06/02/030692782.shtml> (accessed 10 May 2023); Jiakun Pan, Mengyao Wang and Linyue Wu, '"天津大妈"非法持枪案改判缓刑 [The "Tianjin Auntie" Illegal Gun Case Sentenced to Probation]' *BeijingNews* (27 January 2017) <http://news.sohu.com/20170127/n479629288.shtml> (accessed 10 May 2023).

13. The Supreme People's Court, '《最高人民法院统一法律适用工作实施办法》理解与适用 [Understanding and Application of Implementation Measures of Uniform Law Application Work by the Supreme People's Court]'.
14. Ibid.
15. The High People's Court of Inner Mongolia, '解锁法院"黑科技" [Unlock Courts' "Black Technology"]' <https://www.sohu.com/a/517759509_121106854> (accessed 10 May 2023).
16. China Judgment Online, Faxin resource library and the Supreme Court's big data management and service platform are three major legal databases in China. Similar cases are cases that share similarities in the basic facts, the focus of the dispute, and the application of the law. Related cases refer to those where the cases are connected or people involved in the cases are connected. String cases involve a series of different cases but, through the analysis of the means of crime, traces, physical evidence, etc., these cases are put together to solve a crime. Yongfeng Hou, '"法信智推"系统帮法官解类案检索难题目前已收入9000万份文书和1.9亿案件信息 [The system of "Faxin Zhitui" helps judges to solve the problem of case retrieval, which has already collected 90 million judgments and 190 million cases]' <http://ln.people.com.cn/n2/2020/0803/c378317-34200689.html> (accessed 10 May 2023).
17. Zhiyuan Yin, '新疆高院伊犁哈萨克自治州分院：部署类案推送系统，致力于解决"类案不同判"的问题 [Yili Kazakh Autonomous Prefecture Branch of Xinjiang High Court: Deploying Case Push System to Solve the Problem of Different Judgments for Different Types of Cases]' <https://mp.weixin.qq.com/s/JnhokY5SUHGkqTNz5FuWFQ> (accessed 10 May 2023).
18. Ibid.
19. Weimin Zuo, 'Ruhe Tongguo Rengong Zhineng Shixian Leian Leipan (如何通过人工智能实现类案类判) [How to achieve class judgment through artificial intelligence] (2018) *China Law Review* 26.
20. The author interviewed some judges from different regions.
21. Zuo, 'Ruhe Tongguo Rengong Zhineng Shixian Leian Leipan (如何通过人工智能实现类案类判) [How to achieve class judgment through artificial intelligence]'.

22. Xiaobaogong (小包公), '小包公精准对接"规范量刑程序" [Xiaobaogong Precisely Aligned "Standardized Sentencing Procedures"]' <https://mp.weixin.qq.com/s/BR5zgga4lrzy6_hf7K6ckA> (accessed 10 May 2023).
23. Xiaobaogong(小包公), '小包公赋能清远检察院全方位落实科技强检战略 [Xiaobaogong Empowers Qingyuan Procuratorate to Implement A Comprehensive Technology-enhanced Prosecution Strategy]' <https://mp.weixin.qq.com/s/38WMGd89b4NrkRsbCdow2w> (accessed 10 May 2023).
24. Liu Dong, '拥有9大功能！这款人工智能法律软件用户突破20万 [With 9 Major Functions! This AI Legal Software Exceeds 200,000 Users]' *Yangcheng Evening News* (13 October 2022) <https://k.sina.com.cn/article_2131593523_7f0d8933020018uui.html> (accessed 10 May 2023).
25. Yadong Cui, *Artificial intelligence and judicial modernization* (Springer, 2020).
26. Ibid.
27. iFlYTEK, '刘庆峰作为法治论坛唯一企业代表发表主题演讲 [Liu Qingfeng Delivered A Speech As the Only Corporate Representative of the Rule of Law Forum]' <http://www.iflytek.com/news/2016> (accessed 10 May 2023).
28. Weimin Zuo, 'AI Faguan De Shidai Huidaolaima – Jiyu Zhongwai Sifa Rengong Zhineng De Duibi Yu Zhanwang (AI法官的时代会到来吗——基于中外司法人工智能的对比与展望) [Will the Era of AI Judges Come – A Comparison and Outlook Based on Judicial AI in China and Abroad]' (2021) 39 *Tribune of Political Science and Law* 3.
29. Hang Zhen, 'Rengong Zhineng Jieru Liangxing Jizhi: Kunjing, Dingwei Yu Jiegou (人工智能介入量刑机制：困境、定位与解构) [Artificial Intelligence Intervention in Sentencing Mechanism: Dilemma, Positioning and Deconstruction]' [2020] *Journal of Chongqing University* (Social Science Edition) 1.
30. Xiang Ge, 'Sifa Shijian Zhong Rengong Zhineng Yunyong De Xianshi Yu Qianzhan – Yi Shanghai Fayuan Xingzheng Anjian Zhineng Fuzhu Banan Xitong Wei Canzhao (司法实践中人工智能运用的现实与前瞻--以上海法院行政案件智能辅助办案系统为参照) [The Reality and Foresight of Artificial Intelligence Use in Judicial Practice – With Reference to the Intelligent Assisted Case Handling System for Administrative Cases in Shanghai Courts]' (2018) 21 *ECUPL Journal* 67.
31. Lunsheng Wang, 'Dashuju Yu Rengong Zhineng Jishu Yingyong De Fengxian Ji Lunli Guizhi (大数据与人工智能技术应用的风险及伦理规制) [Risks and Ethical Regulation of Big Data and Artificial Intelligence Technology Applications]' (2019) 36 *Studies in Law and Business* 101.
32. Zhen, 'Rengong Zhineng Jieru Liangxing Jizhi: Kunjing, Dingwei Yu Jiegou (人工智能介入量刑机制：困境、定位与解构) [Artificial Intelligence Intervention in Sentencing Mechanism: Dilemma, Positioning and Deconstruction]' (n. 29).
33. Hongmin Liu, '"同案不同判"的实证分析及解决路径 [Empirical Analysis of "Different Judgments in the Same Case" and the Solution Path]' <http://jzzy.hncourt.gov.cn/public/detail.php?id=14604> (accessed 10 May 2023).
34. Ibid.
35. Li Zhang, '坚持辅助审判定位, 积极拥抱司法人工智能 [Adhere to the Positioning of Auxiliary Trial, Actively Embrace Judicial Artificial Intelligence]' <http://www.cac.gov.cn/2019-07/21/c_1124779116.htm> (accessed 11 May 2023).

36. Jiangsu High People's Court, '"江苏法院"同案不同判预警平台 [Jiangsu Court "Early Warning Platform for Different Judgments in the Same Case"]' <https://www.faanw.com/zhihuifayuan/333.html> (accessed 11 May 2023).
37. The Supreme People's Court, 关于规范和加强人工智能司法应用的意见 [The Opinions on Regulating and Strengthening the Applications of Artificial Intelligence in the Judicial Fields].
38. Similar case recommendation serves as case retrieval system to identify similar cases for judges before sentencing. The platform will match the relevant professional knowledge base to the current case and search laws, regulations, rules, etc. from all over the country, for case references, reducing the judge's workload and improving legal application. According to legal rules and sentences of similar cases, the system suggests a sentence to judges. It can also automatically detect writing errors in adjudication documents, such as written errors in verdict results, wrong amount and quantity units, etc. Finally, the warning system will work when the decision made by judges deviates far from the average sentencing range. <https://www.faanw.com/zhihuifayuan/333.html> (accessed on 18 February 2023).
39. Ibid.
40. Ibid.
41. Long Cheng, 'Rengong Zhineng Fuzhu Liangxing De Wenti Yu Chulu (人工智能辅助量刑的问题与出路) [Problems and Solutions of Artificial Intelligence-assisted Sentencing]' (2021) 51 *Journal of Northwest University* (Philosophy and Social Sciences Edition); Yuhao Wu, 'Liangxing Ziyou Cailiangquan De Bianjie: Jiti Jingyan, Geti Juece Yu Biancha Shibie (量刑自由裁量权的边界:集体经验、个体决策与偏差识别) [The Boundaries of Sentencing Discretion: Collective Experience, Individual Decision-Making, and Bias Identification]' (2021) 43 *Chinese Journal of Law* 109.
42. Yanhong Liu, 'Gongsifa Yitihua Shiye Xia Gongxu Liangsu Yuanze De Xingfa Shiyong (公私法一体化视野下公序良俗原则的刑法适用) [The Application of the Principle of Public Order and Good Custom in Criminal Law Based on the Perspective of the Integration of Public Law and Private Law]' (2020) 42 *Modern Law Science* 140.
43. Wenjie Feng, 'Rengong Zhineng Fuzhu Liangxing Gongzheng Quxiang De Shuangchong Goujian (人工智能辅助量刑公正取向的双重构建) [The dual construction of artificial intelligence-assisted sentencing justice orientation]' (2020) 35 *Journal of East China University of Science and Technology* (Social Science Edition) 114; Cheng, 'Rengong Zhineng Fuzhu Liangxing De Wenti Yu Chulu (人工智能辅助量刑的问题与出路) [Problems and Solutions of Artificial Intelligence-assisted Sentencing]'.
44. Wu, 'Liangxing Ziyou Cailiangquan De Bianjie: Jiti Jingyan, Geti Juece Yu Biancha Shibie (量刑自由裁量权的边界:集体经验、个体决策与偏差识别) [The Boundaries of Sentencing Discretion: Collective Experience, Individual Decision-Making, and Bias Identification]'.
45. Cheng (n. 41).
46. Xuejun Sheng and Yue Zou, 'Zhineng Jiqiren Faguan: Haiyou Duoshao Keneng He Bukeneng (智能机器人法官: 还有多少可能和不可能) [Robot Judges: How Many Possibilities and Impossibilities Are There]' (2018) 40 *Modern Law Science* 74.

47. Nu Wang, '"Black Box Justice": Robot Judges and AI-based Judgment Processes in China's Court System' (2020, IEEE International Symposium on Technology and Society (ISTAS)); Han Qin, 'Rengong Zhineng Sifa Caipan Xitong De Xueli Fansi (人工智能司法裁判系统的学理反思) [Theoretical Reflection on AI Judicial Judgment System]' (2021) 15 *Northern Legal Science* 115; Lingyu Meng, 'Cong Suanfa Pianjian Dao Suanfa Qishi: Suanfa Qishi De Zeren Wenti Tanjiu (从算法偏见到算法歧视：算法歧视的责任问题探究) [From Algorithm Bias to Algorithm Discrimination: Research on the Responsibility of Algorithmic Discrimination]' (2022) 24 *Journal of Northeastern University* (Social Science) 1.
48. Wang, '"Black Box Justice": Robot Judges and AI-based Judgment Processes in China's Court System'.
49. Zhanli Sun and Jinhao Hu, 'Rengong Zhineng Yingyun Yu Sifa Shenpan De Wenti Yu Yingdui (人工智能应用于司法审判的问题与应对) [Problems and countermeasures of the application of artificial intelligence in judicial trials]' (2021) 20 *Journal of Zhejiang University of Technology* (Social Science) 405; Meng (n. 47); Hongyan Wu, Di Xiang and Xin Li, *Fairness of Case Retrieval for Chinese Judicial System* (IEEE, 2021).
50. Qin (n. 47).
51. Wang, 'Dashuju Yu Rengong Zhineng Jishu Yingyong De Fengxian Ji Lunli Guizhi (大数据与人工智能技术应用的风险及伦理规制) [Risks and Ethical Regulation of Big Data and Artificial Intelligence Technology Applications]' (n. 31).
52. Yuan and JI, 'Rengong Zhineng Dui Sifa Lingyu De Zhengfu Shuangchong Gongneng (人工智能对司法领域的'正负'双重功能) [The "positive and negative" dual function of artificial intelligence for the judicial field]' (n. 4).
53. Liu (n. 42).
54. Sheng and Zou (n. 46).
55. Wang, '"Black Box Justice": Robot Judges and AI-based Judgment Processes in China's Court System'.
56. Zheng, 'Rengong Zhineng Jishu Zai Sifa Caipan Zhong De Yunyong Ji Guizhi (人工智能技术在司法裁判中的运用及规制) [The Use and Regulation of Artificial Intelligence Technology in Judicial Decisions]'.
57. Ibid.
58. Cheng (n. 41).
59. Lunsheng Wang, 'Dashuju Yu Rengong Zhineng Sifa YIngyong De Huayu Chongtu Jiqi Lilun Jiedu (大数据与人工智能司法应用的话语冲突及其理论解读) [The Discourse Conflict of Judicial Applications of Big Data and Artificial Intelligence and Its Theoretical Interpretation]' (2018) 33 *Legal Forum* 137; Wang, 'Dashuju Yu Rengong Zhineng Jishu Yingyong De Fengxian Ji Lunli Guizhi (大数据与人工智能技术应用的风险及伦理规制) [Risks and Ethical Regulation of Big Data and Artificial Intelligence Technology Applications]' (n. 31).
60. Ji, 'Rengong Zhineng Shidai De Sifaquan Zhibian (人工智能时代的司法权之变) [The Change of Judicial Power in the Era of Artificial Intelligence]'.
61. Yanhong Liu, 'Rengong Zhineng De Kejieshixing Yu AI De Falv Zeren Wenti Yanjiu (人工智能的可解释性与 AI 的法律责任问题研究) [Study on the Explainability of Artificial Intelligence and the Legal Liability of AI]' (2022) 28 *Law and Social Development* 78.

62. Criminal Procedure Law of the People's Republic of China, art 4. (《中华人民共和国刑事诉讼法》第四条).
63. Ji (n. 60).
64. Liu, 'Rengong Zhineng De Kejieshixing Yu AI De Falv Zeren Wenti Yanjiu (人工智能的可解释性与 AI 的法律责任问题研究) [Study on the Explainability of Artificial Intelligence and the Legal Liability of AI]' (n. 61).
65. Wang, 'Dashuju Yu Rengong Zhineng Sifa YIngyong De Huayu Chongtu Jiqi Lilun Jiedu (大数据与人工智能司法应用的话语冲突及其理论解读) [The Discourse Conflict of Judicial Applications of Big Data and Artificial Intelligence and Its Theoretical Interpretation]' (n. 59).
66. Meng (n. 47).
67. Zhou and Wu, 'Rengong Zhineng Sifa Juece De Keneng Yu Xiandu (人工智能司法决策的可能与限度) [The Possibilities and Limits of Artificial Intelligence for Judicial Decision-Making]'.
68. Ji (n. 60).
69. Wang, 'Dashuju Yu Rengong Zhineng Jishu Yingyong De Fengxian Ji Lunli Guizhi (大数据与人工智能技术应用的风险及伦理规制) [Risks and Ethical Regulation of Big Data and Artificial Intelligence Technology Applications]' (n. 31).
70. Ting Yue, 'AI赋能"未来法官助手"苏州中院打造"数字正义"新标杆 [AI-enabled "Future Judge Assistant" Suzhou Central Court creates a new benchmark for "digital justice"]' <http://js.news.cn/20240409/904d131ddb294c2aa8ff3a3548dc41cd/c.html> (accessed 20 April 2024).
71. Ibid.
72. Jiangsu Economic News <https://www.sohu.com/a/769688943_121149620> (accessed 20 April 2024).
73. The SPC has set 2025 and 2030 targets for the integration of AI into the judicial system. The Supreme People's Court, '关于规范和加强人工智能司法应用的意见 [The Opinions on Regulating and Strengthening the Applications of Artificial Intelligence in the Judicial Fields]' <https://www.court.gov.cn/fabu-xiangqing-382461.html> (accessed 11 May 2023).
74. Chen and Li (n. 8).
75. Zuo (n. 28).
76. Xin Wen <https://bjhdfy.bjcourt.gov.cn/article/detail/2021/09/id/6258172.shtml> (accessed 11 May 2023).
77. Ibid.
78. Hong Zhao, '全球教席课堂76讲 Benjamin Liebman：人工智能与司法 [Global Chair Lecture 76 Benjamin Liebman: Artificial Intelligence and Justice]' <https://www.law.pku.edu.cn/xwzx/xwdt/5afe4d2217e241e38efb8e5bbd7a7bab.htm> (accessed 24 April 2024).
79. The Supreme People's Court, 《最高人民法院统一法律适用工作实施办法》理解与适用 *[Understanding and Application of Implementation Measures of Uniform Law Application Work by the Supreme People's Court]*.

REFERENCES

Chen, B.M. and Li, Z., 'How Will Technology Change the Face of Chinese Justice?' (2020) 34 Colum. J. Asian L. 1.

Cheng, L., 'Rengong Zhineng Fuzhu Liangxing De Wenti Yu Chulu (人工智能辅助量刑的问题与出路) [Problems and Solutions of Artificial Intelligence-assisted Sentencing]' (2021) 51 *Journal of Northwest University* (Philosophy and Social Sciences Edition).

Cui, Y., *Artificial intelligence and judicial modernization* (Springer, 2020).

Cui, Y., '司法科技梦: 上海刑事案件智能辅助办案系统的实践与思考 [Judicial Technology Dream: Practice and Reflections on Shanghai's Intelligent Assisted Case Management System for Criminal Cases]' (2018) *People·Rule of Law* 92.

Feng, W., 'Rengong Zhineng Fuzhu Liangxing Gongzheng Quxiang De Shuangchong Goujian (人工智能辅助量刑公正取向的双重构建) [The dual construction of artificial intelligence-assisted sentencing justice orientation]' (2020) 35 *Journal of East China University of Science and Technology* (Social Science Edition) 114.

Ge, X., 'Sifa Shijian Zhong Rengong Zhineng Yunyong De Xianshi Yu Qianzhan – Yi Shanghai Fayuan Xingzheng Anjian Zhineng Fuzhu Banan Xitong Wei Canzhao (司法实践中人工智能运用的现实与前瞻--以上海法院行政案件智能辅助办案系统为参照) [The Reality and Foresight of Artificial Intelligence Use in Judicial Practice – With Reference to the Intelligent Assisted Case Handling System for Administrative Cases in Shanghai Courts]' (2018) 21 *ECUPL Journal* 67.

Ji, W., 'Rengong Zhineng Shidai De Sifaquan Zhibian (人工智能时代的司法权之变) [The Change of Judicial Power in the Era of Artificial Intelligence]' (2018) *Oriental Law* 125.

Liu, Y., 'Gongsifa Yitihua Shiye Xia Gongxu Liangsu Yuanze De Xingfa Shiyong (公私法一体化视野下公序良俗原则的刑法适用) [The Application of the Principle of Public Order and Good Custom in Criminal Law Based on the Perspective of the Integration of Public Law and Private Law]' (2020) 42 *Modern Law Science* 140.

Liu, Y., 'Rengong Zhineng De Kejieshixing Yu AI De Falv Zeren Wenti Yanjiu (人工智能的可解释性与 AI 的法律责任问题研究) [Study on the Explainability of Artificial Intelligence and the Legal Liability of AI]' (2022) 28 *Law and Social Development* 78.

Meng, L., 'Cong Suanfa Pianjian Dao Suanfa Qishi: Suanfa Qishi De Zeren Wenti Tanjiu (从算法偏见到算法歧视: 算法歧视的责任问题探究) [From Algorithm Bias to Algorithm Discrimination: Research on the Responsibility of Algorithmic Discrimination]' (2022) 24 *Journal of Northeastern University* (Social Science) 1.

Qin, H., 'Rengong Zhineng Sifa Caipan Xitong De Xueli Fansi (人工智能司法裁判系统的学理反思) [Theoretical Reflection on AI Judicial Judgment System]' (2021) 15 *Northern Legal Science* 115.

Sheng, X. and Zou, Y., 'Zhineng Jiqiren Faguan: Haiyou Duoshao Keneng He Bukeneng (智能机器人法官: 还有多少可能和不可能) [Robot Judges:

How Many Possibilities and Impossibilities Are There]' (2018) 40 *Modern Law Science* 74.

Stern, R. E. and others, 'Automating Fairness? Artificial Intelligence in the Chinese Courts' (2021) 59 *The Columbia Journal of Transnational Law* 515.

Sun, Z. and Hu, J., 'Rengong Zhineng Yingyun Yu Sifa Shenpan De Wenti Yu Yingdui (人工智能应用于司法审判的问题与应对) [Problems and countermeasures of the application of artificial intelligence in judicial trials]' (2021) 20 *Journal Of Zhejiang University Of Technology* (Social Sciences) 405.

Wang, L., 'Dashuju Yu Rengong Zhineng Sifa YIngyong De Huayu Chongtu Jiqi Lilun Jiedu (大数据与人工智能司法应用的话语冲突及其理论解读) [The Discourse Conflict of Judicial Applications of Big Data and Artificial Intelligence and Its Theoretical Interpretation]' (2018) 33 *Legal Forum* 137.

Wang, L., 'Dashuju Yu Rengong Zhineng Jishu Yingyong De Fengxian Ji Lunli Guizhi (大数据与人工智能技术应用的风险及伦理规制) [Risks and Ethical Regulation of Big Data and Artificial Intelligence Technology Applications]' (2019) 36 *Studies in Law and Business* 101.

Wang, N., '"Black Box Justice": Robot Judges and AI-based Judgment Processes in China's Court System' (IEEE, 2020).

Weng, X. and Rao, S., 'Rengong Zhineng Sifa Juece De Kejieshixing Jiqi Lujing Yanjiu (人工智能司法决策的可解释性及其路径研究) [Research on the Interpretability of Artificial Intelligence Judicial Decision-Making and Its Path]' (2022) *Tribune of Study* 130.

Wu, H., Xiang, D. and Li, X., 'Fairness of Case Retrieval for Chinese Judicial System' (IEEE, 2021).

Wu, X., 'Rengong Zhineng Falv Yingyong De Lilun Zhengyi Yu Xianshi Kunjing (人工智能法律应用的理论争议与现实困境) [Theoretical Controversies and Practical Dilemmas of Legal Applications of Artificial Intelligence]' (2022) FaZhi BoLan 160.

Wu, Y., 'Liangxing Ziyou Cailiangquan De Bianjie: Jiti Jingyan, Geti Juece Yu Biancha Shibie (量刑自由裁量权的边界:集体经验、个体决策与偏差识别) [The Boundaries of Sentencing Discretion: Collective Experience, Individual Decision-Making, and Bias Identification]' (2021) 43 *Chinese Journal of Law* 109.

Yuan, X. and JI, Y., 'Rengong Zhineng Dui Sifa Lingyu De Zhengfu Shuangchong Gongneng (人工智能对司法领域的"正负"双重功能) [The "positive and negative" dual function of artificial intelligence for the judicial field]' (2018) *Guangxi Social Sciences* 100.

Zhen, H., 'Rengong Zhineng Jieru Liangxing Jizhi: Kunjing, Dingwei Yu Jiegou (人工智能介入量刑机制：困境、定位与解构) [Artificial Intelligence Intervention in Sentencing Mechanism: Dilemma, Positioning and Deconstruction]' (2020) *Journal of Chongqing University* (Social Science Edition) 1.

Zheng, X., 'Rengong Zhineng Jishu Zai Sifa Caipan Zhong De Yunyong Ji Guizhi (人工智能技术在司法裁判中的运用及规制) [The Use and Regulation of Artificial Intelligence Technology in Judicial Decisions]' (2020) 32 *Peking University Law Journal* 674.

Zhou, S. and Wu, X., 'Rengong Zhineng Sifa Juece De Keneng Yu Xiandu (人工智能司法决策的可能与限度) [The Possibilities and Limits of Artificial Intelligence for Judicial Decision-Making]' (2019) 22 *ECUPL Journal* 53.

Zuo, W., 'Guanyu Falv Rengong Zhineng Zai Zhongguo Yunyong Qianjing De Ruogan Sikao (关于法律人工智能在中国运用前景的若干思考) [Thoughts on the prospects of using legal AI in China]' (2018) 12 *Tsinghua University Law Journal* 108.

Zuo, W., 'Ruhe Tongguo Rengong Zhineng Shixian Leian Leipan (如何通过人工智能实现类案类判) [How to achieve class judgment through artificial intelligence]' (2018) *China Law Review* 26.

Zuo, W., 'AI Faguan De Shidai Huidaolaima – Jiyu Zhongwai Sifa Rengong Zhineng De Duibi Yu Zhanwang (AI法官的时代会到来吗——基于中外司法人工智能的对比与展望) [Will the Era of AI Judges Come – A Comparison and Outlook Based on Judicial AI in China and Abroad]' (2021) 39 *Tribune of Political Science and Law* 3.

Part III

Challenging Technology

Chapter 10

The Routinisation and Depersonalisation of Justice

Jane Loo and Mark Findlay

A. INTRODUCTION

Recent developments in technology have altered the traditional face of the judiciary and are often represented as positively influencing the openness, accuracy and efficiency of information flow for the judiciary.[1] Technology has enabled enhanced access to online court records and documents ensuring accountability, virtual hearings have facilitated remote or difficult participation promoting court accessibility, and predictive algorithm tools are utilised to identify inconsistencies or trends in case outcomes, enabling greater overall consistency and transparency. Technology has also been increasingly harnessed in court systems for the purpose of case tracking, precedent analysis and writing decisions, promoting the productivity of the Courts.[2] However, even as legal technologies continue to evolve alongside new technological advancements and user demands/needs, it remains important to measure these benefits against a defendant's right of 'access to justice' and their due process rights.

This chapter first elaborates on how digitised justice can worsen the access to justice gap through the 'depersonalisation and routinisation of justice' service delivery.[3] Later, it offers recommendations for the design and deployment of more human-centric and inclusive AI in the judicial process.

B. WHAT IS DEPERSONALISED JUSTICE?

The delivery of justice is depersonalised when technology is deployed to substitute processes or services that presently involve a human actor or person-to-person experience. Take, for instance, when users seek to access court information but are directed towards technologies designed to replace personalised interactivity and services.

One notable example here would be the deployment of smart chatbots. Courts around the world have adopted AI chatbots to handle simple inquiries from the public and these AI chatbots have been fed with various questions and answer pairings, operating procedures and other court information so that when a question is posed by a court user, the bot can present an automated response. While the employment of these chatbots can be useful to manage simple public enquiries and move cases along more efficiently, occasions may arise where a user would require more information than what a chatbot can offer. For instance, when individuals are enquiring on more complex questions, or when certain questions and answer pairings are limited and lacking in important nuances. Similar to the use of other AI systems in the judiciary,[4] reliability, clarity and accuracy is also an issue with these chatbots. Additionally, in cases where users are diverted to chatbots (with no alternative to speak to a human personnel), users may experience frustration, impatience and annoyance[5] when they are unable to receive an appropriate answer to their question. Thus, while automation may arguably lead to more predictability and 'access' in the broader sense, the quality of personalised and individualised justice becomes the casualty since defendants are dealt with as a homogeneous group and could potentially be denied access to legally relevant information from in-person sources that might prove critical for securing their right to a fair trial.

The depersonalisation of justice is especially problematic when it surfaces in sentencing or mitigation decision-making. Traditional court processes value human sensitivity and judges' discretion but when replicated by automation (e.g. through the use of predictive algorithm tools), the algorithm may prioritise efficiency or other utilitarian considerations to the exclusion of basic principles such as fairness or transparency. Take, for example, the use of predictive algorithm tools by some courts for the purpose of making sentencing, probation and bail decisions. These programs make predictions about a defendant's risk of reoffending or fleeing based on variables such as a defendant's criminal record, their failure to attend court, crime severity and other factors deemed relevant or important by the risk prediction tool. However, for the appropriate cases, judges still need to apply their discretion according to individual case particularities to guarantee the doing of justice. The generalisation of certain cases into distinct categories by these predictive tools could potentially devalue and ignore the important role of the human judge. Technology cannot be a substitute for human judgement if justice demands subjective application.

To concretise these critical speculations, the chapter examines the use of electronic guilty pleas and the creation and delivery of automated mitigation pleas in the Singapore Courts.

In Singapore, it is possible to plead guilty by electronic means for some minor traffic offences after an offer of composition has expired.[6] These offences are typically offences committed under the Road Traffic Act or Parking Places Act.[7] A plea of guilt may be entered into at an AXS automatic bill-payment station, and the offender can plead guilty to the offence without needing to attend court.[8] In this expedited process, the accused may, however, lose out on the opportunity to consult a court personnel and it may also trivialise the importance of defendants requiring legal advice. In these cases, the accused may not appreciate the full nature of their plea and punishment because of a lack of information from automated options. This becomes especially problematic when the offence in question carries a possible imprisonment term.[9] What happens after the accused pleads guilty? Will pleading guilty result in a criminal record? The answers to these questions are not always immediately obvious to an unrepresented accused and may demand critical interaction with the legal profession. However, when pleading electronically is presented as an option, the likelihood of an accused person preferring to go to court is sharply reduced since defendants are likely pick the option that is convenient and less intimidating. Additionally, it is important to consider whether such an electronic option might interfere with an accused fully appreciating what they are pleading guilty to and being punished for. When cases are dealt with in such an 'administrative' fashion, the majesty of the courts and the gravity or seriousness of the offence may be lost to the accused. Nonetheless, despite these limitations, digital innovations like electronic guilty pleas are still viewed favourably by some members of the legal profession as helping to speed up the sentencing process, especially for minor offences, thus enhancing court efficiency and optimising court resources.[10] Yet, as emphasised above, electronic guilty pleas cannot provide sufficiently personalised information to equip an accused with enough knowledge to make their judgement. Instead, they are designed to reduce individual choice to a simple 'yes/no' binary. The accused's experience in the conventional plea-bargaining process involving their lawyer and their in-person court attendance is now replaced with a push of a '*guilty*' button. The plea-bargaining process and public justice service delivery are depersonalised because the lawyer, the judge, the live court and its visitors are absent features in this digitised process. The human experience is limited, and any interaction is restricted to the digital screen. When these important characters and features are missing from this 'machine court', it cannot be said that justice is delivered in an impartial, fair, transparent and accountable manner that is productive to a defendant's due process rights.

Moving on to the use of electronic mitigation pleas, the Primary Justice Project at Singapore's Community Justice Centre offers accused persons the opportunity to draft their own e-guided mitigation pleas.[11] After such a plea is drafted, it is reviewed by a lawyer at a fixed fee during a one-hour legal consultation. Access to this e-mitigation platform is, however, only available to accused persons who are signed on to PJP's services.[12] The public has no general access to this service so the quality of this service/tool cannot be verified by the present writers. However, based on publicly available information, it appears that there are no restrictions on the type of cases that can utilise this e-guided option.[13] The CJC previously indicated that a 'mother [had] used the system to draft a mitigation plea for shoplifting'.[14] The outcome of the case is not known but it is notable that there is a mandatory imprisonment term (which may extend up to seven years) for shoplifting offences in Singapore.[15] Poorly drafted mitigation pleas, even with the help of these AI tools, by an unrepresented person so lacking in legal expertise and know-hows could interfere with the case outcome, including the severity of their punishment. While some may argue that such automated document systems are important because they assist the unrepresented litigant to produce legal documents and content through guided interviews[16] at their convenience and a more affordable price range, it must also be considered that these systems could concurrently marginalise an accused's due process protections and expectations for a fair hearing. For example, how is the accused to know what mitigating factors to input in their plea and whether the factors have been correctly applied or conveyed to the judge?

On how justice is depersonalised here, such interfaces fail to convey or may misrepresent to the accused the significance of adequate and individualised legal representation. The lawyer is removed from the legal process and the lawyer's role/expertise in drafting a mitigation plea for their client (that involves careful balancing and weighing of their client's circumstances) is substituted by an algorithm built on a limited dataset. These platforms may tempt the accused into believing that the quality of legal drafting secured is of a sufficient standard and quality as that offered by a human lawyer especially when such platforms are endorsed by official State bodies. Yet, there are always nuances in the facts of any alleged offence and in any individual's particular circumstance. Such variations cannot be adequately captured by standardised questions and answers in automated formats. A one-hour legal review of the plea by a legal professional, while important, may not adequately cover these peculiarities.

Further, the effectiveness and 'quality' of such standardised and repeated mitigation pleas in the mind of the judge as a sentencer also merits reflection. A judge going over hundreds of similar-sounding pleas that are already formatted in a homogeneous way may inadvertently overlook the uniqueness and particularities of each case. Justice is depersonalised because there is the danger that such 'template' documents may interfere with the judge's process or discretion in determining the appropriate individualised and personalised sentence.

C. WHAT IS ROUTINISED JUSTICE?

What about routinised justice that challenges a defendant's right of access to justice? Justice is routinised when certain court processes are automated through digitalisation without regard for individual vulnerability and due process protections. Routinised justice is introduced into the judicial system whenever there is a preference for (more) technology to achieve greater savings in terms of judicial resources and court time. Routinisation interferes with the delivery of impartial, fair, transparent, accountable and non-discriminatory justice.

One way to view routinised justice is likening it to a conveyor belt-type justice that is inserted to distance the accused from their trial. Routinised justice is justice that is processual and mundane; and it is precisely because tech is introduced in the judicial process for such monotonous, routinised and predictable processes and objectives, it is often taken for granted that the court process or service in question *always* protects and guarantees a defendant's right of access to justice. In reality, the nature of access and quality of justice may be completely diluted.

The routinisation of justice delivery goes a step further away from due process protections than depersonalised justice because not only are important personnel in the judicial process 'divorced from the loop', but the defendant or recipient of automated justice is also *excluded*, or 'silenced' from participation in their own proceedings. Justice is routinised whenever a defendant's issues are set up as less deserving of the court's procedural pedantic. The defendant is excluded from their own trial because access to the court system/services is limited or eliminated altogether by the use of 'routine' technologies. In other words, routinised justice is poorly executed justice that neglects to consider the diverse needs of a defendant. For example, justice is routinised when a defendant's digital literacy is lacking but they are forced to (unsuccessfully) adapt to the use of technology since there is a lack of a suitable non-digitised alternative. In this case, critical legal information or assistance may be blocked by the technology itself.

On the surface, routinised justice will outwardly appear to deliver more efficient processes and legal solutions: saving judicial resources, costs and time. Lacking deeper interrogation, this framing and output will motivate the deployment of more technologies that ignore each individual's unique needs in accessing justice. Routinising justice links to depersonalised justice insofar as there is a tendency to also remove individual human interaction and engagement from legal processes to force the defendant into technologised processes that do not necessarily promote their legal interests and rights. The nature of justice on offer is not based on respect for user/defendant needs but one that prefers advancing cost-benefit in administration. Routinised justice is always motivated by a utilitarian cost-benefit frame and convenience.

While routinised justice may come across as more streamlined and, as such, appear to promote access to justice pathways, the delivery and quality of justice itself may be fundamentally lacking. It is true that some of the processes or services 'routinised' are minor or inconsequential on an objective scale of offence seriousness but, particularly in countries where criminal punishments even at the lower end can be substantial, the importance of the outcome to the accused person should not be diminished, so due process rights must always be prioritised.

An example of routinised justice is the use of virtual/online court hearings. These virtual hearings have been employed to meet justice demands in recent years,[17] especially during the recent global health crisis, and will likely play an increasing role in Singapore's digital transformation in legal service delivery. Proponents of online hearings often argue that these hearings are more cost-effective, efficient, and promote better advocacy.[18] However, recourse to these technologies has also created new problems that will impact a defendant's access to justice. For instance, virtual hearings restrict the fluency of dialogues at trial, especially with regard to the presentation of evidence.[19] From a visual perspective, the sharing of legal documents on platforms such as Zoom can relegate the camera feeds of parties to the side or top of the screen where the camera feed of the person giving evidence is minimised, potentially obstructing the court's view of the individual.[20] The integrity of witnesses and their giving of evidence is also challenged by the use of virtual hearings through the unavailability or blocking of non-verbal cues which may be considered revealing by the courts. Digital trials can also render cross-examination difficult due to the lack of a 'frontal encounter'.[21] These online hearings may over or under-emphasise certain interactive gestures, impacting the accurate assessment of witness credibility.[22] Technical failures are also not uncommon[23] and both verbal/non-verbal cues may be distorted by interruptive video streams or the positioning of the video frame.[24]

In this online format, the defendant's participation is routinised as necessary, more efficient and the preferred option. This routinisation is problematic if the court fails to take into account the defendant's unique needs, the defendant is forced to participate against their will and is prevented from negotiating the format the trial should take. Due process safeguards are denied as the trial fails to compensate for how digitalisation might interfere with their physical participation. Additionally, the defendant's participation and presentation of their evidence is now also dependent on their comfort and familiarity with the technology. This digital infrastructure and device(s) contribute another layer of distancing between the accused and the court since technology adds a further realm of professional dependency which the accused must penetrate.

Further, this transition to online justice has the tendency to disregard the atmosphere and solemnity of in-person trials, including the presence of judicial authority.[25] But more than courtroom presentation and traditions, the majesty of the courts is arguably linked to the law's safeguarding of procedural fairness and due process protections. In 2020, a drug trafficker was sentenced to death via Zoom[26] in Singapore, marking the first time capital punishment was delivered remotely in the country. The handling of this case confirms the problems linked to the routinisation of justice. The needs of a defendant are minimised for the promise of more efficiency and speed, and to the extent that the delivery of justice becomes almost clinical, devoid of respect for defendants' ordinary human dignity.

Two other adverse considerations must be interrogated when thinking about the routinisation of justice: namely, *who* is left behind and *what* is at stake.

First addressing the question of *who* is left behind – routinised justice seeks to produce standardised processes that save judicial resources, costs and time. Motivated by this frame, technologies that are deployed tend to ignore vulnerable populations and their unique needs and characteristics in accessing justice. Certain court users, particularly litigants-in-person, may lack access to, or experience difficulty participating in, remote hearings.[27] Some parties may experience financial constraints influencing their ability or means to access digital solutions. Others may lack the necessary digital literacy/know-how to navigate case management systems or enter court applications online. As emphasised, these applications and softwares may appear accessible or simple enough for a defendant to navigate. However, it is precisely because tech is introduced for such monotonous, routinised and predictable processes, it is often taken for granted that a defendant can 'figure it out'. Yet, everyone possesses different levels of digital literacy and confidence when navigating digital solutions and services. A defendant's access to justice is compromised when he is prevented from accessing certain court services or processes due to his limited digital knowledge or comprehension.

Digitised legal aid delivery is an example of a service that could exclude persons who are less digitally equipped in terms of their access to digital tools or know-how. With the move and push towards online legal aid registrations/applications such as Singapore's Legal Aid Bureaus' 'save time go online'[28] messaging, if a defendant is unable to navigate these digitised services, they would be less motivated and inclined to approach critical legal assistance. All of these circumstances, whether independently or cumulatively encountered, produce impediments to access to justice that depreciate the quality of justice service delivery.

What is at stake when justice is so routinised? One unintended consequence of digitalisation and routinised justice is the emergence of cybersecurity threats. In the pursuit for greater judicial efficiency and cost-savings, there is a desire to collect, retain, utilise and repurpose more personal data to be stored in digital formats. Routinisation may inject 'ordinariness' and 'conventionality' in ways of doing things, so individuals would hardly bat an eye or oppose any excessive data collection and retention, even failing clear justification or accountability from a data collector. For example, when data is collected for its own sake contrary to the principle of data minimisation (rather than for a specified justice purpose benefiting the court user) or stored in ways that compromise individual data subject privacy. In these cases, data integrity and security may be at stake. Data that is not appropriately safeguarded will expose defendants to cybersecurity risks and could result in highly sensitive information being leaked, which may have damaging consequences on individual privacy.[29] In 2018, some 223 State Courts online case files in Singapore were retrieved without authorisation due to a loophole in the ICMS system.[30] Data accessed from the files included the names of the accused, their NRIC, addresses, gender, and other information about the offence.[31] With the move towards more digital courts focusing on online case management systems and online dispute resolution platforms, these threats will become even more commonplace at the institutional level. Therefore, when thinking about digitising justice, there is also a need to enhance our digital capabilities and cybersecurity from attacks by malicious actors.

D. PRIORITISING ACCESS TO JUSTICE IN A DIGITISED WORLD

The challenge in digitising justice is employing informed technologies that are also human-centric and inclusive. This means that technologies deployed in the judicial setting must always put people at the centre, respect their human dignity, and conform to ethical AI principles such as fairness, transparency, accountability and explainability. Technologies must also promote human autonomy and respect individual vulnerability to prevent the design/deployment of tech that might discriminate or digitally exclude certain marginalised groups in the judicial process. Legal technologies must work towards capturing the unique needs of groups that are less digitally savvy and groups that are economically and socially prevented from accessing relevant legal digital processes/services.

The cynic might remark that access to justice and the assurances of due process are already so distant for most accused. As such, digitising does not by itself present novel and further complications. In refuting this concession, it is argued here that there is nothing inherent in digitising that must confirm and continue the worst of what is present. In fact, technology can enable fairer outcomes and promote greater access to justice when the values and principles emphasised above are duly respected and incorporated by the designers of legal technologies and stakeholders deploying these technologies. Thus, if digitising justice is to be part of the solution and not just the problem in restricting a defendant's access to justice, then ongoing, advocates of this revolution need to address the negative impacts of digitising such as the depersonalisation and routinisation of justice that can compound problematic institutions and processes in the delivery of justice.

To begin with, countermeasures should be developed within digitised justice to promote defendants' universal access to technology. Not all defendants are digitally literate and are able to confidently navigate digital legal processes or have access to digital tools. These barriers to technology must be addressed. The examples above also reveal how many exclusionist barriers against access to justice are often front-loaded. These barriers tend to present as early on as when an accused person first encounters the criminal process: for example, the push towards online legal aid or legal chatbots assisting with the delivery of legal information. Efforts to address any barriers to justice or exclusionist technology should be concentrated in these processes/services to ensure all defendants have equal access to critical legal information at the earliest possible stage.

Next, adherence to the principles of responsibility and accountability sits well with the general aspirations towards more human-centric and inclusive AI in the judicial process. It is not simply the designers and programmers who need to align and build ethical legal AI models (for example, by ensuring that data used to build models are non-biased or can be monitored for biasedness); lawyers and judicial administrators sponsoring automation must also be alert and should constantly review how certain technologies can interfere with a defendant's access to justice. Technology should not be implemented for technology's sake as this would contribute to the depersonalisation and routinisation of justice. The legal system should not take for granted that all digitised court processes/services will serve the interest of the defendant. As seen in the examples above, certain digitised processes may exclude the defendant from their own trial or even interfere with the defendant's due process rights. Accountability also relates to the expectation that there are persons who can be held responsible for the proper functioning of technologies in the judicial setting. This also means that when things go wrong, defendants can avail themselves to some form of recourse.

Aligned with the above is the importance of presenting automated justice as an option and not the default merely for the sake of efficiency or cost-cutting priorities. Defendants should not feel obliged or pressured to follow the technology but should be given a choice to not engage with certain digitised services and processes if their preference is to opt out. In other words, we need to respect the defendant's human autonomy. For example, defendants should not be pushed to attend virtual hearings even as it grows to become the 'norm' in justice delivery. Instead, they should be given an option to attend in-person hearings if that is what they are acquainted with and comfortable with.

Recognising the problems linked to depersonalised justice, it is important to recall the unique needs and particularities of each person coming before the court. The judicial system should first and foremost resist the temptation of bundling certain categories of defendants into one homogeneous group; the limitations of any standardised mitigation pleas or predictive algorithm should be recognised alongside any broader promise to 'increase access to justice'. Defendants have a right to have their case heard on its own merits and justice should be individualised according to the facts of each defendant's case.

It is also worth noting that cases that are depersonalised or routinised may promote the 'trivial case' narrative as originally theorised by Doreen Mcbarnet.[32] Such a portrayal of triviality may lend to the impression that certain offences are insignificant, mundane and undeserving of the time of the courts. This may further contribute to other undesirable consequences such as the withdrawal of fundamental principles of procedural fairness as seen in the use of electronic guilty pleas. A human-centric approach to justice should not trivialise the legal relevance of each case and its consequences for the accused but ensure that proper court formalities are taken to ensure that a defendant's due process rights are safeguarded.

Finally, to ensure a human-centric approach to justice delivery, the *human* must of course be placed at the forefront of the judicial process. This means recognising the important role of the court personnel in providing court/legal information, the lawyer in providing their relevant legal expertise and drafting skills to their client's case, the judge in applying the law and their informed discretion to certain cases, the court visitor in ensuring that justice is delivered publicly, and the defendant in participating and presenting at their own trial. Whenever technology is deployed, it should assist and not block the judicial process. A human-centric and inclusive approach to justice recognises that the needs and due process rights of the defendant should always be treated as the priority.

NOTES

1. Robert Anderson and others, 'The Impact of Information Technology on Judicial Administration: A Research Agenda for the Future' (1991) 66 *Southern California Law Review* 1761, 1765 <https://heinonline-org.libproxy.smu.edu.sg/HOL/Page?handle=hein.journals/scal66&id=1777&collection=journals&index=> (accessed 24 February 2021).
2. Edgardo Buscaglia and Maria Dakolias, 'Comparative International Study of Court Performance Indicators: A Descriptive and Analytical Account' (Legal and Judicial Reform Unit, The World Bank 1999), 20177 <http://documents1.worldbank.org/curated/en/373641468769467659/pdf/multi-page.pdf> (accessed 23 February 2021).
3. This chapter is a condensed but more updated version of a previously submitted work published on Criminal Law Forum, Springer. For a more in-depth discussion on the depersonalisation and routinisation of justice, and how it contributes to the two tiers of justice, see the authors' full-length paper: Jane Loo and Mark Findlay, 'Digitised Justice: The New Two Tiers?' (2022) 33 Criminal Law Forum 1 <https://link.springer.com/10.1007/s10609-022-09431-x> (accessed 28 September 2022).
4. Kalliopi Terzidou, 'The Use of Artificial Intelligence in the Judiciary and Its Compliance with the Right to a Fair Trial' (2022) 31 *Journal of Judicial Administration* 154.
5. Marie-Claire Jenkins and others, 'Analysis of User Interaction with Service Oriented Chatbot Systems' in Julie A. Jacko (ed.), *Human-Computer Interaction. HCI Intelligent Multimodal Interaction Environments*, vol. 4552 (Springer, Berlin/Heidelberg, 2007) <http://link.springer.com/10.1007/978-3-540-73110-8_9> (accessed 15 April 2023).
6. 'Criminal Procedure Code 2010 (Act 15 of 2010); Criminal Procedure Code (Pleading Guilty by Electronic Means) Regulations 2010' (*Singapore Statutes*

Online, 24 December 2010) <https://sso.agc.gov.sg/SL/CPC2010-S804-2010> (accessed 16 June 2021).

7. Ibid.
8. 'Payment of Court Fines' (*State Courts Singapore,* 11 June 2021) <https://www.stateCourts.gov.sg/cws/CriminalCase/Pages/Payment%20of%20Court%20Fines.aspx> (accessed 16 June 2021).
9. The schedule to the Act stipulates that an accused may plead guilty by electronic means to an offence that is punishable by imprisonment not exceeding three months.
10. Mikayla Brier-Mills, 'Pleading Guilty Online in Queensland: Efficiency at the Expense of Justice' (2015) 35 *Queensland Lawyer* 66 <https://research.bond.edu.au/en/publications/pleading-guilty-online-in-queensland-efficiency-at-the-expense-of> (accessed 16 April 2023).
11. 'Primary Justice Project (PJP)' (*Community Justice Clinic*) <https://cjc.org.sg/services/legal-services/primary-justice-project/> (accessed 1 March 2021).
12. 'Prepare Your Mitigation Plea' (*beta.judiciary.gov.sg,* 3 February 2021) <https://beta.judiciary.gov.sg/criminal/prepare-mitigation-plea> (accessed 8 March 2021).
13. Ibid. Note: limitations may apply once access to the system is granted or after an accused's consultation with the PJP. If this is the case in practice, the e-mitigation option will only be available for certain cases. However, from our knowledge and as reflected on the Singapore Courts website – there are no outright restrictions (on the type of cases that can rely on this option) as reflected on its 'prepare your mitigation plea'.
14. Leonard Lee, 'Innovation in the Pro Bono Scene: An Interview with Leonard Lee' [2018] *Singapore Comparative Law Review* 132 <https://heinonline.org/HOL/LandingPage?handle=hein.journals/singclr1&div=28&id=&page=> (accessed 10 November 2021).
15. 'Penal Code' (*Singapore Statutes Online,* Section 380 (Theft in Dwelling House)) <https://sso.agc.gov.sg/Act/PC1871?ProvIds=pr380-&ViewType=Advance&Phrase=theft&WiAl=1#pr380-> (accessed 10 November 2021). Note: There is also the offence of theft under section 379 punishable with imprisonment for a term which may extend to three years, or with fine, or with both.
16. Helena Whalen-Bridge, 'Automated Document Assembly: Access to Justice and Consumer Risk' (2021) 33 *Singapore Academy of Law* 315 <https://law.nus.edu.sg/trail/wp-content/uploads/sites/9/2022/03/6082_10.-Helena-Whalen-Bridge-Automated-Document-Assembly_Access-to-Justice-and-Consumer-Risk.pdf> (accessed 16 April 2023).
17. 'COVID-19 (Temporary Measures) Act 2020' (*SSO.AGC.GOV.SG*) <https://sso.agc.gov.sg/Act/COVID19TMA2020#pr28-> (accessed 25 February 2021). Section 28(1) provides that an accused will give evidence from a place within a court or a prison in Singapore using remote control technology. Section 28(2) provides that witnesses will similarly give evidence via remote control technology if they are an expert witness or a witness of fact and parties to the proceedings consent.
18. 'The Future of Disputes: Are Virtual Hearings Here To Stay?' (Baker McKenzie; KPMG 2021) <https://www.bakermckenzie.com/-/media/files/insight/publications/2021/02/are-virtual-hearings-here-to-stay--baker-mckenzie-and-kpmg-report_010221.pdf> (accessed 22 April 2023).

19. Aaron Yoong, 'Zooming into a New Age of Court Proceedings' (2020) 19 *Singapore Academy of Law Practitioner* <https://journalsonline.academypublishing.org.sg/Journals/SAL-Practitioner/Advocacy-and-Procedure/ctl/eFirstSALPDFJournalView/mid/589/ArticleId/1531/Citation/JournalsOnlinePDF> (accessed 25 February 2021).
20. Ibid.
21. Ibid.
22. Yoong (n. 19).
23. Ibid.
24. Anne Bowen Poulin, 'Criminal Justice and Videoconferencing Technology: The Remote Defendant' (2004) 78 *Tulane Law Review* 1089, 1108–11 <https://heinonline-org.libproxy.smu.edu.sg/HOL/Page?lname=&public=false&collection=journals&handle=hein.journals/tulr78&men_hide=false&men_tab=toc&kind=&page=1089> (accessed 25 February 2021).
25. Yoong (n. 19).
26. Rebecca Ratcliffe, 'Singapore Sentences Man to Death via Zoom Call', *The Guardian* (20 May 2020) <https://www.theguardian.com/world/2020/may/20/singapore-sentences-man-to-death-via-zoom-call> (accessed 22 April 2023). He was later acquitted of the charge, after the Court considered new evidence that showed the prosecution did not prove its case.
27. Sundaresh Menon, 'The Judiciary's Response to the Exit of the "Circuit Breaker" Period (Message from the Chief Justice)' (29 May 2020) <https://www.stateCourts.gov.sg/cws/Resources/Documents/CJ_Message_Judiciary%27s%20ResponseToExitoftheCircuitBreakerPeriod.pdf> (accessed 25 February 2021).
28. Ministry of Law, Singapore, 'Legal Aid Bureau – Save Time Go Online!' (20 May 2020) <https://www.youtube.com/watch?v=PwYQJi9aCns> (accessed 22 April 2023).
29. Jasmine Ng, Andrew Wong and Jia Qing Yap, 'Legal Tech-Ing Our Way to Justice', *Law Tech Asia* <https://lawtech.asia/legal-tech-ing-our-way-to-justice/> (accessed 24 February 2021).
30. Lydia Lam, '223 State Courts Online Case Files Accessed without Authorisation Due to Loophole', *Channel News Asia* (28 November 2018) <https://www.channelnewsasia.com/news/singapore/223-state-Courts-online-case-files-accessed-without-10976490> (accessed 25 February 2021).
31. Ibid.
32. Doreen McBarnet, 'Magistrates' Courts and the Ideology of Justice' (1981) 8 *British Journal of Law and Society* 181 <https://www.jstor.org/stable/1409720?origin=crossref> (accessed 15 February 2021).

REFERENCES

Anderson, R. and others, 'The Impact of Information Technology on Judicial Administration: A Research Agenda for the Future' (1991) 66 *Southern California Law Review* 1761 <https://heinonline-org.libproxy.smu.edu.sg/HOL/Page?handle=hein.journals/scal66&id=1777&collection=journals&index=> (accessed 24 February 2021).

Brier-Mills, M., 'Pleading Guilty Online in Queensland: Efficiency at the Expense of Justice' (2015) 35 *Queensland Lawyer* 66 <https://research.bond.edu.au/en/publications/pleading-guilty-online-in-queensland-efficiency-at-the-expense-of> (accessed 16 April 2023).

Buscaglia, E. and Dakolias, M., 'Comparative International Study of Court Performance Indicators: A Descriptive and Analytical Account' (Legal and Judicial Reform Unit, The World Bank 1999) 20177 <http://documents1.worldbank.org/curated/en/373641468769467659/pdf/multi-page.pdf> (accessed 23 February 2021).

'COVID-19 (Temporary Measures) Act 2020' (*SSO.AGC.GOV.SG*) <https://sso.agc.gov.sg/Act/COVID19TMA2020#pr28-> (accessed 25 February 2021).

'Criminal Procedure Code 2010 (Act 15 of 2010); Criminal Procedure Code (Pleading Guilty by Electronic Means) Regulations 2010' (*Singapore Statutes Online*, 24 December 2010) <https://sso.agc.gov.sg/SL/CPC2010-S804-2010> (accessed 16 June 2021).

Jenkins, M.-C. and others, 'Analysis of User Interaction with Service Oriented Chatbot Systems' in Julie A. Jacko (ed.), *Human-Computer Interaction. HCI Intelligent Multimodal Interaction Environments*, vol. 4552 (Springer, Berlin/Heidelberg, 2007) <http://link.springer.com/10.1007/978-3-540-73110-8_9> (accessed 15 April 2023).

Lam, L., '223 State Courts Online Case Files Accessed without Authorisation Due to Loophole', *Channel News Asia* (28 November 2018) <https://www.channelnewsasia.com/news/singapore/223-state-courts-online-case-files-accessed-without-10976490> (accessed 25 February 2021).

Lee, L., 'Innovation in the Pro Bono Scene: An Interview with Leonard Lee' [2018] *Singapore Comparative Law Review* 132 <https://heinonline.org/HOL/LandingPage?handle=hein.journals/singclr1&div=28&id=&page=> (accessed 10 November 2021).

'Legal Aid Bureau – Save Time Go Online!' (*YouTube*, 20 May 2020) <https://www.youtube.com/watch?v=PwYQJi9aCns> (accessed 22 April 2023).

Loo, J. and Findlay, M., 'Digitised Justice: The New Two Tiers?' (2022) 33 *Criminal Law Forum* 1 <https://link.springer.com/10.1007/s10609-022-09431-x> (accessed 28 September 2022).

McBarnet, D., 'Magistrates' Courts and the Ideology of Justice' (1981) 8 *British Journal of Law and Society* 181 <https://www.jstor.org/stable/1409720?origin=crossref> (accessed 15 February 2021).

Menon, S., 'The Judiciary's Response to the Exit of the "Circuit Breaker" Period (Message from the Chief Justice)' (29 May 2020) <https://www.statecourts.gov.sg/cws/Resources/Documents/CJ_Message_Judiciary%27s%20ResponseToExitoftheCircuitBreakerPeriod.pdf> (accessed 25 February 2021).

Ng, J., Wong, A. and Yap, J. Q., 'Legal Tech-Ing Our Way to Justice', *Law Tech Asia* <https://lawtech.asia/legal-tech-ing-our-way-to-justice/> (accessed

24 February 2021).
'Payment of Court Fines' (*State Courts Singapore*, 11 June 2021) <https://www.statecourts.gov.sg/cws/CriminalCase/Pages/Payment%20of%20Court%20Fines.aspx> (accessed 16 June 2021).
'Penal Code' (*Singapore Statutes Online, Section 380 (Theft in Dwelling House)*) <https://sso.agc.gov.sg/Act/PC1871?ProvIds=pr380-&ViewType=Advance&Phrase=theft&WiAl=1#pr380-> (accessed 10 November 2021).
Poulin, A. B., 'Criminal Justice and Videoconferencing Technology: The Remote Defendant' (2004) 78 *Tulane Law Review* 1089 <https://heinonline-org.libproxy.smu.edu.sg/HOL/Page?lname=&public=false&collection=journals&handle=hein.journals/tulr78&men_hide=false&men_tab=toc&kind=&page=1089> (accessed 25 February 2021).
'Prepare Your Mitigation Plea' (*beta.judiciary.gov.sg*, 3 February 2021) <https://beta.judiciary.gov.sg/criminal/prepare-mitigation-plea> (accessed 8 March 2021).
'Primary Justice Project (PJP)' (*Community Justice Clinic*) <https://cjc.org.sg/services/legal-services/primary-justice-project/> (accessed 1 March 2021).
Ratcliffe, R., 'Singapore Sentences Man to Death via Zoom Call', *The Guardian* (20 May 2020) <https://www.theguardian.com/world/2020/may/20/singapore-sentences-man-to-death-via-zoom-call> (accessed 22 April 2023).
Terzidou, K., 'The Use of Artificial Intelligence in the Judiciary and Its Compliance with the Right to a Fair Trial' (2022) 31 *Journal of Judicial Administration* 154.
'The Future of Disputes: Are Virtual Hearings Here To Stay?' (Baker McKenzie; KPMG 2021) <https://www.bakermckenzie.com/-/media/files/insight/publications/2021/02/are-virtual-hearings-here-to-stay--baker-mckenzie-and-kpmg-report_010221.pdf> (accessed 22 April 2023).
Whalen-Bridge, H., 'Automated Document Assembly: Access to Justice and Consumer Risk' (2021) 33 *Singapore Academy of Law* 315 <https://law.nus.edu.sg/trail/wp-content/uploads/sites/9/2022/03/6082_10.-Helena-Whalen-Bridge-Automated-Document-Assembly_Access-to-Justice-and-Consumer-Risk.pdf> (accessed 16 April 2023).
Yoong, A., 'Zooming into a New Age of Court Proceedings' (2020) 19 *Singapore Academy of Law Practitioner* <https://journalsonline.academypublishing.org.sg/Journals/SAL-Practitioner/Advocacy-and-Procedure/ctl/eFirstSALPDFJournalView/mid/589/ArticleId/1531/Citation/JournalsOnlinePDF> (accessed 25 February 2021).

Chapter 11

The Lengthening Shadow of the Legal Tech Market on the Supreme Court of India

Varsha Aithala and Siddharth Peter de Souza[1]

A. INTRODUCTION

The Indian legal tech market has the second highest number of startups in the world (after the United States), with over 650 startups, according to a report by the Indian Institute of Management IIM-CIIE in 2022/2023. The market for legal tech is valued at around USD 1.3 billion[2] and more than 8 per cent of legal tech startups in India have received funding to the tune of around USD 55 million.[3] Legal tech is described as being largely in matters related to legal service delivery, process efficiency, access to legal services, and Do-it-Yourself tools that service three customer segments – citizens, legal service providers and the judiciary. The report indicates that the next phase of startups is in the areas of online dispute resolution, litigation finance and court management. Much of this development has taken place rapidly, in the last ten years.

Private sector players, who play a major role in the legal tech market, offer a wide variety of services with the promise of ensuring speedy, efficient and timely delivery of justice services. Coupled with these managerial gains is the neoliberal turn in the justice system, with reducing state influence and encouragement to private institutions and capital to introduce seamlessness to justice delivery.

In parallel with the growth of the legal tech market, conversations have emerged within the Indian judiciary about the role of technology in justice delivery. This includes the use of artificial intelligence in facilitating research, translation, and document review; the rise in online dispute resolution particularly since the COVID-19 pandemic; and increasing infrastructure being developed for e-Courts, amidst general developments around e-governance initiatives of the government.

This chapter locates the growth of the legal tech market within the discourse emerging from the Supreme Court of India's draft e-vision document which was published in 2021,[4] and subsequently revised and published in 2022.[5] We believe this is a significant document because, among other things, the Court outlines and offers a model for how it wishes to fundamentally shift the nature of justice delivery by thinking of justice 'as a service' where justice can be advanced through an 'ecosystem' of actors who provide services to enable or support the delivery of justice. The second section of the chapter explains the contours of India's legal tech market by describing key actors, interventions and growth trends of this market. It also discusses vision of the Court and the role of private sector.

In the absence of clear and specific guidance from the Court, the third section of this chapter offers a typology of the relationship between the Court and the legal tech market. This section examines whether the legal tech market in India is developing in the shadow of the Court, or if this is already an extension of the Court's policy vision. Finally, we examine some of the ethical considerations of the growth of this market, before concluding the chapter.

B. LEGAL TECH AND THE MARKET

I. Description of the legal tech market

In India, the legal tech market is dominated by private service providers who offer interventions such as contract management,[6] legal research, e-discovery, litigation process management, compliance filings (intellectual property rights, tax), lawyer–client matching platforms, online dispute resolution and, in limited cases, legal advice to companies. India's legal tech providers have tended to support traditional institutions like law practices, legal departments, law firms and banking institutions.[7] They have extended the scope of their services to provide support for due diligence processes,[8] and litigation prediction models from natural language processing software which use historical case data[9] to discern patterns in decision-making for predictions on case outcomes. They are also scoping opportunities to create prototype/judgment templates using machine learning-based legal capabilities.[10] Technological interventions are mainly focused to support lawyer's services through automation of manual tasks (workflow management), enhanced research outputs and tools for improving client convenience. 'Even though a firm stands to lose 5% to 40% of its value on a given deal due, for instance, to inefficiency, contracting remains an activity that only some companies do efficiently'.[11] As McKamey identifies, legal tech is largely being seen to *shift*, not supplant the role of legal professionals, who now interact more with technological applications and work collaboratively in their areas of expertise.[12] All this explains the increased interest in their take up.

Despite such advances, however, a majority of Indian lawyers and law firms currently only use technology for limited purposes such as sending emails, time recording, billing,[13] and improving communication using call support and video conferencing. Large law firms and corporate legal teams use legal tech solutions for document management and sharing, data security systems, virtual data rooms and basic document proofing software. Some firms, Shreya Vajpeyi (founder of the blog Prolawgue) argues, have also been working with tech companies to build products for their specific requirements, for instance, specific enterprise resource planning software suitable to their operations, and their strategy is to 'build, not buy'.[14] She believes that the few gains made in the adoption of technology owing to COVID-19 are lost, especially in Tier-2 Indian cities, since there are no drivers for change and little encouragement from the government. Vishnu Kale, who works at a law firm's innovation team, discusses how legal tech in India is largely seen to be focused on technical and procedural interventions, including in terms of improving process management. He suggests, at this point, these interventions are not disruptive, and they would not change the nature of the legal profession and are merely moves to optimise for cost.[15] Some larger Indian law firms have invested in practice management software applications that use cloud computing and AI, and these firms can boast of separate knowledge management teams for working on efficient practice solutions.[16]

Law firms have also invested in the legal innovation ecosystem, for example, Trilegal has supported the 'Agami Prize' which awards both social as well as industry organisations bringing changes to the legal industry.[17] Similar to international trends, Indian law firms have served as incubators[18] for legal tech. Prarambh[19], launched in 2019 by Cyril Amarchand Mangaldas to mentor legal tech startups, has guided three tech start-ups, Conduct, Presolv360, and PropertyChek, through their entire startup journey. Related service providers, such as law firm management consultancies and legal tech/legal design consultancies, play a minor role in this space.

It is therefore clear that law firms and corporate legal departments are playing an important role in the development of the Indian legal tech market.

Despite an emerging market for legal tech products for internal administration and process improvement, this sector lacks major investment. Indian law firms are cost-sensitive, decision-making takes time owing to their business structures and this makes the sales cycle for legal tech products long, and so, products remain expensive.[20] It remains unclear whether the stated benefits of technological transformation flow to individual legal practitioners who form the bulk of this market. As explained above, the role of these tools seems to be limited: currently, they apply AI-enabled processes to help the average law firm associate in matters involving routine, repetitive tasks relating to legal research and document management.

Sachin Malhan, of the non-profit Agami, sees the growth of the legal tech market in India in three phases. The first, where there is an interest in building for problems, entrepreneurs adopted an approach where technology was seen as a solution to fundamental and structural problems in the Indian legal system. The second phase is where legal tech entrepreneurs built for enterprises such as banks seeking dispute resolution systems. The third phase is where entrepreneurs are building for the world, owing to the difficulties of scaling up within the Indian legal tech market.[21] Malhan further states that is consolidation taking place in the market, which remains much smaller in size than in the US.

Despite these advances, an important concern is that the market does not appear to service the common litigant facing an 'everyday' legal problem. The everyday legal problem as Sandefur et al. explain is, 'in the context where many people experience justice problems that they do not recognise as legal or remediable, tools that offer diagnosis of problems involving specific legal aspects … and provide options for response could be particularly valuable. There are very few such tools.'[22] The Hague Institute for Innovation in Law's (HiiL) research suggests that the market for legal tech for the judiciary consists mostly of legal information and advice portals which do not qualify as examples of 'people-centred justice innovations' and do not have scalable, and financially sustainable models. These portals mainly explain technical/legal information and concepts using simple language, but do not really offer solutions to people's problems.[23] An interesting case in point is Legal Zoom which provides consumer-friendly contracts. It consists of an innovative model to service this important segment but struggled to remain profitable due to capital constraints. It raised capital from the public and changed its service delivery model from enabling 'people-centred justice' to supporting small and medium business corporations in order to survive.[24]

In our discussions with subject market experts for this paper, we also discussed what expectations they had from the court in regards to the legal tech market. Kale argues that courts need legal technology to develop as a separate market with its own solutions. Vikas Mahendra, a partner at a law firm, discusses how the nature of discussions with courts often requires that judges are proactive on their own steam to get things done. The informality is a critical element to ensure that courts are able to get solutions that suit their needs. Malhan argues that courts may not be articulating their needs properly and this is where there is a need for curators, and interpreters from the technology sector to understand the court's needs. This will enable renewed collaborations between researchers, designers, lawyers, economists and the courts using open-source design to build practical reference solutions like OpenNyAI which is a collective that develops open-source AI Digital Public Goods that transform how citizens in India experience law and justice.[25] Purushottam Anand, a lawyer and founder of a legal tech firm, argues that when it comes to legal tech it is important that it is examined from different dimensions including, how law understands tech, and how tech can be used as an instrument for law.[26] He also highlights the role of regulation, and argues that industry insiders warn that there is a risk of premature regulation in this rapidly evolving space, which can impose far greater costs than with the current state of lack of guidance. Anand further argues that while policymakers may be unfamiliar with the technology, failure to involve subject experts in the policy consultations could mean genuine requirements are ignored and could present a barrier to the growth of this nascent sector in India.[27]

The next section discusses what the Court sees as its vision for e-justice, and what place the private sector plays in this vision.

II. Private sector and the Court: the vision document

In 2021, the Supreme Court of India released its draft vision document for e-courts for public comments, and it was subsequently finalised in 2022. The goal was to develop open and interoperable digital infrastructure with standards and services to support the integration of services and defined pathways to allow market players to collaborate and analytics-led judicial processes.

The policy document argued for an ecosystem approach to justice delivery which emphasised 'scale, speed and sustainability'.[28] This was heralded as an opportunity to create a multiplier effect for change. The idea was that rather than focus on developing all solutions itself, the judiciary could 'curate the right environment and infrastructure for solutions to emerge rapidly from the ecosystem of public and private actors'.[29] In doing so, the document suggested that 'administration of justice [is to be seen] not just as a sovereign function, but as a service which is provided to the community by different actors'.[30]

We argue that this reflects an important shift in the Court's focus where it is willing to cede its responsibility by making the institutional apparatus available to different actors to ensure 'seamless' justice through exploring a commodified approach to justice delivery.

The vision document provides indications for where the private sector can be involved in the judicial process, including, for instance, in building and co-creating solutions for 'discovery, tracking filings and managing documents'.[31] This encourages the participation of the private sector through finding ways to build complementary technology. Opportunities also exist for 'the development of applications by the private sector that can integrate listing of cases with billing services for lawyers / proactive alerts for litigants'.[32] In its vision for the development of the National Judicial Technological Council, the document supports private sector involvement in the development of digital infrastructures, and for this to be full-time or part-time arrangement, thereby also introducing flexibility in terms of working conditions. In ensuring private sector participation, the vision document also builds support for the existence of off the shelf services, arguing that having licences for algorithms and software makes development cheaper, whereas proprietary software would be more dependent on internal infrastructures.

In keeping with an increasingly techno-centric approach to justice delivery, the former CEO of Niti Aayog and his team introduced the notion of a 'justice stack', aimed 'towards a presence-less, paperless, cashless and consent-based justice delivery'.[33] This approach argues for extending India stack, a program to introduce open APIs and digital public infrastructure to the justice system.[34] It is suggested that, with the justice stack, the emphasis is on making the justice delivery system more productive, efficient and economical in nature.

We believe, this raises critical questions about the 'publicness' of justice delivery and the kind of dependencies which will be created as a consequence of ceding space to private actors in justice delivery.[35]

This approach of the Court also raises some fundamental issues on the view of the Court towards the legal tech market. First, what is the Court's policy/approach to legal tech and how does it respond to the legal tech market? Second, is this a regulated or unregulated market for legal tech services, and who has the responsibility to regulate it? Third, does the Court intervene, and are there clear lines in terms of the permissibility/impermissibility of legal tech in the Indian judiciary?

C. WHAT DOES THIS TELL US ABOUT THE COURT IN RELATION TO LEGAL TECH?

I. Role of the Court in the legal tech market

The last section presented two parallel developments taking place from the Court and from the market that have emerged in India in the last few years. There is a clear overlap in these developments in terms of the motivations of the market and of the Court. Briefly, the focus is on using technology to automate different tasks with the expectation that this will reduce costs, as well as improve accessibility and efficiency of legal tasks.[36]

Given the trajectories of both developments, it becomes important to examine what role the Court sees for itself in relation to the emergence of the legal tech ecosystem. We propose four different ways of examining the relations between the Court and the legal tech market.

A first reading of the Court's vision is to create an ecosystem of actors. If one is to place prominence on this framework, then one can reasonably conclude that the Court sees itself as an active enabler or even a promoter of the legal tech market. In this role, it not only identifies areas where the private sector can intervene but also provides the terms with which the sector can engage with the Court.

A second more cautious reading on the Court's vision is that while the Court has indicated what it intends to do, it has not actively endorsed any legal tech instruments, and therefore the developments taking place with the market are happening in the shadow of the Court, and not with its explicit approval or disapproval.[37] These developments need to be unpacked. They have proceeded to already make inroads in the practice of the law and the market is growing in almost an insurgent manner, due to the lack of any concrete guidance from the Court.[38] In this instance, the lack of clarity from the Court has not dissuaded entrepreneurs but has rather enabled them to push the envelope at the boundaries of illegality.

The third reading of the relationship between the Court and the legal tech market is that the Court itself is an active participant in such a market. The Court has set up an AI Committee and launched three AI tools: Supreme Court Portal for Assistance in Courts Efficiency (SUPACE),[39] Supreme Court Vidhik Anuvaad Software (SUVAAS)[40] and SCI-Interact. The functions of these tools are clearly prescribed. For instance, SUPACE is expected to be used only for the collection and analysis of case data and will not be used to assist judges in decision-making. It is expected only to make information available to the judge faster, and the individual judge retains her autonomy and discretion in decisions. SCI-Interact was launched in 2020 to make all Supreme Court benches paperless and help judges access files, documents and make notes on computers. SUVAAS, launched in 2019, helps translate judicial documents, judgments and orders from English to nine vernacular languages and vice versa, fast and effectively. In its latest iteration, Phase-III of the Supreme Court's eCourts Project is allocated an increased budget outlay of INR 7,210 crores for 2023–27, to 'create a unified technology platform for the judiciary, thus providing a seamless and paperless interface between the courts, the litigants and other stakeholders'.[41] This aims to 'put in place intelligent smart systems enabling data-based decision making for judges and registries while scheduling or prioritizing cases' 'to ensure a smoother user experience by building a "smart" ecosystem'.[42] In this version, the court sees itself also as an active technology developer, whereby it is also creating technology to enable the delivery of legal services.

The fourth possible reading is the role of the Court as a regulator. This is ambiguous. While it is yet unclear if the Court has identified redlines or guardrails for the use of technology in courts, the eCommittee offers a hint in its draft Detailed Project Report on the Implementation of Artificial Intelligence and Blockchain Technology by suggesting that 'AI might be used for Prediction and Forecast, Improving Administrative Efficiency, Automated Filing, Smart Scheduling of Cases, Enhancing the Case Information System & Communicate with litigants through chatbots which may assist in early disposal of cases'.[43] The Indian judiciary appears to self-restrict the use of AI technologies. However, different Supreme Court judges have offered ideas of where they see the use of AI in courts: from focusing on small claims to seeing it as an enabling tool to offering suggestions that it can at best be a research assistant.

In these instances, the Court continues to speak in several voices and, as a consequence, its regulatory capacity is ex-post rather than ex-ante.[44] The regulation therefore, rather than preceding the technology, or providing clear guidelines, instead follows the technology, as a consequence of a policy vacuum.[45]

II. What are the access to justice dimensions of the legal tech market?

The Boston Consulting Group's biannual Digital Government Benchmarking survey in 2018 of more than 14,000 internet users worldwide found that respondents based in India, China and Indonesia indicated the strongest support for government applications of AI, while the citizens surveyed in Switzerland, Estonia and Austria offered the weakest support. However, this survey also found that the majority of those surveyed 'were most supportive of using AI for tasks such as transport and traffic optimization, predictive maintenance of public infrastructure, and customer service activities but did not support AI for sensitive decisions associated with the justice system, such as parole board and sentencing recommendations.'[46]

Technology-determining policy is problematic since it is not clear where one draws the line. The functionalities of technology cannot be limited to just research and process management, and not worrying about decision-making. There is a lot at stake and, as Bachelet of UNHCR argues, there is a need for guardrails to ensure that technology does not cause catastrophic effects on human rights.[47] Due to a lack of clarity in regulation, courts are relied upon to provide guidance on the future direction of the law. Courts also act as guardians of the process by applying commonly accepted constitutional or legal principles, when quasi-judicial or regulatory agencies decide these matters by relying on form, not substance.

AI systems are a potential 'blackbox' for regulation. Their models remove human discretion and make it difficult to determine conscious or unconscious biases in decision-making, particularly for sensitive aspects like access to justice. Zhiyu Li remarks that important questions to consider include: 'Do the developers of legal bots have sufficient knowledge and experience of the law? Is the data that they are using to "train" their algorithms relevant and up to date? Will they inadvertently omit data that could cause key evidence or elements to be filtered out or overlooked by a robot judge or AI software? The decision-making of criminal cases deserves so much attention because oftentimes criminal defendants' freedom and even their lives are at stake.'[48]

One way to decipher this is to ask a basic question: who benefits most from these services? It is not the marginalised populations. 'Comprehending legal text can be challenging due to its verbosity and density and few expert-annotated datasets.'[49] Court documents are complex. Litigants require 'functional literacy' to navigate these – which provides the ability to identify the complexity of a task and the related ability to identify strategies to reduce task complexity. This requirement can extend to language literacy, communication skills, numeracy, and understanding of legal arguments and evidence.[50] For instance, in 2013, Julie Macfarlane, in a seminal study on self-represented litigants (SRLs) in Canadian courts, observed that completing court forms leads to significant frustration among SRLs. The issues ranged from difficulties in determining which court forms were necessary to complete, receipt of contradictory information from court staff about the forms and the language of the forms themselves, which contain legal terms familiar only to judges, lawyers and court staff.[51]

Legal processes are mostly codified, and difficult for everyone to access and understand. They are 'set up for experts', yet expert help is prohibitively expensive.[52] In addition to literacy, people also need to be 'digitally ready' and 'capable' of recognising legal issues and certain about what they need to do and where to access affordable help.[53] In litigation, particularly, criminal litigation, several issues can arise with tech-assisted litigation. Practically, if the tech processes malfunction due to technical difficulties, litigants will need stronger procedural law protections to protect their rights. Currently, available tech solutions do not address these issues.

In 2021, the HiiL conducted a survey on 'Digital Technology and Judicial Reform' covering more than sixty-eight countries. It found that technological innovations mostly serve the government, urban population, lawyers, law firms, and small and medium-sized enterprises. Most importantly, the survey discovered that around 67 per cent of legal tech innovations exclude people with no access to technology.[54] Digital tools, where available, therefore provide limited services for common users, usually limited to information about the law or procedures, or connecting users with lawyers. The report points out that these use tools and technologies such as 'websites, social media, chatbots, telephone, video and other commonly used technologies' and that 'artificial intelligence and advanced technologies such as blockchain are used by a few'.[55] 'Using tools requires access to specific resources and capabilities that some groups and communities are unlikely to have. The same groups often unable to access traditional lawyer assistance – such as people with low incomes, racial minorities, and people with lower levels of education[56] – are also less likely to be able to use digital tools'.[57]

The individual legal practitioner 'advocate' also does not benefit. The 2019 US Survey of Legal Technology for Non-Lawyers suggests that these digital tools are of limited use mainly owing to the legal profession's monopoly on the provision of legal services, which prohibits non-lawyers from providing legal services, as well as 'challenges of coordination in contemporary state court systems' – since 'implementing standardised forms and getting courts to accept them is a herculean task of coordination that requires every court in every county in a state accept a new way of doing its work'. The profession's resistance to change due to its inherent conservatism is, according to Gélinas, 'linked to the function of law as a "stabiliser" of social relations, and the pursuit of the core value of "predictability" through which it notably achieves this function'.[58] Even when rules change formally, clerks, judges and other courthouse staff can persist in older patterns, refusing to recognise documents that are officially approved by the court system. The barriers here are not technological, but human. The report concludes that courts are responsible for this situation.[59] India suffers the same constraints. The argument that legal tech presents the best solution to reduce the access to justice gap therefore remains a myth since available services do not make resolution of legal problems affordable to people. Without sustained efforts to make these work at quality and scale, these are bound to fail.

D. CONCLUSION

There is immense value in the fundamental principles of legitimacy, accountability and transparency that inform the court's functions. Attempts to introduce technology in legal processes without attention to these values and practices are bound to fail.[60]

Courts cannot remain a bystander and need to be acutely conscious that their acts and omissions have repercussions on the development of the Indian legal tech market. Given the complex and rapidly evolving nature of these technologies, building digital data management capabilities for public institutions like courts is important. Collaborations like 'Pucar' are working to develop a multidisciplinary community of innovators to strengthen the capacity of all stakeholders in the justice system.[61]

The utility of technological solutions to remedy problems that Indian courts face cannot be denied. In fact, as Andrew Perlman suggests, 'these tools can be effectively harnessed to promote greater access to legal services to members of the public, and ensure necessary protections for the system'. They have great potential to enhance efficiency and generate impact.[62] But we should stay clear of what Rostain terms 'techno-optimism': which can be illustrated for example in an expectation that self-help technology will improve people's collective capacity to address the legal system's failures.[63] People's aptitude for finding, understanding and using online legal tools effectively is often overestimated. As Kramer and Weinstock point out, the difficulties of integrating technology in highly complex, multilevel judicial organisations and federal contexts need to be examined.[64] Digital exclusion, privacy loss and data misuse are important risks to consider.

Benyekhlef and others in their work sum this up well: 'We cannot assume that there is a necessary or a necessarily positive relationship between court technologies and access to justice: instead, we should proceed with cautious rather than unbridled optimism to ensure that technologies are implemented in such a way as to achieve the positive outcomes that we envision',[65] and that, we argue, is the role of caution that should be employed by the Supreme Court too.

NOTES

1. The authors would like to thank Rachit Sharma at Justice Adda for his invaluable research assistance on the chapter.
2. Shailaja Shukla, 'Beyond the Bench: Promise of Indian Legal Tech Startups: Landscape Study of the Indian Legal Tech Startup Ecosystem' (*IIMA Ventures*, 2022) <https://www.insights.ciie.co/posts/beyond-the-bench-promise-of-indian-legal-tech-startups?utm_source=website&utm_medium=social&utm_campaign=legaltech> (accessed 26 February 2024).
3. Ibid.
4. 'Digital Courts Vision & Roadmap e-Courts Project Phase III' (E-Committee of Supreme Court of India, New Delhi, 2022) <https://cdnbbsr.s3waas.gov.in/s388ef51f0bf911e452e8dbb1d807a81ab/uploads/2023/04/2023042088.pdf> (accessed 15 February 2024).
5. Ibid.
6. Notable examples are Manupatra (MyKase for matter management and Manucontract for contract drafting and management), iPleaders (legal education), Provakil (contract lifecycle management, enterprise legal management and legal collections management solutions), Legistify (legal marketplace), Law Rato (lawyer–client matching), Mattersphere (case management and matter workflow process management).
7. 'Innovation and technology revolutionising the legal landscape in India', *Times of India* (New Delhi, 17 January 2022) <https://timesofindia.indiatimes.com/blogs/voices/innovation-and-technology-revolutionising-the-legal-landscape-in-india/> (accessed 15 February 2024).
8. Saverisk is a risk assessment service provider. It conducts searches of a corporate/individual on the centralised databases like the ministry of corporate affairs, courts and funding websites and due diligence. *Saverisk.com* <https://saverisk.com/> (accessed 13 April 2023).
9. 'Legistify Top 10 Best Legaltech Companies in India 2022' (*Inventiva*, 5 January 2022) <https://www.inventiva.co.in/trends/top-10-legaltech-in-india-2022/> (accessed 14 March 2023).
10. OpenNyAI. Internationally, Kleros is described as 'a decentralised blockchain-based arbitration solution that relies on smart contracts and crowdsourced jurors', mainly used in business contract disputes. It relies on game theory.
11. Tasmia Ansari, 'The Judgment is Out for NLP' (*Analytics India Magazine*, 6 January 2023) <https://analyticsindiamag.com/the-judgment-is-out-for-nlp/> (accessed 13 March 2023).
12. Mark McKame, 'Legal Technology: Artificial Intelligence and the Future of Law Practice' (2017) 22 Appeal 45.
13. App4Legal & SimpleLegal 'Legal Billing Software' (*SourceForge*) <https://sourceforge.net/software/legal-billing/india/> (accessed 13 April 2023).
14. Interview with Shreya Vajpeyi, Founder of Prolawgue.com and member of the Innovation team at one of India's top law firms (July 2023).
15. Interview with Vishnu Kale, Founder of Navya Legal Design and principal associate at a top-tier national law firm (July 2023).
16. Ibid.

17. 'Agami Prizes 2022' (*Agami*) <https://agami.in/prize2022/> (accessed 26 February 2024).
18. Sahil Khan, 'Emergence of Legal Tech Startups in India' (2022) 2 Jus Corpus L.J. 85.
19. 'Prarambh' (*Cyril Amarchand Mangaldas*) <https://www.cyrilshroff.com/prarambh/> (accessed on 19 April 2023).
20. Interviews with Shreya Vajpei and Vishnu Kale (July 2023).
21. Interview with Sachin Malhan, Co-Founder of Agami (July 2023).
22. Rebecca Sandefur, 'Legal Tech for Non-Lawyers: Report of the Survey of US Legal Technologies' (*American Bar Foundation,* 2019), 10 <https://www.americanbarfoundation.org/wp-content/uploads/2023/04/report_us_digital_legal_tech_for_nonlawyers.pdf> (accessed 26 February 2024).
23. The Hague Institute for Innovation in Law, 'Use of Digital Technologies in Judicial Reform and Access to Justice Cooperation' (*HiiL,* 2019), 59 <https://www.hiil.org/wp-content/uploads/2021/11/HiiL-Use-of-digital-technologies-in-judicial-reform-and-access-to-justice-cooperation.pdf> (accessed 26 February 2024).
24. Ibid., 63.
25. *OpenNYAI* <https://opennyai.org/> (accessed 26 February 2024).
26. Interview with Purushottam Anand, Founder of CryptoLegal and Advocate (July 2023).
27. Ibid.
28. E-Committee of Supreme Court of India (n. 4), 22.
29. Ibid., 24.
30. Ibid., 28.
31. Ibid., 45.
32. Ibid., 46.
33. 'Time for a Justice Stack', *Financial Express* (14 July 2021) <https://www.financialexpress.com/opinion/time-for-a-justice-stack/2289629/> (accessed 26 February 2024).
34. India Stack <https://indiastack.org/> (accessed 26 February 2024).
35. Siddharth Peter De Souza, Varsha Aithala and Srishti John, 'The Supreme Court of India's Vision for eCourts: The Need to Retain Justice as a Public Service', *The Hindu Centre* (10 July 2021) <https://www.thehinducentre.com/publications/policy-watch/the-supreme-court-of-indias-vision-for-ecourts-the-need-to-retain-justice-as-a-public-service/article64936007.ece> (accessed 26 February 2024).
36. Natasha Dow Schull, *The Folly of Technological Solutionism: An Interview with Evgeny Morozov* (Public Books) <https://www.publicbooks.org/the-folly-of-technological-solutionism-an-interview-with-evgeny-morozov/> (accessed 2 June 2021); Siddharth Peter de Souza and Maximilian Spohr, *Technology, Innovation and Access to Justice: Dialogues on the Future of Law* (Edinburgh University Press, 2020).
37. Julia Black, 'Decentring Regulation: Understanding the Role of Regulation and Self Regulation in a "Post-Regulatory" World' (2001) 54 *Current Legal Problems* 103.
38. One could argue that the lack of guidance takes a similar form to judicial evasion, where, through a lack of decision-making by the court, there are developments that take place due to inaction. Gautam Bhatia, 'Judicial Evasion and the Status Quo: On SC Judgments', *The Hindu* (10 January 2019) <https://www.the

hindu.com/opinion/lead/judicial-evasion-and-the-status-quo/article25953052.ece> (accessed 31 August 2021).

39. National Informatics Centre, 'Launching of AI Portal – SUPACE by Hon'ble Shri Justice Sharad Arvind Bobde (Chief Justice of India and Patron-in-Chief, AI Committee)' (6 April 2021) <https://webcast.gov.in/events/MTI1MQ--/session/MzE1MA> (accessed 13 April 2023).
40. Supreme Court of India, *Press Release for Law Day Celebration* <https://main.sci.gov.in/pdf/Press/press%20release%20for%20law%20day%20celebratoin.pdf> (accessed 13 April 2023).
41. Press Information Bureau, 'e-Courts Phase-III aims to usher in a regime of maximum ease of justice by moving towards digital, online and paperless courts through digitization of entire court records' (1 August 2024) https://pib.gov.in/PressReleseDetailm.aspx?PRID=2040232 (accessed 5 August 2024).
42. Ibid.
43. Press Information Bureau, *Use of Advance Technology at Courts* (7 April 2022) <https://pib.gov.in/PressReleaseIframePage.aspx?PRID=1814536> (accessed 13 April 2023).
44. See Law Rato case at Allahabad HC: 'Allahabad HC Takes Up The Issue Of Online Portals Advertising, Soliciting For Lawyers' *LiveLaw* (15 October 2018) <https://www.livelaw.in/allahabad-hc-takes-up-the-issue-of-online-portals-advertising-soliciting-for-lawyers-read-order/> (accessed 26 February 2024). Siddharth Peter de Souza, 'AI and the Indian Judiciary: The Need for a Rights-Based Approach' (2024) <https://www.thehinducentre.com/incoming/ai-and-the-indian-judiciary-the-need-for-a-rights-based-approach-html-version/article68917505.ece> (accessed 8 January 2025).
45. Lyria Bennett Moses, 'How to Think About Law, Regulation and Technology: Problems with "Technology" as a Regulatory Target' (2013) 5(1) *Law, Innovation and Technology* 1–20 <https://papers.ssrn.com/abstract=2464750> (accessed 29 June 2022).
46. Miguel Carrasco, Steven Mills, Adam Whybrew and Adam Jura, 'The Citizen's Perspective on the Use of AI in Government' *BCG* (1 March 2019) <https://www.bcg.com/publications/2019/citizen-perspective-use-artificial-intelligence-government-digital-benchmarking> (accessed 26 February 2024).
47. 'Urgent action needed over artificial intelligence risks to human rights', *United Nations News* (15 September 2021) <https://news.un.org/en/story/2021/09/1099972> (accessed 26 February 2024).
48. Andrew Singer, 'All rise for the robot judge: AI and blockchain could transform the courtroom' *Magazine by Cointelegraph* (13 March 2023) <https://cointelegraph.com/magazine/all-rise-for-robot-judge-ai-blockchain-transform-courtroom/> (accessed 16 March 2023).
49. Ibid. Brousalis and Mathews (n. 25).
50. Ibid.
51. Amy Salyzyn, Lori Isaj, Brandon Piva and Jacquelyn Burkell, 'Literacy Requirements of Court Documents: An Underexplored Barrier to Access to Justice' (2017) 33(2) *Western Yearbook of Access to Justice* 1–48 <https://ir.lib.uwo.ca/fimspub/158/> (accessed 26 February 2024).
52. Salter and Thompson (n. 25).
53. Kate M. Murray, 'Achieving Digital Equity in Access to Justice' (Legal Services

Society of British Columbia, October 2021) <https://legalaid.bc.ca/sites/default/files/inline-files/Murray_2021_LABC_Achieving_Digital_Equity_Final_Report.pdf> (accessed 26 February 2024).
54. Ibid., p. 60.
55. Kanan Dhru, Manasi Nikam and Maurits Barendrecht, 'Use of Digital Technologies in Judicial Reform and Access to Justice Cooperation' (*The Hague Institute for Innovation in Law*) <https://www.hiil.org/research/digital-technology-and-judicial-reform/> (accessed 26 February 2024).
56. Legal Services Corporation, *The Justice Gap: Measuring the Unmet Civil Legal Needs of Low-income Americans* (Washington, DC: Legal Services Corporation, 2017) <https://www.lsc.gov/sites/default/files/images/TheJusticeGap-FullReport.pdf> (accessed 26 February 2024).
57. Sandefur (n. 22).
58. Fabien Gélinas, 'Continuity and Technological Change in Justice Delivery', in Karim Benyekhlef and others (eds), *eAccess to Justice* (University of Ottawa Press, 2016), p. 256.
59. Sandefur (n. 22).
60. Pierre Noreau, 'The Old … and the New? Elements for a General Theory of Institutional Change: The Case of Paperless Justice', in Karim Benyekhlef and others (eds), *eAccess to Justice* (University of Ottawa Press, 2016), p. 274.
61. Summary of Interview with Sachin Malhan, Co-Founder at Agami (July 2023); 'AgamiScape' (*Agami*) <https://agami.in/agamiscape/> (accessed 26 February 2024).
62. Andrew Perlman, 'The Twenty-First Century Lawyer's Evolving Ethical Duty of Competence', *The Professional Lawyer* 22:4 (2014).
63. Tanina Rostain, 'Techno-Optimism & Access to the Legal System' (2019) 148(1) *Daedalus* 93–7 <https://doi.org/10.1162/daed_a_00540> (accessed 26 February 2024).
64. Benyekhlef, *eAccess to Justice* (n. 56), p. 260.
65. Ibid., p. 165.

REFERENCES

'Best Legal Billing Software in India', *SourceForge* <https://sourceforge.net/software/legal-billing/india/> 'Time for a Justice Stack', *Financial Express* (14 July 2021) <https://www.financialexpress.com/opinion/time-for-a-justice-stack/2289629/>

'Urgent action needed over artificial intelligence risks to human rights', *United Nations News* (15 September 2021) <https://news.un.org/en/story/2021/09/1099972>

Ansari, Tasmia, 'The Judgment is Out for NLP', *Analytics India Magazine* (6 January 2023) <https://analyticsindiamag.com/the-judgment-is-out-for-nlp/>

Bhatia, Gautam, 'Judicial Evasion and the Status Quo: On SC Judgments', *The Hindu* (10 January 2019) <https://www.thehindu.com/opinion/lead/judicial-evasion-and-the-status-quo/article25953052.ece>

Black, Julia, 'Decentring Regulation: Understanding the Role of Regulation and Self Regulation in a "Post-Regulatory" World' (2001) 54 *Current Legal Problems* 103.

Brousalis, Kristina and Mathews, Julie, 'A Framework for Ontario: Introducing a Working Legal Capability Matrix' (2016) Community Legal Education Ontario (CLEO) <https://cleoconnect.ca/wpcontent/uploads/2019/06/working-legal-capability-matrix.September-2016.final_.pdf>

Carrasco, Miguel, Mills, Steven, Whybrew, Adam and Jura, Adam, 'The Citizen's Perspective on the Use of AI in Government', *BCG* (1 March 2019) <https://www.bcg.com/publications/2019/citizen-perspective-use-artificial-intelligence-government-digital-benchmarking>

de Souza, Siddharth Peter and Spohr, Maximilian (eds), *Technology, Innovation and Access to Justice: Dialogues on the Future of Law* (Edinburgh University Press, 2020).

de Souza, Siddharth Peter, Aithala Varsha and John, Srishti, 'The Supreme Court of India's Vision for eCourts: The Need to Retain Justice as a Public Service', *The Hindu Centre* (10 July 2021) <https://www.thehinducentre.com/publications/policy-watch/the-supreme-court-of-indias-vision-for-ecourts-the-need-to-retain-justice-as-a-public-service/article64936007.ece>

Dhru, Kanan, Nikam, Manasi and Barendrecht, Maurits, 'Use of Digital Technologies in Judicial Reform and Access to Justice Cooperation', The Hague Institute for Innovation in Law (2021) <https://www.hiil.org/research/digital-technology-and-judicial-reform/>

Gélinas, Fabien, 'Continuity and Technological Change in Justice Delivery', in Karim Benyekhlef and others (eds), *eAccess to Justice* (University of Ottawa Press, 2016)p. 256.

Khan, Sahil, 'Emergence of Legal Tech Startups in India' (2022) 2 Jus Corpus L.J. 85.

Legal Services Corporation, 'The Justice Gap: Measuring the Unmet Civil Legal Needs of Low-income Americans' (Washington, DC: Legal Services Corporation, 2017) <https://www.lsc.gov/sites/default/files/images/TheJusticeGap-FullReport.pdf>

McKamey, Mark, 'Legal Technology: Artificial Intelligence and the Future of Law Practice' (2017) 22 *Appeal* 45.

Moses, Lyria Bennett, 'How to Think About Law, Regulation and Technology: Problems with "Technology" as a Regulatory Target' (2013) 5(1) *Law, Innovation and Technology* 1–20 <https://papers.ssrn.com/abstract=2464750>

Murray, Kate M., 'Achieving Digital Equity in Access to Justice', Legal Services Society of British Columbia (October 2021) <https://legalaid.bc.ca/sites/default/files/inline-files/Murray_2021_LABC_Achieving_Digital_Equity_Final_Report.pdf>

Narayanan, Badri and Maheshwari, Vrinda, 'Innovation and technology revolutionising the legal landscape in India', *Times of India* (New Delhi, 17 January 2022) <https://timesofindia.indiatimes.com/blogs/voices/innovation-and-technology-revolutionising-the-legal-landscape-in-india/>

National Informatics Centre, 'Launching of AI Portal – SUPACE by Hon'ble Shri Justice Sharad Arvind Bobde, Chief Justice of India and Patron-in-Chief, AI Committee' (6 April 2021) <https://webcast.gov.in/events/MTI1MQ--/session/MzE1MA>

Nishi, 'Legistify Top 10 Best Legaltech Companies in India 2022', *Inventiva* (5 January 2022).

Rostain, Tanina, 'Techno-Optimism & Access to the Legal System' (2019) 148(1) *Daedalus* 93–7 <https://doi.org/10.1162/daed_a_00540>

Salter, Shannon and Thompson, Darin, 'Public-Centred Civil Justice Redesign: A Case Study of the British Columbia Civil Resolution Tribunal' (2016–2017) 3 *McGill Journal of Dispute Resolution* 133 <https://ssrn.com/abstract=2955796>

Salyzyn, Amy, Isaj, Lori, Piva, Brandon and Burkell, Jacquelyn, 'Literacy Requirements of Court Documents: An Underexplored Barrier to Access to Justice' (2017) 33(2) *Western Yearbook of Access to Justice* 1–48 <https://ir.lib.uwo.ca/fimspub/158/>

Sandefur, Rebecca, 'Legal Tech for Non-Lawyers: Report of the Survey of US Legal Technologies', American Bar Foundation (2019), 10 <https://www.americanbarfoundation.org/wp-content/uploads/2023/04/report_us_digital_legal_tech_for_nonlawyers.pdf>

Schull, Natasha Dow, 'The Folly of Technological Solutionism: An Interview with Evgeny Morozov', *Public Books* (9 September 2013) <https://www.publicbooks.org/the-folly-of-technological-solutionism-an-interview-with-evgeny-morozov/>

Sebastian, Manu, 'Allahabad HC Takes Up The Issue Of Online Portals Advertising, Soliciting For Lawyers' *LiveLaw* (15 October 2018) <https://www.livelaw.in/allahabad-hc-takes-up-the-issue-of-online-portals-advertising-soliciting-for-lawyers-read-order/>

Shukla, Shailaja, 'Beyond the Bench: Promise of Indian Legal Tech Startups: Landscape Study of the Indian Legal Tech Startup Ecosystem', *IIMA Ventures* (2022) <https://www.insights.ciie.co/posts/beyond-the-bench-promise-of-indian-legal-tech-startups?utm_source=website&utm_medium=social&utm_campaign=legaltech>

Singer, Andrew, 'All rise for the robot judge: AI and blockchain could transform the courtroom' *Magazine by Cointelegraph* (13 March 2023) <https://cointelegraph.com/magazine/all-rise-for-robot-judge-ai-blockchain-transform-courtroom/>

Supreme Court of India, E-Committee 'Digital Courts Vision & Roadmap e-Courts Project Phase III' (New Delhi, 2022) <https://cdnbbsr.s3waas.gov.in/s388ef51f0bf911e452e8dbb1d807a81ab/uploads/2023/04/2023042088.

pdf>

The Hague Institute for Innovation in Law, 'Use of Digital Technologies in Judicial Reform and Access to Justice Cooperation' (HiiL, 2019), 59 <https://www.hiil.org/wp-content/uploads/2021/11/HiiL-Use-of-digital-technologies-in-judicial-reform-and-access-to-justice-cooperation.pdf>

Chapter 12

A Case of Digital Rights Discourse and Advocacy within Nepali Judiciary

Rita Baramu

The usage of legal tech is a comparatively new phenomenon, with gradual development within the field of the judiciary in Nepal. As digital technology is pervasive in every sector possible these days, the judiciary system in Nepal is also stepping ahead with different digital components in its daily administration. Starting from the replacement of handwritten documents and typewriters with computers in 1998,[1] now it has evolved into different kinds of software applications for virtual hearing practice. Today legal tech consists of several software applications and systems too, such as digital attendance, email correspondence, publication of daily cause list,[2] online case status, websites of courts and bar, case management system (CMS), e-library, video conferences and many more facilities. Adding to the list, the ten-year IT master plan for the court, training[3] on digital evidence and the effective implementation of legal tech for human resources can be highlighted too. During the COVID pandemic, the Supreme Court of Nepal also began online hearings[4] for a brief period, which can be considered one of the milestones in the history of the Nepali judiciary in the light of digital tech and its usage in the legal system. However, the return to in-person procedures, and the documentation of such procedures being scarcely covered by the media, has therefore meant that the public is mostly unaware of such development.

It is a well-known fact that the judiciary system entails different entities such as courts, lawyers, Bar Associations, Judges, and laws. Similarly, law firms, citizens/clients, and legal provisions of the country also play a role as stakeholders in this system. However, the existing Cis-het Brahmanical Patriarchy has a significant impact on who gets to sit at the table of delivering justice and who is on the receiving end, how accessible and fair the process is for them, especially for women and the marginalised group.

Within this scenario, legal tech has already arrived and been accepted as a supportive tool to facilitate the justice delivery procedure. It is also predictable that judiciaries will continue implementing and adding various digital tech applications in future. This is because the government and private sector have been working together for the establishment of an e-governance system in Nepal, including a digital economy, e-commerce, online education and so on with the development of digital infrastructures.[5] The private sector and individuals have played an influential role in the development of such digital infrastructures in Nepal. This kind of private sector influence persists and will continue within the judiciary and legal tech's application. Therefore, civil society, including law scholars and activists, also has an important role to play in regard to knowledge production and advocacy from a digital rights perspective, keeping women and marginalised groups at the centre of the legal tech application and justice discourse. Here, 'digital rights' mean human rights applicable within the digital landscape: freedom of expression, privacy, right to information, right to association. Nonetheless, digital rights should be inclusive and guided by the feminist principle of the internet.[6]

Civil society organisations in Nepal and activists have yet to figure out the digital rights discourse within the legal system, and advocacy intervention is needed on the matter. The digital rights discourse is somehow being initiated in general from relevant civil society organisations but is lacking in relation to the judiciary, even among human rights activists, lawyers and CSOs. Therefore, to identify this gap and initiate discussion on how digital rights advocacy should look, and what impacts the application of legal tech leaves within the whole judiciary system – especially to the marginalised communities in the Nepali context – this study was conducted with the following objectives:

- To map out what and how the court is implementing legal tech at different levels for justice delivery.
- To navigate issues of access to justice, privacy and security within the application of this legal tech while providing justice, especially for women and marginalised groups in Nepal.
- To find out digital rights concerns in civil society and that activists need to be aware of while working towards human rights and justice for women and marginalised groups.

For the purpose of this study, media monitoring and literature review through desk study were done at first to map the scenario and kinds of legal tech being used in the justice system. Additionally, a qualitative research approach was applied in which purposive and snowball sampling was done for primary data collection. In total, five key person informants (lawyers, law scholars, activists and government officers at the Supreme Court) were approached for the in-person and semi-structured interviews to find out how these legal techs are being used as well as to evaluate their effectiveness and impact.

However, during the study, the researcher was not able to reach out to multiple stakeholders to assess the phenomenon from an intersectional perspective. Since Nepal is gradually moving forward to the implementation of legal tech in the judiciary system, and various gaps still exist in the digital rights discourse, the researcher could not find any digital rights activists or civil society stakeholder working on the same issue.

A. MAPPING PROVISIONS AND SYSTEMS RELATED TO LEGAL TECH IN COURTS AND JUDICIARY

The use of digital technology in courts and for judicial systems is envisioned through different laws, policies and plans. In this section, a few landmark initiatives and policies related to them will be presented as it is important to understand the recent advent of legal tech and its usage in Nepal.

Supreme Court Guideline 2016, in section 124 and 125 outlines the usage of IT in court and judiciary activities. It allows the Court to develop its own website, useful software and all digital infrastructures for judicial proceedings.[7] The District Court Guideline 2017 followed the same envisioning of digital infrastructures and necessary outputs for the district-level courts. Similarly, the fourth five years Strategic Plan (2020-2025) envisions the establishment of e-judiciary by using ICT for court management for effective and citizen-centric service. It aimed to enhance public access to justice through e-court by establishing and implementing automated court management and judge support systems. It further proposes to establish court-owned data centres, data recovery centres, a single window or integrated e-court systems, usage of digital signatures, encryption of data and so on (ibid.).

The ICT initiative was earlier envisioned through the Judicial five-year strategic plan in 2004–2009. The current Judicial five-year strategic plan 2020–2025 aims to have an institutional improvement in hearing and decision-making from the court and to increase the public's access to justice by using ICT, effective legal support mechanisms,[8] and establishing necessary infrastructures.

Beyond the Supreme Court's plan and initiatives, there also were projects like Enhancing Access to Justice through Institutional Reform[9] by the United Nations Development Programme (UNDP) that supported the Ministry of Law and stakeholders for legal reforms and access to justice in general. Their outcomes included digitisation of a total of 9,045 cases during the project phase. Similarly, another project also supported private firms to develop software for courts, as mentioned by one of the staff of the Supreme Court.

Some laws that included or allowed the use of digital technology in court procedures were also found while mapping out the legal framework in the context of legal tech usage in the court. The entire provisions of the Electronic Transaction Act 2008 are aimed to authenticate and regulate electronic transactions carried out by any means of ICT.[10] The Evidence Act 1973 has accepted audio-visuals and digital output including digital signatures as evidence during trials.[11] Similarly, section 109 of the Criminal Code 2017[12] and section 182 of the Civil Code 2017[13] also elaborate on the use of audio-video materials in legal proceedings including the virtual witness-keeping practice.

B. CURRENT STATUS OF LEGAL TECH, ITS USAGE AND PURPOSE IN THE COURT

Within the judiciary system all over the world, people complain that the courts and justice system are hard to access, the process is very lengthy as well as the judiciary being corrupted.[14] This scenario is similar in the present case too. The impeachment case of a former chief justice[15] has also shed light regarding how tangled yet serious the case of corruption within the judiciary is. The influence, interference and interconnection between the court and political authorities as an open secret has put the judiciary in crisis, says scholar Bikram Timilsina.[16] The aftermath of this incident brought about a lottery system for judges in case delegation until the automated system is implemented to establish the transparency and accountability of the court.[17] However, the intended outcome of transparency, accountability and fast justice delivery is not yet guaranteed or proven.

Given this context of judiciary reformation discourse, the present writer reached out to a couple of people working in the legal sector to further investigate what legal tech is and how it is being used in court in order to deliver quick and efficient justice. In this chapter, the findings and observations will be presented around this issue.

In an interview with IT personnel of the Supreme Court, it was found that the Supreme Court has its own data storage system in its periphery whereas all the other governmental data is stored in Singhadurbar, the central administrative area for the executive works of the state. All kinds of software as per judicial needs are developed, managed and implemented by the twenty-four members of the internal team within the Supreme Court and 124 people in total all over Nepal. The work is not outsourced to other private companies. The IT person claimed the privacy and security of the data is a serious concern and it is being taken care of by the Supreme Court. Proof of the data security maintained by the Supreme Court is that its website and tech infrastructure were safe and sound even during the recent incident of government servers and websites going down.[18] However, in another conversation with a trans rights activist Rukshana Kapali, she mentioned facing technical glitches in the Supreme Court's website and its server being down at crucial times[19] during her case's proceeding related to her identity and right to education.[20]

Similarly, the Case Management Software recently developed by the Supreme Court is installed to integrate and manage all kinds of cases from District-High Courts to the Supreme Court. In this software, a unique registration number and case number is provided to each case, and the Supreme Court can access all sorts of information needed for a case's update using that number, said the IT personnel. It is supposed to make the case management task easier, faster, effective, and cater to the public/clients given how cases assigned to particular judges can go undecided if the judges retire or the cases are re-appealed, and so on. There is another software in the making to digitise entire cases from the beginning, which is approximately 36 lakhs (3.6 million) in number from all over Nepal (ibid.). One of the initiatives is to make the courts paperless. The Supreme Court also provides a daily cause list[21] to update a case's status whether registered, hearing ongoing or decided, to the related parties. It is done through a website and SMS system. This initiative is believed to reduce fraud by lawyers too where they are found demanding higher charges from their clients in the name of 'handling' cases catering to client's time availability and needs, say IT personnel.[22]

The Supreme Court is developing decision implementation software in which decisions of cases, including the punishment or financial charges for the guilty, could be updated. This software's access will later be provided to entities such as the passport department, police and other related government agencies so that they are aware of the court's decision and can take immediate or further action against the alleged culprit (ibid.). For example, if anyone is guilty of any crime and applied for a police record, the Department of Police can check this software and identify the person and their history to eventually decide whether or not to provide the clearance certificate to them. This sort of legal tech has indeed a positive and moral intention but, when it comes to application, or say the software is not updated regularly or the digital footprint is there, it could hamper citizens' right to a dignified life or even the right to be forgotten in digital spaces.

For future initiatives, the Supreme Court is going to establish systems such as courtroom technology or an online case registration system. First, the online registration is aimed at writ petition in which law firms will be given access to the procedures. They are hoping to expand the service to other types of cases too. Further, they are planning to link the registration process to financial apps such as e-Sewa or Khalti for clients to pay for the court's respective services online. It is aimed at the public's hassle-free experience while registering cases and in terms of increasing access to the initial process. Another kind of software to interlink and integrate the service of government lawyers, police and the Supreme Court is in the planning phase. This will bring all the criminal and civil cases into one integrated system where each entity could know the status of the case and act as per their jurisdictive rights (ibid.).

C. RIGHT TO ACCESS TO JUSTICE

Every person has the right to access to justice, which is also accepted as a human rights issue.[23] However, rights to access legal justice for women and people from marginalised communities are found to be very limited in Nepal, which is a serious concern. Overall, the justice delivery system is not as rapid as it is supposed to be. According to the recent news report by Kantipur Television, a total of 29,107 cases are on the to-be-decided list and waiting,[24] of which 16,922 cases have been ongoing for more than two years and 4,563 for more than five years. If the 'justice delayed is justice denied' phrase is to be considered, all of these cases' parties are directly and indirectly denied their rights to justice.

Besides the court's inability to solve and decide the accumulated cases over time, there is Nepal's socio-economic foundation, which comes into play when people, especially women, poor and from marginalised backgrounds, have to go through legal proceedings and are unable to get justice easily or denied at different levels by the state's authorities. A case report also shows how it is very difficult to get justice in sexual violence cases and how the survivors have to go through different levels of harassment and hardships in pursuit of justice.[25]

Research by Body & Data regarding online violence and relevant laws also found that there are sociocultural barriers for women and queer individuals trying to access the justice system.[26] The barriers usually come in the form of manipulation, silencing or threats to victims in the name of case reconciliation before court procedures. The onus of proof on the victim, victim blaming and backfiring on the victim through slander are other barriers after the case is filed. A survivor who filed a rape case against a national cricket player recently shared in interview[27] that the player, who is very powerful and influential, has seven lawyers on his side and they debate for thirty-five minutes even if they speak for five minutes each, whereas she has only two lawyers, who can speak for ten minutes only (five minutes each). She is also unable to pay for her lawyers due to her low economic status. This interview also proves how lack of power, influence and access makes the justice process very difficult, unequal and unpleasant for women, poor and marginalised survivors.

The statute of limitation is also another factor that blocks survivors from the road to justice if they are not able to file the case within the legal timeline. There is probability that a survivor dealing with trauma due to the violence that occurred against them could not have taken immediate action to access justice.

Additionally, the existing digital divide from accessing justice[28] is also difficult to cross for women, poor and marginalised people, who do not have access to information about legal parameters or structures. There are incidents and discourse around women and girl children being deprived of the use of information and technology in Nepal in the name of morality and decency.[29] Although such deprivation is claimed to be for their own protection, it is actually the cis-het Brahmanical patriarchy that is in the background wanting to control sexuality and freedom of women, to protect the existence of the status quo and the establishment. Similarly, people with disabilities often find it challenging to access digital information and infrastructures due to inaccessible designs and structures.[30]

In this sense, it is clearly seen that women and marginalised groups have less access to information and technology. And even if the information related to a case from its hearing date to the decision is publicly available through the court's website and SMS (as claimed by the authorities) or the tech infrastructure is very informative, easy and protects their right to access and information from the user's perspective, such infrastructures cannot work efficiently unless the digital divide and lack of access to the internet and devices is addressed in Nepal.

During an interview with activist Rukshana Kapali, she mentioned that things are digital as well as manual in court these days. In her experience, one has to submit both printed and soft copies of the documents to the court and, although everything is claimed to be digital, the signature process after the case's decision is done manually. Also, the court does not provide digital copies of the decision. One has to request a copy of such a decision, after which they will get a photocopied version of the printed version, that too only after paying tax. She added that, although such copies are comprehensible for her compared to handwritten documents, which had chances of being misinterpreted as different people have different handwritings; for people with disabilities, the whole process is very inaccessible. If they give a printed document, it is not in braille, or, if it is digital, it is not an accessible version at all, she added.

As mentioned earlier, the Supreme Court started an online hearing procedure to continue the work of justice delivery for the public despite the crisis during the COVID-19 pandemic). However, it could not run as successfully as imagined due to the trust issues of clients towards their lawyers. They did not take virtual hearing as seriously and real as physical hearing because it is still a new thing for non-tech people. When it comes to online expression, presence or even online violence, it seems elusive compared to real-life experiences for many. Although the pleasure or harm received through online activities is real, it still is not accepted as real-life experience by many.

On the other side, lawyers or accused parties tend to escape the online hearing in the name of 'slow internet' or 'technical problem' to delay the procedure, according to an internal source. Therefore, online hearings could work efficiently only if both parties are equally responsible and eager to settle with the proceeding no matter what the decisions and consequences are. However, remote areas or district courts such as Dipayal and Kanchanpur have been practising virtual hearings as their geographical status is far away from the Supreme Court located in the capital, and virtual hearings are helpful for them to connect with the case's processing and all, says the Supreme Court officer.

Staff also stressed that the development and installation of software alone is not enough when it comes to legal tech applications in justice delivery. The issue of its implementation by lawyers, judges, staff or related parties is equally important for the smooth functioning and targeted outcome. They explained that the entire responsibility of implementing the system falls upon them after developing such software, which is a very adverse situation and should in fact come under the auspices of the management department. Even if they train others on the interface and its application after the software is released, the willingness to learn and follow instructions for the functional aspect of the software is low from the implementation team. This is due to the lack of digital literacy and enthusiasm to adopt new technologies in their work, along with the lack of work integrity and desire to provide quality work and enough reward/encouragement from the government, which is a pervasive problem in Nepal. 'Who do you think is willing to digitise all those dusty papers stored for years if there are no extra incentives or rewards from the management?' asked the staff.

In such a scenario, it is essential to ask: will digital/legal tech actually be able to facilitate and provide the actual justice sought and demanded? Or is it just another illusionary promise that has been given to us by the authorities within the parameters of the neoliberal, tech-solutionist approach currently reigning the world?

D. PRIVACY AND SECURITY CONCERNS

Privacy as a human rights issue protects us from unwanted interference from others by helping us to manage our boundaries with the outer world.[31] As per human rights treaties, it is related to individual autonomy, which is guaranteed by Article 12 of the UDHR[32] and Article 17 of the ICCPR.[33] Nepal's current Constitution in Article 28 also ensures the right to privacy of citizens, while there is the Individual Privacy Act 2018 which lays the ground for the protection of an individual's right to privacy both online and offline.

Besides these legal frameworks and treaties, privacy is a crucial phenomenon for our dignified and autonomous life with agency and freedom, which is also referred to by different scholars who voice our rights to exercise privacy. In her article 'When our body becomes data, where does that leave us?',[34] Anja Kovacs talks about different nuances of privacy both online and offline in a socio-political context, where she highlights that privacy is especially important for women and individuals from oppressed and marginalised groups. She provides examples of Dalit individuals' autonomy to be anonymous in the bigger city than the villages where their caste status is well known; trans-sex workers' agency to choose sex work as their profession and maintain privacy; or women's abortion or STD issues that they want to keep private due to the societal judgement and vilification. All of these examples, and her argument for protection of privacy, prove how the privacy concern is very important to people, mostly the marginalised or oppressed groups, and how they are vulnerable in terms of their life and livelihood when their privacy and anonymity is violated.

Meanwhile, the privacy issue is equally important and should be considered and addressed accordingly when we are talking about being online and using technology. Also during this study, issues of privacy, data privacy and security came across, which will be thoroughly discussed.

During the interview with IT personnel, the researcher was told that neither the public nor any other party except the system manager has access into the server and data centre of the Supreme Court. If the IT staff are using the software, their activity log is recorded so that the administration or the IT staff themselves can check what they are doing. Similarly, every activity log by working staff is recorded into the software and can be observed by the administration. Due to such a system, the IT personnel claimed that the data is very private and secured; but, somehow, if staff make any mistake at their end, for example, uploading incorrect decisions or information, that can be tracked and the staff could be made liable for their mistake.

As mentioned above, the private sector was involved in the initial phase of digitalisation and digitisation of the judiciary in different stages in collaboration with development projects related to judiciary reform. Currently, the Supreme Court IT management team also consists of a consultant who worked on the same project and is continuing the same work of software updates, management and implementation at Supreme Court.[35] This raises the concern of data privacy and security as there had been similar concerns of data privacy over government-collected data in which private consultants were given access to the data.[36]

However, the Supreme Court IT personnel member assured the interviewer of his integrity, honesty and dignity towards his work and expressed that he is also aware of the possible charges and liability in case of fraud or privacy violation. Another concern is the lack of sufficient budget from the government to protect and manage the system from privacy and security aspects as per the IT consultant.[37]

The software being developed and implemented, such as case management or decision implementation, should be able to protect the privacy of people, especially victims from vulnerable groups. The court follows the practice of closed-door hearings in sensitive cases. The name of victims is anonymised in the legal documents. This trend should be followed in all the available software at the Supreme Court to protect the privacy of victims; and the staff there claimed that the software has such provisions and practice of keeping the names private in sensitive cases. However, a lawyer working with an NGO that supports women and marginalised in access to justice procedure mentioned the gap in the privacy of the information of lawyers in every step of the legal procedures from filling up forms during the litigations to asking for copies of final decisions. They mentioned that lawyers' names are explicitly published in the list offline and online, which is a serious case of privacy violation. It is a serious concern especially when it comes to lawyers who side with women and marginalised victims in sensitive cases such as sexual assault. Also, the system by default promotes transparency and the right to information that undermines an individual's right and choice to remain undisclosed. As privacy is an individual's choice to manage their boundary, lawyers should have the agency to choose where and to whom to reveal (or not) their names. In this case, the legal system does not seem to care about the agency of individual lawyers although it somehow does care about victims' privacy.

Overall, privacy and security of data are very important to ensure access to justice through the means of technology. Relevant actors, whether the government's lawyers, administrators, IT personnel or anyone involved in the system, should strive to make the process easier and beneficial to all, especially women and individuals at the margins while in the journey of seeking and accessing justice.

E. CONCLUSION

The usage of legal tech within the judiciary system in Nepal is increasing. Things are being digitised and digitalised gradually under the concept of a paperless/digitalised court which is supported and addressed by different policies, plans and legal measures. Similarly, different kinds of software, systems and tech are developed and implemented as well as planned to aim for efficient, quick and people-centric justice delivery.

Additionally, people's right to justice by exercising their agency and autonomy to remain private both online and offline is an important issue. This should be considered and addressed within the digital system being developed and implemented for people-centric justice delivery. However, there is also Nepal's socio-political landscape, which is cis-het Brahmanical patriarchal and oppressive to women, queer and marginalised folks and plays an adverse role in making these groups more vulnerable and deprives or denies them of the justice they seek. Therefore, the idea of suggesting and applying tech usage for any kind of services, including judicial proceedings, needs to be handled very carefully and sensitively given all these hegemonic socio-political complications already thriving among people and their social realities. Otherwise, the usage of legal tech will be useless for the people who are already suffering. Their right to a dignified life will be far-fetched even if the legal tech application has good intentions such as effective, easy, people-centric and quick justice delivery, elimination of frauds from authorities, hassle-free experience for the public, and so on. Meanwhile, if a Supreme Court owned data storage centre is functional, it can be assumed and understood that separation of power is quite assured between the judiciary and the executive when it comes to handling cases of political authority and public concerns as well as civil cases. This is yet another topic to research and find out about rather than using assumptions as a basis.

Additionally, an evaluation is needed in the long run to assess if the good intentions of such legal tech usage is real or not and whether these legal techs are able to achieve their aim of people-centric justice delivery or not.

Civil societies on the other side should also be aware of the application and implication of the legal tech being used within the judiciary. They should play the role of observers as well as be able to organise against the idea of tech solutionism if it is doing more harm than good to the public, especially towards those who are at the bottom of the social hierarchies.

NOTES

1. 'न्यायपालिकामा सूचना प्रविधिको प्रयोग र प्रभावकारीता' (*Lekalighar*, 25 July 2021) <www.dhanulekali.com/2021/07/blog-post_88.html> (accessed 10 March 2023).
2. 'Supreme Court of Nepal: Daily Cause List' (*Supreme Court of Nepal*) <https://supremecourt.gov.np/lic/sys.php?d=reports&f=daily_public> (accessed 1 March 2023).
3. 'Training on Cyber Crime and Digital Evidence' (*National Judicial Academy, Nepal*) <https://njanepal.org.np/training/326> (accessed 1 March 2023).
4. 'Supreme Court also begins online hearing' (*OnlineKhabar English*, 18 May 2021) <https://english.onlinekhabar.com/supreme-court-also-begins-online-hearing.html> (accessed 1 March 2023).
5. 'How Nepal Is Making Digital Economy a Possibility' (*Khalti*, 31 July 2018) <https://blog.khalti.com/fintech-trends/digital-economy-nepal/> (accessed 16 February 2024).
6. 'Sexuality, Feminism, Activism, and the Internet we dream of' (GenderIT.org, 13 April 2014) <https://genderit.org/feminist-talk/sexuality-feminism-activism-and-internet-we-dream> (accessed 2 August 2024).
7. Interview with Supreme Court Authorities, Nepal (13 February 2023) on file with author.
8. Ibid.
9. 'Enhancing Access to Justice through Institutional Reform Project (A2j)' (*UNDP*) <www.undp.org/nepal/projects/enhancing-access-justice-through-institutional-reform-project-a2j> (accessed 2 March 2023).
10. Electronic Transaction Act 2008 (Nepal). The Electronic Transaction Act 2008 is Nepal's very first act that recognised usage of ICT and digital infrastructures. It was promulgated for the authentication, regularisation, of the recognition, validity and reliability of generation, production, processing, storage, communication and transmission of electronic records and transactions.
11. Evidence Act 1973 (Nepal). In sections 2, 6, 13, 18, 35 and 37 of the Evidence Act, there is mention of digital evidence such as digital signatures, audio-visual means, digital publications or documents being considered as strong evidence during criminal trials.
12. Criminal (Code) Act 2017 (Nepal), s. 109. Section 109 of the Criminal Code Act mentions that if the witness cannot be present during the trials due to their disability status or if they are children, the procedure will be conducted through videoconferencing.

13. Civil (Code) Act 2017 (Nepal), s. 182. Section 182 of the Civil (Code) Act mentions that if the witness could not be present if they are a child or out of the country or due to their disability, the procedure will be conducted through videoconferencing.
14. Dory Reiling, *Technology for justice: How information technology can support judicial reform* (Leiden University Press, 2009).
15. 'Nepal's chief justice, suspended for months, prepares to return to Supreme Court – Nepal Live Today' (*Nepal Live Today,* 7 December 2022) <www.nepal livetoday.com/2022/12/07/nepals-chief-justice-suspended-for-months-prepares-to-return-to-supreme-court/> (accessed 2 March 2023).
16. Poreg, 'Nepal Judiciary in Crisis' (*Policy Research Group*) <www.poreg.org/nepal-judiciary-in-crisis/> (accessed 2 March 2023).
17. Binod Ghimire, 'What's the lottery system for assigning cases and does it really work?' *The Kathmandu Post* (19 November 2021) <https://kathmandupost.com/national/2021/11/19/what-s-the-lottery-system-for-assigning-cases-and-does-it-really-work> (accessed 2 March 2023).
18. 'Government websites going down question Nepal's cybersecurity status. What are solutions anyway? – OnlineKhabar English News', *OnlineKhabar English News* (30 January 2023) <https://english.onlinekhabar.com/nepal-government-websites-down.html> (accessed 2 March 2023).
19. Interview with Rukshana Kapali and with lawyers (15 February 2023) on file with author.
20. Rukshana Kapali, 'रिट निवेदन (Writ Petition)' <https://minchyaameyju.wordpress.com/writ-petitions/> accessed (2 May 2023).
21. 'Supreme Court of Nepal: Daily Cause List' (*Supreme Court of Nepal*) <https://supremecourt.gov.np/lic/sys.php?d=reports&f=daily_public> (accessed 1 March 2023).
22. Interview with Supreme Court Authorities, Nepal (13 February 2023) on file with author.
23. UNHCR, 'Access to Justice', *Handbook for the Protection of Internally Displaced Persons* (UNHCR 2007) 241–254 <www.unhcr.org/4794b4e12.pdf>.
24. Kantipur TV HD, 'Kantipur Samachar' (15 February 2023) <www.youtube.com/watch?v=vOvsxG3eN7o> (accessed 2 March 2023).
25. Sagar Chand, 'Justice is a dream deferred for survivors of rape and sexual violence in Nepal – OnlineKhabar English News', *OnlineKhabar English News* (1 February 2023) <https://english.onlinekhabar.com/justice-rape-sexual-violence-in-nepal.html> (accessed 2 March 2023).
26. Shubha Kayastha and Rita Baramu, *Mapping Laws relevant to Online Violence in Nepal* (Body & Data 2021) <https://bodyanddata.org/wp-content/uploads/2021/12/OnlineGBVLawsMapping-min.pdf> (accessed 16 February 2024).
27. Basanta Basnet, 'प्रधानमन्त्रीज्यू- सन्दीप लामिछानेलाई भेट्नुभयो, मलाई भेट्नुहुन्न?' *Online Khabar* (25 February 2023) <www.onlinekhabar.com/2023/02/1268776> (accessed 2 March 2023).
28. Sakar Pudasaini, 'Addressing Nepal's digital divide', *Nepali Times* (11 January 2022) <www.nepalitimes.com/opinion/addressing-nepals-digital-divide/> (accessed 2 March 2023).

29. Shailee Chaudhary, 'Internet Access, Digital Rights and Privacy in Madhesh | Body & Data' (*Body & Data*, 7 October 2021) <https://bodyanddata.org/internet-access-digital-rights-and-privacy-in-madhesh/> (accessed 2 March 2023).
30. Jalasha Sapkota, 'Let's Strive to Make Our Digital Platforms Accessible for All | Body & Data' (*Body & Data*, 31 October 2022) <https://bodyanddata.org/lets-strive-to-make-our-digital-platforms-accessible-for-all/> (accessed 2 March 2023).
31. What Is Privacy?' (*Privacy International*, 23 October 2017) <www.privacyinternational.org/explainer/56/what-privacy> (accessed 2 March 2023).
32. UN General Assembly, *Universal Declaration of Human Rights*, 10 December 1948, 217 A (III), Art. 12.
33. UN General Assembly, *International Covenant on Civil and Political Rights*, 16 December 1966, United Nations, Treaty Series, vol. 999, p. 171, Art. 17.
34. Anya Kovacs, 'When our bodies become data, where does that leave us?' (*Internet Democracy Project*, 15 June 2020) <https://internetdemocracy.in/reports/when-our-bodies-become-data> (accessed 2 March 2023).
35. Interview with Supreme Court Authorities, Nepal (n. 7).
36. S. Sapkota, 'Panic Spikes as PM's IT Guru Ali Has Access to People's Private Data', *My Republica* (4 April 2020) <https://myrepublica.nagariknetwork.com/news/panic-spikes-as-pm-s-it-guru-ali-has-access-to-people-s-private-data/> (accessed 16 February 2024).
37. Interview with Supreme Court Authorities, Nepal (n. 7).

REFERENCES

'Enhancing Access to Justice through Institutional Reform Project (A2J)' (UNDP) <www.undp.org/nepal/projects/enhancing-access-justice-through-institutional-reform-project-a2j> (accessed 1 March 2023).

'Government websites going down question Nepal's cybersecurity status. What are solutions anyway?' *OnlineKhabar English News* (30 January 2023) <https://english.onlinekhabar.com/nepal-government-websites-down.html> (accessed 1 March 2023).

'How Nepal Is Making Digital Economy a Possibility' (Khalti, 31 July 2018) <https://blog.khalti.com/fintech-trends/digital-economy-nepal/> (accessed 1 March 2023).

'Nepal's chief justice, suspended for months, prepares to return to Supreme Court', *Nepal Live Today* (7 December 2022) <www.nepallivetoday.com/2022/12/07/nepals-chief-justice-suspended-for-months-prepares-to-return-to-supreme-court/> (accessed 1 March 2023).

'Supreme Court also begins online hearing', *OnlineKhabar English* (18 May 2021) <https://english.onlinekhabar.com/supreme-court-also-begins-online-hearing.html> (accessed 1 March 2023).

'Supreme Court of Nepal: Daily Cause List' (Supreme Court of Nepal) <https://supremecourt.gov.np/lic/sys.php?d=reports&f=daily_public> (accessed 1 March 2023).

'Training on Cyber Crime and Digital Evidence' (National Judicial Academy, Nepal) 'न्यायपालिकामा सूचना प्रविधिको प्रयोग र प्रभावकारीता' (Lekalighar, 25 July 2021) <www.dhanulekali.com/2021/07/blog-post_88.html> (accessed 1 March 2023).

Basnet, B., 'प्रधानमन्त्रीज्यू- सन्दीप लामिछानेलाई भेट्नुभयो, मलाई भेट्नुहुन्न?' *Online Khabar* (25 February 2023) <www.onlinekhabar.com/2023/02/1268776> (accessed 1 March 2023).

Chand, S., 'Justice is a dream deferred for survivors of rape and sexual violence in Nepal' *OnlineKhabar English News* (1 February 2023) <https://english.onlinekhabar.com/justice-rape-sexual-violence-in-nepal.html> (accessed 1 March 2023).

Chaudhary, S., 'Internet Access, Digital Rights and Privacy in Madhesh' (Body & Data, 7 October 2021) <https://bodyanddata.org/internet-access-digital-rights-and-privacy-in-madhesh/> (accessed 1 March 2023).

Civil (Code) Act 2017 (Nepal), s. 182.

Criminal (Code) Act 2017 (Nepal), s. 109.

Ghimire, B., 'What's the lottery system for assigning cases and does it really work?' *The Kathmandu Post* (19 November 2021) <https://kathmandupost.com/national/2021/11/19/what-s-the-lottery-system-for-assigning-cases-and-does-it-really-work> (accessed 1 March 2023).

Kapali, R., 'रिट निवेदन (Writ Petition)' <https://minchyaameyju.wordpress.com/writ-petitions/> (accessed 1 March 2023).

Kantipur TV HD, 'Kantipur Samachar' (15 February 2023) <www.youtube.com/watch?v=vOvsxG3eN7o> (accessed 1 March 2023).

Kayastha, S. and Baramu, R., *Mapping Laws Relevant to Online Violence in Nepal* (Body & Data, 2021).

Poreg, 'Nepal Judiciary in Crisis' (Policy Research Group) <www.poreg.org/nepal-judiciary-in-crisis/> (accessed 1 March 2023).

Pudasaini, S., 'Addressing Nepal's digital divide', *Nepali Times* (11 January 2022) <www.nepalitimes.com/opinion/addressing-nepals-digital-divide/> (accessed 1 March 2023).

Reiling, D., *Technology for Justice: How Information Technology Can Support Judicial Reform* (Leiden University Press, 2009).

Sapkota, J., 'Let's Strive to Make Our Digital Platforms Accessible for All' (Body & Data, 31 October 2022) <https://bodyanddata.org/lets-strive-to-make-our-digital-platforms-accessible-for-all/> (accessed 1 March 2023).

Sapkota, S., 'Panic Spikes as PM's IT Guru Ali Has Access to People's Private Data', *My Republica* (4 April 2020) <https://myrepublica.nagariknetwork.com/news/panic-spikes-as-pm-s-it-guru-ali-has-access-to-people-s-private-data/> (accessed 1 March 2023).

UNHCR, 'Access to Justice' in *Handbook for the Protection of Internally Displaced Persons* (UNHCR 2007) 241–254.

Electronic Transaction Act 2008 (Nepal).

Evidence Act 1973 (Nepal).

Chapter 13

Lessons from Pakistan's Judicial Techno-Solutionism

Aimen Taimur

A. INTRODUCTION

According to Digital Rights Watch,[1] Evgeny Morozov's book[2] *To Save Everything, Click Here: The Folly of Technological Solutionism* is where the term 'techno solutionism' first gained popularity. The idea is a critique of the post-modern urge to use technical solutions to everyday problems without fully appreciating their negative effects or considering how they can work against us in the long term. Similar issues can be found if the same criticism is applied to the employment of technologies in courts. The paper chapter will look at how Pakistani courts have tried to use technology to speed up adjudicative procedures and how to evaluate the advantages and disadvantages of such technology for both litigants and the courts.[3]

To ensure that its 225.2 million citizens have access to justice[4] and raise its position on the Rule of Law Index,[5] Pakistan has made a number of improvements to its judicial system. Following the formation of the National Judicial Automation Committee (NJAC), which is led by a senior Supreme Court Judge,[6] new initiatives have been created in this regard.

NJAC recently called for the creation of an artificial intelligence cell to develop algorithmic cataloguing of case law for the development of an AI-driven data analytics platform and a comprehensive cross-linking of cases for digital database integration across other institutions.[7] This was done in collaboration with the National Centre of Artificial Intelligence (NCAI) at the National University of Sciences and Technology (NUST). These sophisticated databases produce data that is meant to be used by algorithms that can assist judges in drafting judgments using predictive text programming, as well as for updating statistics for policymakers.

Yet it must be acknowledged that the adoption of cutting-edge technologies has sometimes felt a bit like a reflexive response to an impetuous desire to modernise.[8] For instance, there have been serious data protection issues over the development of online case repositories for AI platforms because no attempt has been made to secure the identity of vulnerable litigants. Although using new technologies in the courtroom and behind the bench has been centred on the noble goal of ensuring that everyone has access to justice, there does seem to be an imbalance due to the fact that the majority of people, including court staff who are not tech experts, lack digital literacy. As a result, there is discrimination between individuals who understand how online systems function and have a basic comprehension of the digital world and others who do not. This is related to the fact that sufficient employee training, impact analyses, and policy consultations should have taken place prior to the real-time implementation of automation plans.

B. FROM PAPER TO DIGITAL

In the past, paper-based record-keeping and correspondence were the norm in official settings. Digitalisation, however, seemed to be the only practical answer that brought about a new era of judicial reforms in light of the escalating environmental issues and the burden of keeping vast amounts of paper records. With some deviations based on the national resources of each individual government at the time,[9] this mass digitisation of Asian judiciaries could be observed in the late 1990s and early 2000s. Pakistan is a special case study because, despite the majority of its court records being on paper, there have been irregular spurts of patchy digitisation, in which some court records have been converted to digital form by unofficial, privately owned online repositories.[10] That said, since they are neither owned nor controlled by the Courts themselves, they do contain a number of errors, such as inaccurate citations and missing passages from reported judgments. They are nevertheless frequently used by law schools, students, firms and court personnel despite their slow, unfriendly interfaces. The only official versions of these court repositories are available in limited numbers on the websites of the Supreme Court and the provincial High Courts.

This inconsistent strategy has been extremely troublesome since it has led to a system that supports both the drawbacks of a legal environment that is not digitally advanced and the drawbacks of attempts to digitally advance without having proper quality control in place. The journey of Pakistan's efforts to improve digitisation is rife with irritating real-time problems, giving it the worst of both worlds. The development of a case law management system and ensuing plans to release software applications that would automate judicial procedures heavily rely on fundamental pre-work like the building of databases. However, the databases need data, which must then be processed and formatted into sets that can be read.

The earliest known legal paper records for Pakistan date from 1947, making them about seventy-four years old. Many records, including several renowned landmark rulings, have disintegrated and are no longer readable because paper cannot withstand the test of time. Even though efforts were made to gather these paper documents so that their remnants could be promptly scanned and uploaded for the online case repository, it was found that the paper had become almost translucent over time and that when double-sided documents were scanned, the text overlapped and became illegible. Additionally, there was a lack of knowledge in place to deal with deteriorating, damaged records that would shatter at the slightest touch, which led to the termination of these efforts to preserve historical judgments.

Consequently, the next best solution for the court staff would be to manually type the judgments but lack of administrative interest and human resources has resulted in yet another incomplete project. As time goes on, paper records are becoming harder to maintain but no attention is being given to record preservation. This is a recurring theme within most technological projects undertaken by the Judiciary, that is, enthusiastic adoption without prior impact assessments nor the necessary maintenance protocols in place and then eventual abandonment.[11]

C. PAKISTAN'S EXPEDITIOUS JUSTICE INITIATIVE

Pakistan suffers from a major backlog of cases in courts of all levels.[12] On the High Court level, the Lahore High Court and the Sindh High Court have made the most prominent attempts in recent years to inculcate the use of technologies within judicial administrative functions to speed up administrative processes.[13] In cooperation with the Punjab Information Technology Board (PITB), a budget of approximately PKR 197.5 million was allotted to purchase computers and other supplies in 2011.[14] During his tenure as Chief Justice of the Lahore High Court, Justice Syed Mansoor Ali Shah did advocate for a categorised and publicly accessible system of case flow management, along with the upgradation of the official High Court website. Surprisingly, this development was faced with protest from some factions of lawyers who deemed this system to be inflexible and a means to restrict their choice to present their clients at their discretion. The outcry is evidence that technology can provide for more procedural equity to prevent the misuse of power by lawyers who would usually keep applying for adjournments on frivolous grounds while charging their clients over an extended period.[15] There is now a national case flow management system known as e-CFMS. This idea was inspired by its success in the United States[16] and solidly helped make the case for the Pakistani Judiciary to develop its own case flow management system so that the ever-increasing cases can be managed within an appropriate time frame.[17]

However, the most revolutionary change came from the Sindh High Court while Justice Mushir Alam was the Chief Justice until his elevation to the Supreme Court in 2013. Not only was the High Court equipped with a fully functioning case flow information system[18] but also a live roster of the sitting judges. Recently, it has also developed a biometric identification branch allowing lawyers to easily submit and register their cases online, which simultaneously double-checks the ID cards of the litigants and their lawyers due to a shared database with the National Database and Registration Authority (NADRA). The real-time tracking of the judicial roster also ensures that judges are not on extended leaves and are presiding over the hearings that they ought to be present for.[19] Having a publicly available case flow management system[20] also provides for various individuals to know the time and day that they would need to be in court. The concept of E-summons has also been introduced to ensure that the case disposal rate is not stagnated by the absence of litigants and their legal representatives. This also ties into the vision that the Sindh High Court is working towards: to go completely digital by 2030, where most if not all court procedures will be automated.[21]

To address the slow pace of case disposal at the Supreme Court, under the very able direction of Justice Mushir Alam,[22] after his elevation to the Supreme Court of Pakistan as the Senior Puisne Judge, the processing of appeals was aimed to be resolved via the implementation of the successful model of technological upgradation as launched in the Sindh High Court. The outcome of this is that the Supreme Court has finally developed a more organised approach towards the creation and implementation of new technologies within its institution.

In the Supreme Court of Pakistan, the National Judicial Automation Committee was established in 2009 to oversee technology-centred projects. Its composition was carefully decided, including senior members of the Judiciary to ensure that tech-focused development plans and problems are dealt with seriously. However, through time, its output became negligible. The National Judicial Automation Committee was therefore reconstituted in September 2016 by the Chief Justice of Pakistan and the Chairman of the National Judicial (Policy Making) Committee under the Ordinance (LXXI) of 2002.[23] Broadly, the Committee is composed of a chairman (from the Supreme Court) and six

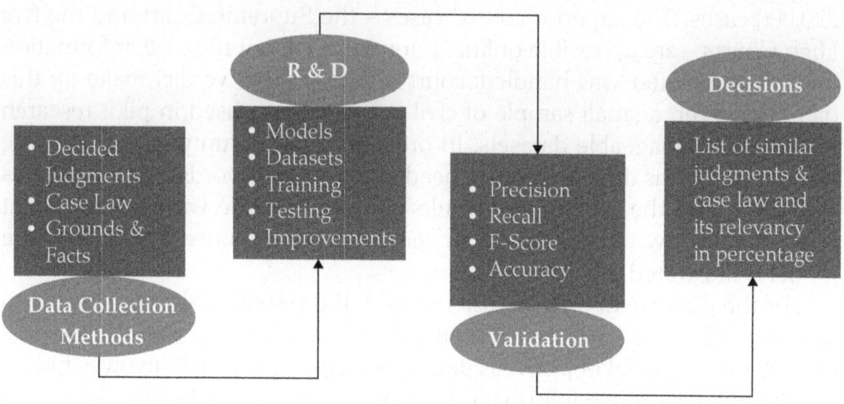

Figure 13.1 High-level flow pilot model depicts the flow of information from the point of input to the suitable output to be used within judgment drafting

members from each of the High Courts and the Federal Shariat Court. Further to the judicial staff, the Committee also has one sub-committee for standardisation of nomenclature for the IT staff and a sub-committee of IT experts for standardisation and integration of IT Systems for the Judiciary. The mandate of the National Judicial Automation Committee is the planning, execution, monitoring and financial assessment for the automation of the court system. It also coordinates with the National Centre of Artificial Intelligence (NUST) and the National Information Technology Board (NITB).

D. ARTIFICIAL INTELLIGENCE AND THE JUDICIARY

A new influx of scientific and technical advancements has been centred on artificial intelligence. The latest round of judicial reforms has been influenced by advances in artificial intelligence, which have been considered almost like strategic resources. According to the National Judicial Automation Committee's agenda, it was determined that producing judgments is a difficult task that requires information from a variety of sources, including decided cases, legal academic journals and other resources.[24] Automation of this function would therefore aid in case disposition rates and uniformity of decisions made on the same factual and legal grounds. In order to implement the idea, it was also suggested that various national knowledge databases be integrated. This would save the time needed for the manual process of retrieving case law from law digests.

The availability of data, dataset preparation, processing power, infrastructure and trained resources must all be met for this plan to be put into practice. Between 2015 and 2019, there were over 3.0 million cases registered in Pakistan, and 2.97 million cases were determined there on average per year. Out of the 2.97 million, the superior courts alone decided about 220,000 cases. The superior courts' cases – the Supreme Court and the five High Courts – are accessible online. Information about the case, information on how the matter was handled, court orders and the verdict make up this data. However, a small sample of civil law cases was used in pilot research to produce manageable datasets. In order to create a running model, more data cleaning was done to remove head notes and keywords. The model was evaluated, and the preliminary results showed promise with a 30 per cent relevancy that was scaled to 70 per cent with adjustments. The flow of the model is illustrated in Figure 13.1.[25]

For the purpose of orderly case retrieval, the system is also anticipated to automatically mark cases based on the classification (civil, criminal, services, etc.). Another crucial objective is data anonymisation, which involves hiding the plaintiffs' sensitive information, such as their names and residences, in case law databases that are available to the general public.

The goal is eventually to create a system capable of commenting on the performance of judicial officers, particularly those in subordinate courts, in order to serve as a quality control tool. This opens a discussion on how a similar development would limit judges' ability to make decisions. The role of a judge is too sacred and significant to be scrutinised by an algorithm.[26] Since common law frameworks are based on the principles of consistency and the preservation of judicial precedent, it is likely that an algorithm may flag a judgment as worrisome if it departs from the judicial approach used in earlier, comparable cases.

The duty of judges is to determine how a law may be applied in a certain circumstance, which gives the law important flexibility[27] and guarantees that the factual context is taken into account; this can be used to overturn, distinguish from and modify judgments.[28] The dread of being judged by strict computational systems would put unwarranted additional strain on court employees, which will ultimately be counterproductive. Contrarily, on a more positive note, performance reviews will be much more objective and standardised, which leads to the conclusion that AI-based reviews should maybe be limited to the judicial officers' procedural performance rather than tight substance scrutiny of judgments.

The fact that this project has not yet advanced because auto-tagging of verdicts and document verification has not been enabled is cause for concern. Additionally, a system that can evaluate the calibre of earlier judgments when offering drafting recommendations to judges, or even an algorithm with a considerably more complex level of intelligence, is required to effectively detect opposing evidence. It is not yet ready to be utilised as a tool for making judgment recommendations or creating documents in its current state because there is no adequate user procedure. Another reason the database is worthless in the current edition is because, as was already indicated, the whole body of existing case law has not been digitally preserved. Unfortunately, the initiative has not been pursued since the retirement of Justice Mushir Alam, who led it in the first place. All the earlier testing and investment will be lost if the project is not swiftly resumed since the private market, which offers comparable services, is developing at a faster rate than internal developments.

E. SOUTH ASIAN COURTS AS UNIQUE TERRITORY

Asia was the first area to experience an extended lockdown due to COVID-19, which originated in China. As a result, the region was forced to lead the way in implementing policies to secure the operation of its public offices in order to restore some sense of normalcy in these extraordinary circumstances. Before the catastrophic events of 2019,[29] the worry of case pendency was a frequently acknowledged barrier for most judiciaries. This resulted in Video Link Hearings[30] and the conversion of numerous procedures to online alternatives in a judicial setting. Although this increased reliance on technology had to be pushed, it must be said that most courts lacked the procedures required to ensure orderly sessions. Particularly in the early stages of the pandemic, there were no models to follow. Under the leadership of Chief Justice Gulzar Ahmed, the Pakistani Supreme Court made sure that courts remained open even while infection rates were at their highest. This was accomplished by announcing a 'smart lockdown'. The courts would have had the luxury of conducting all hearings online if technology innovation had been prioritised and the protocols for using technologies in courtrooms had been well-practised. As was the case in Pakistan, there was no established basis on which technology could be confidently used to completely automate a public service and be a substitute for in-court pre-pandemic proceedings. Similarly, throughout South Asia, the digitisation of court functions was not necessarily seen as being essential to the proceedings but rather as an alternative to administrative functions.[31]

Digital illiteracy is another issue in South Asia's more economically underdeveloped regions.[32] The elderly and litigants in rural areas are most affected by this problem. There is a clear gap between the judicial solutionist argument and the end user, or the typical litigant. Even while the use of smartphones and the improvement of internet connectivity is a process that is still in progress, it is not yet possible to construct a completely online environment for litigant interaction. In fact, it would deprive people of the ability to exercise their rights if they lacked access to reliable internet (which is the case for the majority of people since rural areas have a larger population density) or the right technology to access judicial websites. The reliance on an entirely online environment for litigants, it is said, would obstruct access to justice and widen the gap between those who can afford to purchase and learn how to use new technology and those who cannot.[33]

South Asia has long been recognised as a renowned leader in innovation and technology. Asia is an ecosystem unto itself that transcends and to some extent fails to be confined by the mostly European and American conceptions of technology regulation, being the industrial backbone for big tech businesses. Geographical and socio-economic diversity makes it difficult to create an all-encompassing system. Cyberspace may provide the impression of continuity, but this is not how it works in practice. Even if we were to apply cutting-edge technology within Pakistan that goes beyond the meta-narrative of simplifying the job of the courts to administer fundamental judicial functions, the cultural variations and the very conceptualisation of justice may differ too greatly from one another to be technologically integrated. The native methods of resolving disputes, such as *jirgas*[34] and *panchayats*[35] serve as an illustration of this. Since the existence of these types of grassroots out-of-court settlements[36] depends on their non-conformance to the mainstream judicial sector, we cannot force these indigenous traditions[37] to be a part of the automation trend. The strength of the aforementioned argument, however, is limited to the assertion that the native modes of conflict resolution function within acceptable parameters. The format is significantly different, even though the law of the land relied upon is the same as that which is relied upon in the official court system. The intersectional constraints of technology solutionism are thus made apparent.[38]

F. THE FUTURE

It is important to realise that integrating technology into current systems should not be mistaken for progress if doing so slows down or interferes with the delivery of justice, which is the primary objective of the judicial system.[39] There is no one model that can be used to use technology in every court system because each one has its own difficulties and would need a different form of technological support.[40] However, there are some lessons that can be taken away from Pakistan's efforts to employ technology to modernise its judiciary. It is important to realise that integrating technology into current systems should not be mistaken for progress if doing so slows down or interferes with the delivery of justice, which is the primary objective of the judicial system.

The first stage in any development is to make sure that it complies with the established constitutional provisions and human rights laws. This includes an emphasis on cybersecurity, data protection and privacy.[41] Dealing with sensitive data necessitates a higher level of responsibility while handling it. The courts must also take on the role of a data management organisation if they begin employing technology to automate more of their processes. In this role, they will be accountable for any data breaches and purposeful or unintentional abuses of litigants' privacy. The courts must inform persons who depend on their services of the specific, publicly accessible gazetted norms that would determine their liability should they fail to act in accordance with the highest standards of data protection.[42]

Since ChatGPT's introduction and the range of applications it provides, its effects on the judiciary are already apparent, as demonstrated by the case of a Colombian judge who used ChatGPT to ask a question before making a decision regarding a state welfare issue.[43] It is imperative to make sure that the judiciaries are outfitted with the necessary regulatory protections for the maintenance of the rule of law and fairness because it is only a matter of time before this practice expands and reaches Asian judiciaries.[44] Either the judiciaries must develop secure, reliable AI systems, or they must establish internal rules that prioritise human rights and specify the morals and regulations to be followed when utilising these new operating systems. Impact assessments[45] need to be prioritised in both cases, with adequate resources and time allocated, to avoid unpleasant shocks once automated systems are implemented.[46]

NOTES

1. 'Techno solutionism – very few things actually need to be an app' (*Digital Rights Watch*, 25 March 2021) <https://digitalrightswatch.org.au/2021/03/25/technosolutionism/> (accessed 16 February 2024).
2. 'The Folly of Technological Solutionism: An Interview With Evgeny Morozov' (*Public Books*, 9 September 2019) <https://www.publicbooks.org/the-folly-of-technological-solutionism-an-interview-with-evgeny-morozov/> (accessed 16 February 2024).
3. This chapter would not have been possible without the support and guidance of Justice (r.) Mushir Alam, who retired as the Senior Puisne Judge at the Supreme Court of Pakistan. Being a Judicial Law Clerk under his mentorship, the present writer learned about the practicalities of court technologies and got an authentic insight into the realities of techno-solutionism. His resolve to engage new technologies for enhancing access to justice and upholding the rule of law despite a multitude of obstacles has inspired this chapter and continues to motivate the author's research.
4. Asian Development Bank, 'Pakistan's Access to Justice Program Completion Report' (2009).
5. World Justice Project, 'Rule of Law Ranking – Pakistan' (2021) <https://worldjusticeproject.org/rule-of-law-index/country/2021/Pakistan/> (accessed 16 February 2024).
6. Justice (r.) Iftikhar Chaudhry, Keynote address at the concluding session of National Judicial Conference (2011) <http://www.pljlawsite.com/2011art24.html> (accessed 16 February 2024).
7. Law and Justice Commission of Pakistan, *Law and Justice Commission Newsletter (January–June 2020)* (2020) <http://ljcp.gov.pk/nljcp/assets/dist/Publication/jj2020.pdf> (accessed 16 February 2024).
8. LJCP (n. 7), 21–3.
9. Faqir Hussain, 'Judicial System of Pakistan' (*Supreme Court of Pakistan*) <https://www.supremecourt.gov.pk/downloads_judgements/all_downloads/Judicial_System_of_Pakistan/thejudicialsystemofPakistan.pdf> (accessed 16 February 2024).
10. *Pakistan Law Site* <https://www.pakistanlawsite.com/Login/MainPage> (accessed 16 February 2024).
11. Ziaullah Ranjha, 'How Far Can the Pakistani Justice System Be Changed with Technology', *The Friday Times* (24 July 2022) <https://thefridaytimes.com/24-Jul-2022/how-far-can-the-pakistani-justice-system-be-transformed-with-technology> (accessed 16 February 2024).
12. M. Shah Alam, 'Problems of Delay and Backlog Cases', *The Daily Star* (25 February 2010) <https://archive.thedailystar.net/suppliments/2010/02/ds19/segment3/delay.html> (accessed 16 February 2024).
13. Z. Ranjha (n. 11).
14. 'The Journey of Automating Lahore High Court Hits its Final Stage' (*Punjab Information Technology Board*, 2015) <https://pitb.gov.pk/journey_automating_lahore> (accessed 16 February 2024).

15. R. U. Shah and others, 'Causes for Delay in Civil Justice' (2014) 6 *Pakistan Journal of Criminology* <http://www.pjcriminology.com/wp-content/uploads/2019/01/4-15.pdf> (accessed 16 February 2024).
16. R. Hoffman, 'Case and case flow management', Paper presented at Law and policy reform at the Asian development bank: Challenges in implementing access to justice reforms, Michigan, United States (2005).
17. J. P. Coolsen, 'Case Management Innovation in a Large, Urban Trial Court: the Critical Importance of Legal Stakeholder Attitudes' [2008] *The Justice System Journal* 70.
18. Z. A. K. Sherwani, 'Case flow management system and court automation' (International Judicial Conference, Islamabad, 2006).
19. 'Automation of Federal Courts and Tribunals' (*Ministry of Law and Justice*) <https://molaw.gov.pk/ProjectDetail/ZDZjYzY3ZDAtZTQ2OS00NGRhLTliNmItMzJmMzdiYTY3ZDE0> (accessed 16 February 2024).
20. Justice Rahmat Hussain Jafferi, 'Use of Information Technology IT in Courts' (Beijing, 25–28 October 2010) <http://www.apjrf.com/PakistanPresentationatBeijing2010.pdf> (accessed 16 February 2024).
21. 'E-Courts Project Vision 2030' (*eNotices*) (*High Court of Sindh*) <https://enotices.sindhhighcourt.gov.pk/> (accessed 16 February 2024).
22. 'Chairmen IT' (*High Court of Sindh*) <https://www.sindhhighcourt.gov.pk/IT_Chairmen.php> (accessed 16 February 2024).
23. 'National Judicial (Policy Making) Committee' (*Law and Justice Commission Pakistan*) <http://www.ljcp.gov.pk/NJPMC.html?BD1C26EABB74a6d00CG=GMYF> (accessed 16 February 2024).
24. Maxi Scherer, 'Artificial Intelligence and Legal Decision Making: The Wide Open? A study examining international arbitration' [2019] 318 QSML Legal Studies Research Paper <https://sifocc.org/app/uploads/2020/04/Artificial-Intelligence-and-Legal-Decision-Making-The-Wide-Open-Maxi-Scherer-041119.pdf> (accessed 16 February 2024).
25. Expeditious Justice Initiative, 'AI and Judiciary: High Level Meeting of the Global Judicial Integrity Network' (Doha, 24– 27 February 2020).
26. J. Iqbal, 'The Role of the Judiciary as a Catalyst of Change' (International Judicial Conference, Islamabad, 2006); S. M. Irshad, 'Eradication of Corruption: Initiatives and Strategies' (National Judicial Conference, Islamabad, 2011).
27. The issue of ex-parte decision is taken up by Superior Courts differently in different instances. In some cases, the Supreme Court justified the orders passed by the courts ex-parte (*M. Idrees* v. *Shamim Akhtar*, 1980; *Rehmat Ali* v. *Javed Ur Rehman*, 1985) while in others they were set aside on grounds that the party was not given proper opportunity of hearing and technicalities have to be avoided for substantial justice (*Ashiq Hussain Shah* v. *Province of Punjab*, 2003; *Nouroz Khan* v. *Haji Qadoor*, 2005). The Civil Procedure Code is quite clear about this issue in its Order IX Rule 6, wherein it has declared that a court may proceed ex parte in a case where the judge has found that summons is properly and timely served on the defendant but its contextual interpretation shows how the courts may use their discretion to decide according to what may be procedurally necessary in each case without being bound by prior approaches.
28. Ibid.

29. M. K. Lakho, 'Social reasons for and repercussions of judicial delays in subordinate courts of Karachi: the need for sociological analysis' (2021) 44(2) *Sri Lanka Journal of Social Sciences* 181 <https://sljss.sljol.info/articles/10.4038/sljss.v44i2.7928> (accessed 16 February 2024).
30. D. L. F. de Vocht, 'Trials by video link after the pandemic: the pros and cons of the expansion of virtual justice' (2022) 8 China-EU Law J. 33 <https://link.springer.com/article/10.1007/s12689-022-00095-9> (accessed 16 February 2024).
31. S. P. de Souza., V. Aithala and S. John, 'The Supreme Court of India's Vision for e-Courts: The Need to Retain Justice as a Public Service' [2021] 14 Policy Watch No. 14 <https://www.thehinducentre.com/publications/policy-watch/article35229520.ece> (accessed 16 February 2024).
32. ASEAN, 'Digital Literacy in Education Systems Across Asia: Key insights and opinions of young people' (*UNICEF*, 2021) 6 https://www.unicef.org/eap/media/7766/file/Digital%20Literacy%20in%20Education%20Systems%20Across%20ASEAN%20Cover.pdf> (accessed 16 February 2024).
33. Amir Kullah, 'Delays, costs and glorious uncertainty – how judicial procedure hurts the poor' in S. Gangopadhyay (ed.), *Economic reforms for the poor* (New Delhi, Konark Publishers, 2000), pp. 298–343.
34. Barakatullah Advocate and Imran Ahmad Sajid, 'Jirga System in Pakhtun Society: An Informal Mechanism of Dispute Resolution' (2013) 5(2) *Pakistan Journal of Criminology* <http://www.pjcriminology.com/wp-content/uploads/2019/01/4-19.pdf> (accessed 16 February 2024).
35. Abid Ghafoor Chaudhry and others, 'Perception of Local Community and Biradari on Panchayat: An Exploratory Anthropological Study of Biradari in Village Saroki, District Gujranwala, Pakistan' (2014) 4(2) *Advances in Anthropology* <https://www.scirp.org/journal/paperinformation?paperid=46091> (accessed 16 February 2024).
36. Ibid.
37. Ibid.
38. S. Akhtar and others, 'Study of informal justice system in Pakistan: Evaluation report. Karachi: Sindh Judicial academy & UNICEF' (The Sindh Judicial Academy 2008) <https://sja.gos.pk/assets/publication/Misc/Report%20Informal%20Justice%20System%20in%20Pakistan.pdf> (accessed 16 February 2024).
39. S. Hamid, 'An overview of the judicial system of Pakistan and how far has it succeeded in providing justice and establishing rule of law: Report' (Justice, accountability and international experience. Islamabad: Pakistan institute of legislative development and transparency (PILDT), 2007).
40. G. M. Khan, 'Speedy justice – how?' [1988] *Pakistan Legal Decision XL* 228.
41. H. Abbas, 'Pakistan 2020: A Vision for Building a Better Future (Washington, DC, Asia Society Pakistan Study Group, 2011).
42. Supreme Court of Pakistan Rules, 1980 (the rules allow for the highest appellate court to make its own internal protocols under the guidance of the sitting judges).
43. L. Taylor, 'Colombian judge says he used ChatGPT in ruling', *The Guardian* (2023) <https://www.theguardian.com/technology/2023/feb/03/colombia-judge-chatgpt-ruling> (accessed 16 February 2024).
44. AI and the Rule of Law: Capacity Building for Judicial Systems' (*UNESCO*) <https://www.unesco.org/en/artificial-intelligence/rule-law/mooc-judges> (accessed 16 February 2024).

45. J. Dusik, A. Bond and B. Sadler, 'Should We Have Impact Assessments for Disruptive Technologies' (International Institute for Sustainable Development, 2019).
46. W. P. Grimm and others, 'Artificial Justice: The Quandary of AI in the Courtroom' (Judicature International – Duke Law School, 2022) <https://scholarship.law.duke.edu/cgi/viewcontent.cgi?article=1004&context=judicature_intl> (accessed 16 February 2024).

REFERENCES

Abbas, H., 'Pakistan 2020: A Vision for Building a Better Future' (Asia Society Pakistan Study Group, Washington, DC, 2011).

Akhtar, S., Alam, M., Shafiq, M. S. and Detho, I. A., 'Study of Informal Justice System in Pakistan: Evaluation Report' (Sindh Judicial Academy and UNICEF, Karachi, 2008).

Alam, M. S., 'Problems of Delay and Backlog Cases' (2010) *The Daily Star* (25 February 2010) <https://archive.thedailystar.net/suppliments/2010/02/ds19/segment3/delay.html>

ASEAN, 'Digital Literacy in Education Systems Across Asia: Key Insights and Opinions of Young People' (2021) <https://www.unicef.org/eap/media/7766/file/Digital%20Literacy%20in%20Education%20Systems%20Across%20ASEAN%20Cover.pdf>

Asian Development Bank, 'Pakistan's Access to Justice Program Completion Report' (2009).

Barkatullah and Sajid, I., 'Jirga System in Pakhtun Society: An Informal Mechanism of Dispute Resolution' (2013) *Pakistan Journal of Criminology* <http://www.pjcriminology.com/wp-content/uploads/2019/01/4-19.pdf>

Chaudhry, A., Ahmed, A., Khan, S. and Hussain, S., 'Perception of Local Community and Biradari on Panchayat: An Exploratory Anthropological Study of Biradari in Village Saroki, District Gujranwala, Pakistan' (2014) 4(2) *Advances in Anthropology* 53–58.

Chaudhry, Justice (r.) Iftikhar, 'Keynote Address at the Concluding Session of National Judicial Conference' (2011) <http://www.pljlawsite.com/2011art24.htm>

Coolsen, J. P., 'Case Management Innovation in a Large, Urban Trial Court: The Critical Importance of Legal Stakeholder Attitudes' (2008) *The Justice System Journal* 70–90.

de Souza, S. P., Aithala, V. and John, S., 'The Supreme Court of India's Vision for e-Courts: The Need to Retain Justice as a Public Service' (2021) Policy Watch No. 14 <https://www.thehinducentre.com/publications/policy-watch/article35229520.ece>

de Vocht, D. L. F., 'Trials by Video Link after the Pandemic: The Pros and Cons of the Expansion of Virtual Justice' (2022) *China-EU Law Journal* 8, 33–44.

Digital Rights Watch, 'Techno Solutionism – Very Few Things Actually Need to Be an App' (2021) <https://digitalrightswatch.org.au/2021/03/25/technosolutionism/>

Dusik, J., Bond, A. and Sadler, B., 'Should We Have Impact Assessments for Disruptive Technologies?' (International Institute for Sustainable Development, 2019).

Expeditious Justice Initiative, 'AI and Judiciary: High-Level Meeting of the Global Judicial Integrity Network' (Doha, 24–27 February 2020).

Gangopadhyay, S., 'Delays, Costs and Glorious Uncertainty: How Judicial Procedure Hurts the Poor' in S. Gangopadhyay (ed.), *Economic Reforms for the Poor* (Konark Publishers, New Delhi, 2000).

Grimm, W. P. et al., 'Artificial Justice: The Quandary of AI in the Courtroom' (Judicature International – Duke Law School, 2022) <https://scholarship.law.duke.edu/cgi/viewcontent.cgi?article=1004&context=judicature_intl>

Hamid, S., 'An Overview of the Judicial System of Pakistan and How Far Has It Succeeded in Providing Justice and Establishing Rule of Law: Report' (Pakistan Institute of Legislative Development and Transparency, Islamabad, 2007).

Hoffman, R., 'Case and Case Flow Management', Paper presented at Law and Policy Reform at the Asian Development Bank: Challenges in Implementing Access to Justice Reforms, Michigan, United States (2005).

Hussain, F., 'Judicial System of Pakistan' (Supreme Court of Pakistan) <https://www.supremecourt.gov.pk/downloads_judgements/all_downloads/Judicial_System_of_Pakistan/thejudicialsystemofPakistan.pdf>

Iqbal, J., 'The Role of the Judiciary as a Catalyst of Change', Paper presented at the International Judicial Conference, Islamabad (2006).

Irshad, S. M., 'Eradication of Corruption: Initiatives and Strategies', Paper presented at the National Judicial Conference, Islamabad (2011).

Justice Rahmat Hussain Jafferi, 'Use of Information Technology IT in Courts' (Presented in Beijing 25–28 October 2010) <http://www.apjrf.com/PakistanPresentationatBeijing2010.pdf>

Khan, G. M., 'Speedy Justice – How?' (1988) *Pakistan Legal Decision XL* 228.

Lakho, M. K., 'Social Reasons for and Repercussions of Judicial Delays in Subordinate Courts of Karachi: The Need for Sociological Analysis' (2021) *Sri Lanka Journal of Social Sciences* 181–97.

Ministry of Law and Justice, 'Automation of Federal Courts and Tribunals' <https://molaw.gov.pk/ProjectDetail/ZDZjYzY3ZDAtZTQ2OS00NGRhLTliNmItMzJmMzdiYTY3ZDE0>

Pakistan Law Site <https://www.pakistanlawsite.com/Login/MainPage>

Public Books, 'The Folly of Technological Solutionism: An Interview with Evgeny Morozov' (2021) <https://www.publicbooks.org/the-folly-of-technological-solutionism-an-interview-with-evgeny-morozov/>

Punjab Information Technology Board, 'The Journey of Automating Lahore High Court Hits its Final Stage' (2015) <https://pitb.gov.pk/journey_automating_lahore#:~:text=The%20budget%20allocated%20was%20PKR197,courts%20with%20essential%20IT%20equipment>

Ranjha, Z., 'How Far Can the Pakistani Justice System Be Changed with Technology?' *Friday Times* (2022).

Scherer, M., 'Artificial Intelligence and Legal Decision Making: The Wide Open? A Study Examining International Arbitration' <https://sifocc.org/app/uploads/2020/04/Artificial-Intelligence-and-Legal-Decision-Making-The-Wide-Open-Maxi-Scherer-041119.pdf>

Shah, R. U. et al., 'Causes for Delay in Civil Justice' (2014) 6 *Pakistan Journal of Criminology* 49–60 <http://www.pjcriminology.com/wp-content/uploads/2019/01/4-15.pdf>

Sherwani, Z. A. K., 'Case Flow Management System and Court Automation', Paper presented at the International Judicial Conference, Islamabad (2006).

Taylor, L., 'Colombian judge says he used ChatGPT in ruling' (2023) *The Guardian* <https://www.theguardian.com/technology/2023/feb/03/colombia-judge-chatgpt-ruling>

UNESCO, 'AI and the Rule of Law: Capacity Building for Judicial Systems' <https://www.unesco.org/en/artificial-intelligence/rule-law/mooc-judges>

World Justice Project, 'Rule of Law Ranking – Pakistan' (2021) <https://worldjusticeproject.org/rule-of-law-index/country/2021/Pakistan>

Chapter 14

Digital Rights in Southeast Asia: Civil Society's Legal Tactics and Courts' Roles

Letitia Visan and Emilie Palamy Pradichit

A. INTRODUCTION

Technology plays an increasingly important role in every facet of people's lives, and, with its rise, human rights understanding has changed. While the digital age has opened new spaces for the enjoyment of human rights, such as the right to freedom of expression, it has also brought a range of new threats and risks to them. Technological developments not only enable individuals to use new information and communications technologies that improve lives, strengthen justice and boost productivity but also enhance the capacity of governments, businesses and individuals to undertake surveillance and interception, which may violate or abuse human rights. For this very reason, regulatory systems need to adapt to counteract the ways they can be exploited to threaten fundamental human rights and freedoms in the digital space. The responsibility to uphold and protect digital rights, dispersed across multiple layers of society, lies with a range of stakeholders. From states to businesses, to civil society, to international organisations, to academia, each of them has a specific role; and, unless they abide by their role, there is little prospect of living in a society where digital rights are respected for all.

While states face the challenge of reforming their laws to keep pace with the digital revolution, civil society is confronted with ensuring that new rules meet international standards and represent an appropriate adaptation of offline rules to online contexts, which all too often is not the case. Protecting the space for civic engagement and activities is not particularly straightforward nor easy to achieve in an environment of weak rule of law, where online democracy is under attack, which is the case in the Southeast Asia region.[1] In many countries across the region, the very concept of the rule of law is something the powerful are constantly negotiating, as we experience the expansion of authoritarian regimes. Authorities have utilised new and old legislation and government-aligned courts to punish critics and silence the outspoken. This view gains currency from the intensification of repression against opposition voices, both through legal and extrajudicial means, but tougher enforcement through the courts indicates the ever-shrinking room for discourse. In the struggle for the rule of law and in holding the authorities accountable for the respect for human rights, civil society plays a significant role.

This chapter explores how civil society actors (CSAs) are approaching courts to guarantee digital rights in Southeast Asia, by analysing five cases initiated by CSAs from across the region. The secondary purpose of studying these cases is to determine how well the courts have conceptualised digital rights and how much expertise is required for them to act on these matters. The chapter concludes with recommendations for states to defend internet freedom as a vital form of democracy, and to protect and enhance civic space; and for civil society to promote and ensure good governance, while contributing to the promotion, protection and advancement of human rights online.

B. HOW CIVIL SOCIETY IS APPROACHING COURTS TO FACILITATE AND GUARANTEE DIGITAL RIGHTS IN SOUTHEAST ASIA

Southeast Asia is a heterogeneous regional setting comprising a number of countries with differing sizes, levels of development and governance systems. A multi-tiered judicial system exists in many of the countries in the region, but its effectiveness in preserving people's rights and freedoms is often compromised by its vulnerability to executive pressure.

Southeast Asia has over 400 million internet users and a booming digital economy, and the internet penetration rate ranges from around 70 per cent in all countries but Laos, Myanmar and Timor-Leste.[2] In fact, the digital space has become an integral part of people's everyday lives and has expanded the democratic and civic space, which are essential for ensuring freedom of expression and political participation, among others. Yet, it has brought with it immense challenges in protecting human rights and democracy.

While the remarkable power of the internet to enable millions of people to express their opinions, organise, share and receive information is obvious, the actions of governments in Southeast Asia in recent years have demonstrated just as clearly how the internet has given states unprecedented power to stem the flow of information and opinion through technical means, with rapid and widespread effect. The declining internet freedom was documented in the Freedom on the Net 2022 Report by Freedom House, which reveals that none of the eight countries monitored in the region have an online sphere rated as 'free'.[3] On top of inadequate safeguards to protect digital rights, the legal systems have repeatedly proved inadequate, with judges handing down decisions that legitimised governments to suppress already curtailed digital rights.

In this chapter, cases show how CSAs petitioned courts and called upon them to review the constitutionality or legal conformity of provisions, driving collective action to defend digital rights and resist authoritarianism. Although their success in bringing strategic litigation to quash online repression has been limited to a certain extent, nonetheless these cases show the tenacity of civil society in defending digital rights and its courageous and proactive role in approaching the courts to guarantee these rights.

I. Thailand

With the rise of digital dictatorship, which Prayuth's regime has sparked, respect for digital rights is being lost.[4] Thailand has a restrictive political environment, and blocking and punishing opinions deemed critical of the monarchy and the government are frequent. Over 200 people are currently charged with lèse-majesté under the Criminal Code, which enshrines the crime of defamation against the monarchy and sets out draconian penalties.[5] The authorities also frequently charge activists and netizens with sedition and violations of the Computer Crime Act,[6] which gives officials broad powers to prosecute online expression.[7] Hundreds of people are guilty until proven innocent and detained, and courts, which suffer from politicisation and corruption,[8] regularly deny them bail.[9]

To counter digital rights restrictions, civil society actors have had to find alternative forms of resistance, including building regional solidarity and reaching out to the international community to call on the Thai government to respect its human rights obligations and protect democratic values.[10] Youth pro-democracy activists have even resorted to unconventional outlets to show their grievances.[11] In addition, civil society has turned to the judiciary, petitioning courts to uphold digital rights. A landmark case from 2021 shows dogged civil society's success in approaching courts and pushing back against digital repression.

On 29 July 2021, the Prime Minister promulgated a regulation under section 9 of the Emergency Decree on Public Administration in Emergency Situations B.E. 2548 (2005),[12] which would have authorised the suspension of internet services for those who share content that may 'instigate fear', 'mislead' or affect security.[13] It also required internet service providers (ISPs) to identify IP addresses accused of producing content deemed illegal, report the details to the government, and immediately suspend internet service to that IP address. In front of this, civil society did not stand idly by while their liberties were attacked. On 2 August of the same year, a group of human rights lawyers and twelve Thai media companies filed a petition before a civil court challenging the regulation.[14]

On 6 August, in extremely positive news, the Civil Court issued a judgment strongly in favour of upholding and advancing the human rights of people online. In its decision, the court ruled that a prohibition relating to 'content that may instigate fear among the people' is ambiguous and may lead to an unnecessarily broad interpretation affecting freedoms of expression and the press guaranteed by the constitution. Additionally, it held that 'the importance of the internet access is recognised throughout the society, particularly, in the current situation of Coronavirus Disease (COVID-19) pandemic', which Thailand was going through at that time. The court confirmed that regulations requiring ISPs to cease providing internet services for owners of content violating the regulation results in an impermissible blockage of communication channels and is unconstitutional. Furthermore, it determined that the regulation would place a disproportionate burden on the people to interpret and comply with the law.[15] The court issued an emergency order that prevented the Prime Minister from enforcing the regulation, whereupon the government issued a regulation repealing it.[16] The regulation's quashing marked a positive step for freedom of expression online in Thailand and for the role of civil society as a key player in contributing to the realisation of digital rights.

In a more recent development, civil society actors in Thailand have once again demonstrated their importance as agents of change for enhancing accountability and promoting fundamental rights. For the first time in Southeast Asian history, eight Thai citizens jointly filed a lawsuit against NSO Group, the Israeli company that developed the Pegasus spyware,[17] for violating their rights after their phones were infected by Pegasus over the past two years.[18] The lawsuit was dismissed by a civil court in Bangkok on the grounds that the cases could not be combined. Following this, Yingcheep Atchanon, one of the individuals who had originally filed the lawsuit in November, stated he would bring a new lawsuit with himself as the plaintiff.[19] In June 2023, Yingcheep Atchanont, alongside an activist, filed a lawsuit against nine Thai government agencies, demanding 2,500,000 baht in compensation for alleged privacy violations due to the government's reported use of Pegasus spyware. The Court ruled that the case was outside its jurisdiction and declined to proceed. As of now, the case is awaiting appeal.[20] The decision is likely to echo far beyond Thailand when it is handed down.

II. Indonesia

In Indonesia, freedom of expression, including online, is protected in the constitution and other laws, but the right is routinely curtailed in practice. Digital repression is rampant and includes disruptions to internet access, criminalisation of people's online activities, as well as digital attacks against civil society, especially critical groups such as journalists, activists and human rights defenders.[21] Moreover, the new Criminal Code passed in December 2022 poses a massive threat to human rights, as it contains problematic provisions which are bound to push Indonesia deeper into authoritarianism, leaving no space for civil liberties and threatening freedom of expression.[22] Although the judiciary has occasionally shown its independence, the court system is rife with corruption and is subject to political influence.[23] In a case related to internet shutdown episodes, courts reached opposing conclusions, with the final court failing to uphold digital rights.

Disrupting internet services during times of social unrest is a classic authoritarian tactic, and the Indonesian government used it in August and September 2019 during protests in Papua and West Papua. Following this, a coalition of civil society groups filed a lawsuit against the government for purposely shutting down the internet.[24] The petitioners argued that the government's action to shut down the internet violated press freedom and the right to information, as journalists were unable to report and inform the public about the protests. In what was then a victory, the Jakarta State Administrative Court held on 3 June 2020 that internet shutdowns were 'a violation of the law by government bodies or officials'. It held that the Electronic Information and Transactions (ITE) Law, which the government relied on in court to argue that the internet shutdown was in compliance with it, should only be used to restrict online information or documents that are 'unlawful', not to terminate access in its entirety. The court ruled that 'any decision that limits people's right to information should be made in accordance with the law and not merely based on the government's discretion'.[25] Nevertheless, the victory for human rights lasted a fleeting moment. In October 2021, the Constitutional Court found that it is constitutionally acceptable for the government to block and throttle the internet in times of social strife, overturning the precedent established in the previous court decision. The court explained that the government has the responsibility to 'prevent[...] the dissemination and use of electronic information and/or electronic documents that have prohibited contents in accordance with statutory provisions'.[26] In effect, the court held that the decision to block internet access was lawful and 'within reason', given the threat to public order.[27]

Therefore, in its decision, the court focused on the arguments concerning the legality and proportionality of the restrictions. The limitation of this approach was that the court recognised deference to the state in its assessment, and this created the implication that shutdowns may sometimes be justified and proportionate. The ruling has set a dangerous precedent for online freedoms. Worse still, it perpetuates authoritarian rule and aids and abets the consolidation of power. Without internet access, activists, dissidents and opposition parties are cut off from each other, making it difficult for them to organise and mobilise their ideals and capabilities.[28] The court also shrugged off the potential of long-term internet shutdowns to take on the characteristics of apartheid by excluding specific populations from public participation in a highly interconnected and digitised world.[29] Such judgment has the potential to reverberate globally.

Dictatorship is far from being a distant memory in Indonesia and is even expanding. At the same time, the fight against digital repression is also increasing, oftentimes led by civil society organisations (CSOs).

On 30 November 2022, Indonesian CSOs filed a lawsuit against the Ministry of Communication and Informatics with the Jakarta State Administrative Court, over its decision to block access to a number of online platforms that had violated the law by failing to register with the government.[30] The civil society group alleged that the termination of access violated economic rights, hindered journalists' work, and prevented the public from obtaining information. The court's decision, in this case, will set a significant precedent for human rights online.

III. The Philippines

The Philippines has taken a turn towards authoritarianism over the past years and the decline in internet freedom has occurred amidst an erosion of political and civil rights under ex-president Rodrigo Duterte.[31] Following the May 2022 elections, the ascent of President Bongbong Marcos, son of ousted dictator Ferdinand Marcos, exacerbated this, as it revived memories of large-scale human rights abuses and corruption that the Philippines had to endure only several decades ago.[32] The former president's government has been notable for diminishing the independence of the judiciary, which has been plagued by inefficiency, corruption and intimidation.[33]

Similar to Thailand and Indonesia, civil society groups approached courts to guarantee the respect of digital rights, showing at the same time resistance to attempts to crack down on rights and civil liberties. In July 2020, former president Duterte signed into law the Anti-Terrorism Act of 2020.[34] Almost all advocacy actions, including speeches and publications, fell under the law's broad definition of 'terrorism', which prompted civil society groups from different sectors to file thirty-seven petitions with the Supreme Court challenging the law's constitutionality and preventing its implementation.[35] The groups expressed concern over the Act's broad scope and its potential for use by state authorities as another instrument to persecute opponents and limit free speech. In fact, one of the common themes of the petitions was threats to free speech posed by many provisions under the law, such as the one on inciting terrorism.

The Supreme Court's decision from December 2021 was highly controversial. The Court upheld the constitutionality of the law, keeping most of its repressive provisions, and only striking down two provisions: section 4, which allowed 'advocacy, protest, dissent, stoppage of work, (and) industrial or mass action' to be classed as terrorism; and section 25, which empowered the Anti-Terrorism Council to designate people and groups as terrorists at the request of other countries or international organisations.[36] Lawyers in the country put the ruling in the crosshairs. While some considered it a 'small victory'[37] and others a 'consolation',[38] they unanimously agreed that the upheld provisions continue to pose a threat to human rights defenders, activists, members of marginalised groups, and others wrongly accused of terrorism, by giving the government sweeping, unrestrained authority and leaving room for arbitrary enforcement.[39] To illustrate, the vague prohibition on 'inciting to commit terrorism' in section 9 may have important implications and ramifications for the right to freedom of opinion and expression, as it extends criminalisation beyond acts or threats of lethal violence to acts protected under international law. In April 2022, the Supreme Court dismissed the six appeals filed by petitioners to reverse its ruling on their pleas against the law, due to the 'lack of substantial issues and arguments raised by the petitioners'.[40]

The court's decision, in this case, is particularly important because the law is presumed to have received the most criticism of any piece of legislation in Philippine history.[41] The Constitutional Court has failed to protect not only civil liberties and human rights but also procedural rights and the rule of law, as democratic space shrinks. In the prevailing climate of impunity and attacks on human rights defenders, the court's decision portends peril for them, as the law grants excessive and unchecked powers to the government.

IV. Malaysia

Malaysia's legal framework is made up of a great number of repressive laws, such as the Sedition Act, and provisions that aim to impose censorship and punish those exercising their right to freedom of expression, including online.[42] In addition to inadequate protections, the judicial system has proved to be weak at times, compromised by executive influence,[43] failing to rule in respect of fundamental rights.

On 17 September 2014, law professor Azmi Bin Sharom[44] challenged the constitutionality of the 1948 Sedition Act, hereinafter the Act.[45] He contended that the Parliament alone, and not any other bodies, had the authority to enact laws restricting freedom of speech and expression. He claimed the Act was unconstitutional since it was passed during the British colonial era, before independence, being therefore not an Act of the Parliament of Malaysia. On 6 October 2015, the Federal Court ruled that the Act is constitutional, thus compatible with Article 10 of Malaysia's Federal Constitution, which guarantees the right to freedom of speech and expression. The court determined that the assessment of what is 'necessary or expedient' in balancing fundamental rights with security interests lies with Parliament, and not with the courts.[46] The holding, in this case, is particularly disconcerting, in light of the elusive nature of the Sedition Act provisions that allow for investigation and prosecution, if not conviction, of virtually any utterer whose speech is not to authorities' liking.

With this ruling, the Federal Court, in its position as the highest judicial authority in Malaysia, defied international human rights law that protects freedom of speech and legitimised the government to continue using this Act as a tool to quell it. At the same time, the decision has brought into question the judiciary's ability to safeguard fundamental rights, especially considering the illiberal and undemocratic nature of the Act, which has been used to suppress legitimate dissent in Malaysia, both offline and online.[47]

In Southeast Asia, where the path to democracy is onerous and many countries are heading towards authoritarianism,[48] civil society – recognised for its role as a check and balance on compliance with international human rights standards – is particularly important. The cases presented in this chapter highlight civil society's crucial role in bringing human rights claims to court, leading to contentious and far-reaching verdicts, while also providing lessons on how to meaningfully seek and effect change through litigation in domestic courts. This is despite the fact that civil society has frequently struggled with poorly capacitated court systems lacking independence.

In the case of civil society challenging Regulation No. 29 in Thailand, the Civil Court demonstrated a thorough understanding of the importance of access to internet services for society. Although it did not make an explicit reference to digital rights in its judgment, it did note that a particular clause that forbade the dissemination of information that may instigate fear among people led to a superfluous and unnecessary deprivation of people's rights and freedoms. Thus, it highlighted the revolutionary impact that technology has on human rights. Despite civil society's approach to courts and their intention to assist them in upholding and guaranteeing digital rights in the other instances from Indonesia, the Philippines and Malaysia, the final court's decision in each case flagrantly failed to take into account and uphold human rights. These cases indicate that courts, overall, have loosely conceptualised digital rights, with some not even peripherally considering the impact of technology on human rights, and hence overlooking the implications that their rulings might have on digital rights.

To effectively conceptualise digital rights in Southeast Asia, a comprehensive and nuanced approach is imperative. This involves the formulation of clear digital rights frameworks that are consistent with international human rights standards while being responsive to local cultural contexts. Given the increasing significance of the online space – particularly in authoritarian regimes where it frequently serves as a crucial platform for expression – it is essential that legal protections robustly encompass freedom of expression, privacy, and data protection. Additionally, fostering digital literacy and continuously updating legal frameworks to address emerging technological advancements are integral to this endeavour.

C. CONCLUSION AND RECOMMENDATIONS

A set of recommendations for states to defend internet freedom, protect and enhance civic space, and for civil society to ensure good governance, is provided below.

I. Recommendations to states to defend internet freedom as a vital form of democracy, and protect and enhance civic space

1. Promote and advance internet freedom as a key element to contribute to the development of democracy. Support programmes aimed at bolstering judicial independence and improving technical literacy among judges and other members of the judiciary.
2. Ensure that limits to rights, including the rights of freedom of expression and association, are legal and proportionate.
3. Recognise and strengthen the role of the judiciary in upholding digital rights. In particular, ensure that the judiciary contributes to influencing the understanding of digital rights, addressing gaps in legislative guarantees of these rights, and ensuring accountability for violations of these rights.
4. Considering the significant role CSA actors play in society and in defending democracy and the rule of law, offer them institutional support to stay alert and react to deviations from the rule of law.
5. Develop or reinforce legal frameworks to ensure that the rights of citizens, including online, and civil society organisations are protected.
6. Improve and strengthen legal frameworks that allow citizens and civil society organisations to form and operate.
7. Protect online civic space and strengthen access to information frameworks.

II. Recommendations to civil society to promote and ensure good governance and the protection of human rights

1. Set up an independent multi-stakeholder body with the cooperation of various sectors to monitor and provide recommendations on trends in and individual cases of digital rights abuses.
2. Support the independent evaluation and analysis of substantive aspects, including the use of the principles of necessity and proportionality through established global standards, and the impact of responses on society and economy.
3. Hold implementing authorities and officials liable for the misuse of their powers or information obtained, while carrying out their duties in the existing legal framework.
4. Reinforce the power of individuals to play a greater role in making online spaces more free, secure and inclusive.
5. Strengthen solidarity for underprivileged people.
6. Promote a civilised environment for free online expression.
7. Continue to increase knowledge of digital rights through training and capacity-building programmes.
8. Continue disseminating information to the public on various legal violations to make them more aware of existing problems and require adherence to laws from the public institutions.

NOTES

1. 'WJP rule of law index' (*World Justice Project*, 2022) <https://worldjusticeproject.org/rule-of-law-index/global/2022/historical> (accessed 12 November 2022).
2. 'Data Reportal' (*Data Reportal*, 16 February 2022) <https://datareportal.com/reports/tag/Southeastern+Asia> (accessed 12 November 2022).
3. 'Freedom on the Net report' (*Freedom House*, 2022) <https://freedomhouse.org/countries/freedom-net/scores> (accessed 12 November 2022).
4. 'Digital Rights in Thailand: Joint Submission to the UN Universal Periodic Review (UPR) For Thailand's Third UPR Cycle 39th Session of The UPR Working Group' (*Manushya Foundation*, 25 March 2021) <https://www.manushyafoundation.org/digital-rights-joint-upr-submission> (accessed 12 November 2022); 'Dictating the Internet: Curtailing Free Expression and Information Online in Thailand' (ICJ, April 2021) <https://icj2.wpenginepowered.com/wp-content/uploads/2021/06/Thailand-Dictating-the-Internet-FoE-Publication-2021-ENG.pdf> (accessed 12 November 2022); 'Digital Rights in Thailand: Thailand's Third Universal Periodic Review Cycle' (*Manushya Foundation*, 9 September 2021) <https://www.manushyafoundation.org/thailand-third-upr-cycle-factsheet-digital-rights> (accessed 12 November 2022).
5. Thai Lawyers for Human Rights, 'Statistics of persons prosecuted under Section 112 "Defamation of the King" in 2020–23' (*TLHR*, 1 April 2022, last updated 25 January 2023) <https://tlhr2014.com/archives/23983> (accessed 25 January 2023).
6. Computer Crime Act B.E. 2550 (2007).
7. The Computer Crime Act (CCA) is notorious for being a tool to prosecute online dissent. More than 154 people have been charged under the CCA in 174 cases, from the start of political demonstrations in July 2020 to October 2022. 'Thailand Computer Crime Act: Restricting Digital Rights, Silencing Online Critics', *Engage Media* (8 June 2022) <https://engagemedia.org/projects/thailand-freedom-expression/> (accessed 15 November 2022); Thai Lawyers for Human Rights, 'October 2022: The total number of politically charged persons is 1,864 people in 1,145 cases' (*TLHR*, 3 November 2022) <https://tlhr2014.com/archives/50215> (accessed 25 January 2023).
8. '2022 Index of Economic Freedom' (*The Heritage Foundation*, January 2022) <https://www.heritage.org/index/country/thailand> (accessed 14 November 2022); 'Freedom in the World 2022 Thailand' (*Freedom House*, 2022) <https://freedomhouse.org/country/thailand/freedom-world/2022> (accessed 14 November 2022).
9. iLaw, 'The right to bail: right that is often exempted for activists facing section 112 accusations' (*iLaw*, 14 February 2021) <https://www.ilaw.or.th/node/5819> (accessed 29 November 2022); 'Thai court revokes bail for two monarchy reform activists' (*Thai PBS World*, 9 January 2023) <https://www.thaipbsworld.com/thai-court-revokes-bail-for-two-monarchy-reform-activists/> (accessed 13 January 2023); Online Reporters, 'Two hunger strikers granted bail' (*Bangkok Post*, 7 February 2023) <https://www.bangkokpost.com/thailand/general/2501176> (accessed 8 February 2023).
10. In November 2021, in response to the Constitutional Court ruling that calls for Royal Reform are an attempt to overthrow the monarchy – which could have

an overarching impact on online speech – thousands of people protested in Bangkok, asking for monarchy reform, and three representatives of the protestors submitted a letter opposing absolute monarchy to the German Embassy. 'Protesters submit statement opposing absolute monarchy to German embassy' (*Bangkok Post*, 14 November 2021) <https://www.bangkokpost.com/thailand/politics/2215223/protesters-submit-statement-opposing-absolute-monarchy-to-german-embassy> (accessed 29 November 2022). The concerning civic space in the country as well as the limited space for free speech also drove CIVICUS to send a joint letter to the Thai Minister of Justice urging Thailand to end prosecution of pro-democracy activists and protesters, drawing attention to the growing number of cases of lèse-majesté prosecutions, including for online speech. 'Thailand: Halt prosecution of pro-democracy activists and protesters' (*CIVICUS*, 17 June 2021) <https://www.civicus.org/index.php/media-resources/media-releases/open-letters/5118-thailand-halt-prosecution-of-pro-democracy-activists-and-protesters> (accessed 29 November 2022). Such concerns were also brought under the international community's scrutiny by civil society organisations during Thailand's third UPR Cycle Review, when Thailand's human rights record was examined by UN Member States in November 2021. 'Digital Rights in Thailand: Joint Submission to the UN Universal Periodic Review (UPR) For Thailand's Third UPR Cycle 39th Session of The UPR Working Group' (*Manushya Foundation*, 25 March 2021) <https://www.manushyafoundation.org/digital-rights-joint-upr-submission> (accessed 12 November 2022).

11. Subel Rai Bhandari, 'Young Thai activists adapt, get creative in protesting for monarchy reform', *Benar News* (8 March 2022) <https://www.benarnews.org/english/news/thai/adaptive-protests-03082022143956.html> (accessed 13 November 2022).
12. ข้อก ำหนด ออกตำมควำมในมำตรำ ๙ แห่งพระรำชก ำหนด กำรบริหำรรำชกำรใน สถำนกำรณ์ฉุกเฉิน พ.ศ. ๒๕๔๘ (ฉบับที่ ๒) [Regulation Issued under the Royal Act Emergency Decree on Public Administration in Emergency Situations B.E. 2548 (2005) (No. 29)] <https://ratchakitcha.soc.go.th/pdfdownload/?id=138D170S0000000000100> (accessed 13 November 2022); 'Regulation Issued under the Royal Act Emergency Decree on Public Administration in Emergency Situations B.E. 2548 (2005) (No. 29)' (*Manushya Foundation*, 2021) <https://www.manushyafoundation.org/_files/ugd/a0db76_973c580f6ab6408193184683e2bb388e.pdf> (accessed 13 November 2022).
13. 'Joint Statement Thailand: Stop Weaponizing "COVID-19" to Censor Information "Causing Fear" and Crack Down on Media and Internet Service Providers' (*Manushya Foundation*, 4 August 2021) <https://www.manushyafoundation.org/joint-statement-stop-weaponizing-covid19-to-censor-information> (accessed 12 November 2022); 'Thailand: Immediately Repeal Emergency Regulation that Threatens Online Freedoms' (*Human Rights Watch*, 3 August 2021) <https://www.hrw.org/news/2021/08/03/thailand-immediately-repeal-emergency-regulation-threatens-online-freedoms> (accessed 12 November 2022).
14. Online Reporters, 'Court accepts petition against internet blocking', *Bangkok Post* (2 August 2021) <https://www.bangkokpost.com/thailand/general/2158731/court-accepts-petition-against-internet-blocking> (accessed 14 November 2022).

15. 'Press Release' (*The Civil Court*, 6 August 2021) <https://civil.coj.go.th/cms/s41/u392/6408/PR640806en.pdf> (accessed 14 November 2022).
16. 'Thai Civil Court forced Prayut to Repeal his Regulation No. 29 censoring the Truth online!' (*Manushya Foundation*, 10 August 2021) <https://www.manushyafoundation.org/post/thai-civil-court-forced-prayut-to-repeal-his-regulation-no-29-censoring-the-truth-online> (accessed 16 February 2024).
17. Pegasus spyware is zero-click mobile surveillance software designed to infiltrate iOS and Android devices to secretly collect information.
18. 'Thai activists file lawsuit against NSO Group for privacy violations using Pegasus spyware' (*iLaw-freedom*, 15 November 2022) <https://freedom.ilaw.or.th/node/1138?fbclid=IwAR1Am1v6u4uFCId7LDC4T_lzqa8JVtCC9ea29AP1vFyuFJCjBackKfhUFoE> (accessed 16 February 2024); 'Pegasus victims sue NSO in Thailand: It's time for spyware accountability' (*Access Now*, 15 November 2022) <https://www.accessnow.org/thailand-pegasus-lawsuit/> (accessed 24 November 2022).
19. Rina Chandran, Thomson Reuters Foundation, 'Activists suing govt over Pegasus spyware', *Bangkok Post* (14 February 2023) <https://www.bangkokpost.com/thailand/general/2506436/activists-suing-govt-over-pegasus-spyware> (accessed 14 February 2023).
20. 'Thai Activists Sue Government Over Alleged Use of Pegasus Spyware' <https://thediplomat.com/2023/06/thai-activists-sue-government-over-alleged-use-of-pegasus-spyware/> and 'Thai Civil Court dismisses case against NSO Group over the use of Pegasus spyware in Thailand' <https://prachataienglish.com/node/11215>.
21. Safenet Voice, 'Digital Rights Situation Report Indonesia 2021: In Indonesia, Digital Repression Keep Continues' (*SAFEnet*) <https://safenet.or.id/2022/03/in-indonesia-digital-repression-is-keep-continues/> (accessed 28 November 2022).
22. 'Indonesia's New Criminal Code Is a Massive Threat to Human Rights' (*Manushya Foundation*, 9 December 2022) <https://www.manushyafoundation.org/post/indonesia-s-new-criminal-code-is-a-massive-threat-to-human-rights> (accessed 15 December 2022); 'Indonesia: New Criminal Code Disastrous for Rights' (*Human Rights Watch*, 8 December 2022) <https://www.hrw.org/news/2022/12/08/indonesia-new-criminal-code-disastrous-rights> (accessed 15 December 2022).
23. '2022 Index of Economic Freedom' (*The Heritage Foundation*, January 2022) <https://www.heritage.org/index/country/thailand> (accessed 14 November 2022).
24. Fendi Widianto, 'Monitoring the ruling vs 2019 internet shutdowns in Papua and West Papua' (*Coconet*, 12 June 2020) <https://coconet.social/2020/papua-internet-shutdown-indonesia/index.html> (accessed 14 November 2022).
25. Safenet Voice, '[Press Release] Jakarta PTUN Declares Termination Of Internet Access In Papua And West Papua Violates The Law' (*SAFEnet*) <https://safenet.or.id/2020/06/jakarta-ptun-declares-termination-of-internet-access-in-papua-and-west-papua-violates-the-law/> (accessed 14 November 2022); 'Court rules the internet shutdowns in Papua and West Papua were illegal' (*Access Now*, 3 June 2020) <https://www.accessnow.org/court-rules-the-internet-shutdowns-in-papua-and-west-papua-are-illegal/> (accessed 14 November 2022).

26. Global Voices South East Asia, 'Indonesian court allows internet blocking amid social unrest' (*Global Voices advox*, 9 November 2021) <https://advox.globalvoices.org/2021/11/09/indonesian-court-allows-internet-blocking-amid-social-unrest/> (accessed 14 November 2022).
27. Agustinus Beo Da Costa and Stanley Widianto, 'Indonesian internet blocks amid social unrest lawful, court rules' (*Reuters*, 27 October 2021) <https://www.reuters.com/business/media-telecom/indonesian-internet-blocks-amid-social-unrest-lawful-court-rules-2021-10-27/> (accessed 14 November 2022).
28. The UN has repeatedly condemned the use of internet shutdowns to intentionally and arbitrarily prevent or disrupt access to or dissemination of information online. See e.g.: Report of the Special Rapporteur on the promotion and protection of the right to freedom of opinion and expression (30 March 2017), UN Doc. A/HRC/35/22; Resolution adopted by the Human Rights Council on 5 July 2018, The promotion, protection and enjoyment of human rights on the Internet (17 July 2018), UN Doc. A/HRC/RES/38/7; Report of the Special Rapporteur on the promotion and protection of the right to freedom of opinion and expression (9 October 2019), UN Doc. A/74/486; UN Human Rights Council (14 July 2020), UN Doc. A/HRC/44/L.18/Rev.1; 'Internet shutdowns: UN report details "dramatic" impact on people's lives and human rights' (*United Nations*, 23 June 2022) <https://www.ohchr.org/en/press-releases/2022/06/internet-shutdowns-un-report-details-dramatic-impact-peoples-lives-and-human> (accessed 14 November 2022).
29. 'Digital apartheid' was first coined by General Colin Powell. Paula Barnard-Ashton and others, 'Digital apartheid and the effect of mobile technology during rural fieldwork' (2008) SCIELO <http://www.scielo.org.za/scielo.php?script=sci_arttext&pid=S2310-38332018000200004&lng=en&nrm=iso> (accessed 7 January 2023).
30. Jakarta State Administrative Court 424/G/TF/2022/PTUN.JKT (30 November 2022) <https://sipp.ptun-jakarta.go.id/index.php/detil_perkara> (accessed 19 December 2022).
31. 'Freedom on the Net 2022 Philippines' (*Freedom House*, 2022) <https://freedomhouse.org/country/philippines/freedom-net/2022> (accessed 15 December 2022).
32. Rebecca Ratcliffe, 'Philippines election Q&A: why did Marcos Jr win and what can we expect from his presidency?' *The Guardian* (London, 10 May 2022) <https://www.theguardian.com/world/2022/may/10/philippines-election-qa-why-did-macros-jr-win-and-what-can-we-expect-from-his-presidency> (accessed 15 December 2022).
33. '2022 Index of Economic Freedom' (*The Heritage Foundation*, January 2022) <https://www.heritage.org/index/country/philippines> (accessed 14 November 2022); 'Judicial independence in Philippines is under threat, says UN human rights expert' (*United Nations*, 1 June 2018) <https://www.ohchr.org/en/press-releases/2018/06/judicial-independence-philippines-under-threat-says-un-human-rights-expert> (accessed 15 December 2022).
34. The Anti-terrorism Act of 2020; UN Special Procedures, 'Comments on The Anti-Terrorism Act of 2020' (29 June 2020) OL PHL 4/2020.
35. Rey Panaligan, '37 petitions filed with SC against Anti-Terrorism Act', *Manila Bulletin* (8 October 2020) <https://mb.com.ph/2020/10/08/37-petitions-filed-with-sc-against-anti-terrorism-act/> (accessed 15 December 2022).

36. Supreme Court En Banc Decision on G.R. No. 252578, et al. (Atty Howard M. Calleja et al. v. Executive Secretary et al. (7 December 2021).
37. Lian Buan, 'Supreme Court ruling "eases fears" on anti-terror law "but still dangerous" – lawyers' (*Rappler*, 9 December 2021) <https://www.rappler.com/nation/lawyers-statements-supreme-court-ruling-anti-terrorism-law/> (accessed 15 December 2022).
38. Lian Buan, '"We don't deserve mere consolation from Supreme Court" – lawyers vs anti-terror law' (*Rappler*, 10 December 2021) <https://www.rappler.com/nation/lawyers-reaction-supreme-court-ruling-anti-terrorism-law-consolation-we-do-not-deserve/> (accessed 15 December 2022).
39. 'Anti-Terror Act remains dangerous and fundamentally flawed' (*Amnesty International Philippines*, 9 December 2021) <https://www.amnesty.org.ph/2021/12/anti-terror-act-remains-dangerous-and-fundamentally-flawed/> (accessed 15 December 2022).
40. Lian Buan, 'Appeals roll for another shot to void feared anti-terror law' (*Rappler*, 2 March 2022) <https://www.rappler.com/nation/motion-reconsideration-roll-another-shot-void-anti-terrorism-law/> (accessed 15 December 2022); Kristine Joy Patag, 'Supreme Court upholds decision leaving Anti-Terror Act mostly intact' (*Philstar GLOBAL*, 26 April 2022) <https://www.philstar.com/headlines/2022/04/26/2176912/supreme-court-upholds-decision-leaving-anti-terror-act-mostly-intact> (accessed 15 December 2022).
41. Franco Jose C. Baroña, 'SC rules on terror cases drafted', *Manila Times* (18 December 2022) <https://www.manilatimes.net/2022/12/18/news/national/sc-rules-on-terror-cases-drafted/1870716> (accessed 13 January 2023).
42. 'Freedom on the Net 2022 Malaysia' (*Freedom House*, 2022) <https://freedomhouse.org/country/malaysia/freedom-net/2022> (accessed 15 November 2022).
43. '2022 Index of Economic Freedom' (*The Heritage Foundation*, January 2022) <https://www.heritage.org/index/country/malaysia> (accessed 14 November 2022).
44. Anisah Shukry and The Malaysia Insider (contributor), 'Azmi Sharom strikes first as court allows review of Sedition Act' (*The Edge Markets*, 1 October 2014) <https://www.theedgemarkets.com/article/azmi-sharom-strikes-first-court-allows-review-sedition-act> (accessed 14 November 2022).
45. Sedition Act 1948, a relic of British colonial rule, criminalises any conduct with a 'seditious tendency', including a tendency to 'excite disaffection' against or 'bring into hatred or contempt' the ruler or government. It does not require the prosecution to prove intent, and provides for up to three years' imprisonment and/or a fine of 5000 Ringgit for those found guilty of a first offence. Subsequent offences may be punished with up to five years' imprisonment. The use of the Sedition Act to suppress dissent in Malaysia has received significant criticism from the UN. See e.g.: UN Special Procedures (10 May 2019) AL MYS 2/2019; 'Malaysia Sedition Act threatens freedom of expression by criminalising dissent' (*United Nations*, 8 October 2014) <https://www.ohchr.org/en/press-releases/2014/10/malaysia-sedition-act-threatens-freedom-expression-criminalising-dissent?LangID=E&NewsID=15144> (accessed 14 November 2022). During its third UPR cycle, Malaysia received several recommendations for the revise and repeal of the Sedition Act. See e.g.: <https://www.ohchr.org/en/hr-bodies/upr/m-yindex> (accessed 14 November 2022).

46. 'Malaysia: Sedition Act upheld in further blow to free expression' (*Ifex*, 13 October 2015) <https://ifex.org/malaysia-sedition-act-upheld-in-further-blow-to-free-expression/> (accessed 15 November 2022).
47. The Act gives authorities sweeping powers to target those who oppose them. Malaysian authorities have cast a wide net of repression in their use of the Sedition Act, targeting a range of individuals including rights activists, journalists, lawyers and opposition politicians. 'Malaysia: Repeal the Sedition Act' (*Article 19*, 27 July 2022) <https://www.article19.org/resources/malaysia-repeal-the-sedition-act/> (accessed 15 November 2022); 'Malaysia 2021' (*Amnesty International*) <https://www.amnesty.org/en/location/asia-and-the-pacific/south-east-asia-and-the-pacific/malaysia/report-malaysia/> (accessed 15 November 2022); 'Freedom on the Net Malaysia' (*Freedom House*, 2022) <https://freedomhouse.org/country/malaysia/freedom-net/2022> (accessed 15 November 2022).
48. 'Global State of Democracy Report 2022: Forging Social Contracts in a Time of Discontent' (*International IDEA*) <https://idea.int/democracytracker/gsod-report-2022> (accessed 15 November 2022).

REFERENCES

'2022 Index of Economic Freedom' (The Heritage Foundation, January 2022).

'Anti-Terror Act remains dangerous and fundamentally flawed' (Amnesty International Philippines, 9 December 2021).

Anti-Terrorism Act of 2020.

'Court rules the internet shutdowns in Papua and West Papua were illegal' (Access Now, 3 June 2020).

'Data Reportal' (Data Reportal, 16 February 2022).

'Dictating the Internet: Curtailing Free Expression and Information Online in Thailand' (ICJ, April 2021).

'Digital Rights in Thailand: Joint Submission to the UN Universal Periodic Review (UPR) For Thailand's Third UPR Cycle 39th Session of the UPR Working Group' (Manushya Foundation, 25 March 2021).

'Freedom in the World 2022 Thailand' (Freedom House, 2022).

'Freedom on the Net 2022 Malaysia' (Freedom House, 2022).

'Freedom on the Net 2022 Philippines' (Freedom House, 2022).

'Global State of Democracy Report 2022: Forging Social Contracts in a Time of Discontent' (International IDEA).

'Indonesia's New Criminal Code Is a Massive Threat to Human Rights' (Manushya Foundation, 9 December 2022).

'Joint Statement Thailand: Stop Weaponizing "COVID-19" to Censor Information "Causing Fear" and Crack Down on Media and Internet Service Providers' (Manushya Foundation, 4 August 2021).

'Judicial independence in Philippines is under threat, says UN human rights expert' (United Nations, 1 June 2018).

'Malaysia 2021' (Amnesty International).

'Malaysia: Repeal the Sedition Act' (Article 19, 27 July 2022).

'Malaysia: Sedition Act upheld in further blow to free expression' (Ifex, 13 October 2015).

'Pegasus victims sue NSO in Thailand: It's time for spyware accountability' (Access Now, 15 November 2022).

'Press Release' (The Civil Court, 6 August 2021).

'Thai Civil Court forced Prayut to Repeal his Regulation No. 29 censoring the Truth online!' (Manushya Foundation, 10 August 2021).

'Thailand: Halt prosecution of pro-democracy activists and protesters' (CIVICUS, 17 June 2021).

'UN Special Procedures "Comments on The Anti-Terrorism Act of 2020"' (29 June 2020) OL PHL 4/2020.

'WJP rule of law index' (World Justice Project, 2022).

ข้อก ำหนด ออกตำมควำมในมำตรำ ๙ แห่งพระรำชก ำหนด กำรบริหำรรำชกำร ในสถำนกำรณ์ฉุกเฉิน พ.ศ. ๒๕๔๘ (ฉบับที่ ๒) [Regulation Issued under the Royal Act Emergency Decree on Public Administration in Emergency Situations B.E. 2548 (2005) (No. 29)].

Baroña, F. J. C., 'SC rules on terror cases drafted', *Manila Times* (18 December 2022).

Buan, L., 'Appeals roll for another shot to void feared anti-terror law', *Rappler* (2 March 2022).

Buan, L., 'Supreme Court ruling "eases fears" on anti-terror law "but still dangerous" – lawyers', *Rappler* (9 December 2021).

Buan, L., '"We don't deserve mere consolation from Supreme Court" – lawyers vs anti-terror law', *Rappler* (10 December 2021).

Cabañes, J. V. A. and Ong, J. C., *The Politics of Digital Media in the Philippines* (2020).

Chachavalpongpun, P. (ed.), *Routledge Handbook of Contemporary Thailand* (2019).

Chib, A. and Abdul Wahab, J., 'Internet in Malaysia: Development, Challenges, and Opportunities' (2020).

Citron, D., *The Fight for Privacy: Protecting Dignity, Identity, and Love in the Digital Age* (2022).

Coronel, S. S. (ed.), *Southeast Asian Cyberactivism: Freedom of Expression and Democratization* (2012).

Costa, A. B. D. and Widianto, S., 'Indonesian internet blocks amid social unrest lawful, court rules' (Reuters, 27 October 2021).

Jones, M. O., Sonay, A. and Thompson, M. (eds), *Digital Authoritarianism in the Middle East and Southeast Asia* (2023).

Karpf, D., *Digital Resistance in the Internet Age* (2020).

Karpf, D., *Speech Police: The Global Struggle to Govern the Internet* (2019).

Online Reporters, 'Court accepts petition against internet blocking', *Bangkok Post* (2 August 2021).

Panaligan, R., '37 petitions filed with SC against Anti-Terrorism Act', *Manila Bulletin* (8 October 2020).

Patag, K. J., 'Supreme Court upholds decision leaving Anti-Terror Act mostly intact', *Philstar GLOBAL* (26 April 2022).
Ratcliffe, R., 'Philippines election Q&A: why did Marcos Jr win and what can we expect from his presidency?' *The Guardian* (London, 10 May 2022).
Report of the Special Rapporteur on the promotion and protection of the right to freedom of opinion and expression (30 March 2017), UN Doc. A/HRC/35/22.
Report of the Special Rapporteur on the promotion and protection of the right to freedom of opinion and expression (9 October 2019), UN Doc. A/74/486.
Safenet Voice, 'Digital Rights Situation Report Indonesia 2021: In Indonesia, Digital Repression Keep Continues' (SAFEnet).
Safenet Voice, '[Press Release] Jakarta PTUN Declares Termination Of Internet Access In Papua And West Papua Violates The Law' (SAFEnet).
Shukry, A. and The Malaysia Insider (contributor), 'Azmi Sharom strikes first as court allows review of Sedition Act' (The Edge Markets, 1 October 2014).
Tkacheva, O. and others, 'Internet Freedom and Political Space' (2013).
UN Human Rights Council, 'Resolution adopted by the Human Rights Council on 5 July 2018, The promotion, protection and enjoyment of human rights on the Internet' (17 July 2018), UN Doc. A/HRC/RES/38/7.
UN Human Rights Council, 'Internet shutdowns: UN report details "dramatic" impact on people's lives and human rights' (United Nations, 23 June 2022).
UN Special Procedures (10 May 2019) AL MYS 2/2019.

Index

EU Authorised Representative:
Easy Access System Europe Mustamäe tee 50, 10621 Tallinn, Estonia
gpsr.requests@easproject.com

Printed and bound by CPI Group (UK) Ltd, Croydon, CR0 4YY
14/09/2026
02216781-0005